A Black Elite

Recent Titles in
Contributions in Afro-American and African Studies
Series Advisers: John W. Blassingame and Henry Louis Gates, Jr.

Writing "Independent" History: African Historiography, 1960–1980
Caroline Neale

More Than Drumming: Essays on African and Afro-Latin American Music
and Musicians
Irene V. Jackson, editor

More Than Dancing: Essays on Afro-American Music and Musicians
Irene V. Jackson, editor

Sterling A. Brown: Building the Black Aesthetic Tradition
Joanne V. Gabbin

Amalgamation!: Race, Sex, and Rhetoric in the Nineteenth-Century American
Novel
James Kinney

Black Theatre in the 1960s and 1970s: A Historical-Critical Analysis of
the Movement
Mance Williams

An Old Creed for the New South: Proslavery Ideology and Historiography,
1865–1918
John David Smith

Wilson Harris and the Modern Tradition: A New Architecture of the World
Sandra E. Drake

Portrait of an Expatriate: William Gardner Smith, Writer
LeRoy S. Hodges, Jr.

Race, Politics, and Culture: Critical Essays on the Radicalism of the 1960s
Adolph Reed, Jr.

The White Press and Black America
Carolyn Martindale

Africa and the West: The Legacies of Empire
Isaac James Mowoe and Richard Bjornson, editors

A BLACK ELITE

A Profile of Graduates of UNCF Colleges

Daniel C. Thompson

Contributions in Afro-American
and African Studies, Number 98

GREENWOOD PRESS
NEW YORK • WESTPORT, CONNECTICUT • LONDON

Library of Congress Cataloging-in-Publication Data

Thompson, Daniel C. (Daniel Calbert)
  A Black elite.

  (Contributions in Afro-American and African studies,
ISSN 0069-9624 ; no. 98)
  Bibliography: p.
  Includes index.
  1. Afro-American college graduates.   2. Afro-Americans
—Social conditions.   3. Afro-Americans—Economic
conditions.   I. Title.   II. Series.
E185.8.T48   1986   305.8'96073   85–27308
ISBN 0–313–25291–2 (lib. bdg. : alk. paper)

Library of Congress Catalog Card Number: 85–27308
ISBN: 0–313–25291–2
ISSN: 0069–9624

First published in 1986

Greenwood Press, Inc.
88 Post Road West, Westport, Connecticut 06881

Printed in the United States of America

The paper used in this book complies with the
Permanent Paper Standard issued by the National
Information Standards Organization (Z39.48–1984).

10 9 8 7 6 5 4 3 2 1

In memory of

W.E.B. Du Bois (1868–1963)
Charles S. Johnson (1893–1956)
E. Franklin Frazier (1894–1962)

and to my wife, Barbara

Contents

Tables

Foreword

The Black experience in the Republic of America has been deeply informed and inspired by a love affair with education. Black people, for a variety of reasons, and from the dark and tragic night of slavery, have had boundless faith in the power, centrality, and creative and higher possibilities of education—the liberation and cultivation of the mind and the sense of wonder, with all the richness, joy, beauty, and awesome consequences inherent in and flowing therefrom. Education has been an article of faith for Black people.

This profound and enduring commitment to and passion for education, was due, in no small part, to the tragic exclusion and estrangement of Blacks from other avenues and forms of power and social progress—economic, political, and social; and occupational opportunities, rewards, institutions, and processes.

Moreover, Blacks have viewed education as perhaps the key to upward social mobility, security, and Black liberation. And, intuitively, Blacks perceived education as a generator and sustainer of self-esteem, dignity, and the sense of self-worth so tragically negated by a radically racist society whose very essence is a denial of the equal and common humanity of Blacks.

So runs a central theme of this remarkable book by the eminent scholar, Dr. Daniel C. Thompson.

This is a unique and landmark study. It is a perceptive, comprehensive, exhaustive, major contribution to our knowledge, understanding, and appreciation. It is a significant contribution to the literature of the area. The author brings impressive credentials to his task.

Dr. Thompson is a distinguished scholar who has written extensively on such topics as Black colleges, Black leadership, the sociology of the Black experience, the Black family, and the Black middle class. He is uniquely qualified to do this study of the graduates of UNCF colleges. A lifetime of distinguished scholarship, writing, and reflection is brought to bear on the subject. This book reflects Dr. Thompson's distilled wisdom and rich perspective. He takes the broad, long, and total view of Black college graduates in American society. Where appropriate, he illuminates the data by using the comparative racial view. To make the material more meaningful and intelligible, he does not hesitate to use the historical approach to avoid the tyranny of the moment.

This is a first-rate book on a topic that is basic and timely, which portrays perennial meaning, significance, and relevance.

While the UNCF colleges constitute the research sample of this study, the study, by extension and implication, involves much more. The UNCF graduates "may be regarded as quintessential representatives of the Black-college educated in American society generally," as the author states. This is no narrow undertaking. It casts a wide net.

In exploring the careers of graduates of UNCF colleges, the study deals with a variety of phenomena: UNCF colleges, parents, socio-economic status, income, educational levels, Black social life and organizations, curricula, the persistence of racism, job satisfaction, political participation and leadership, civil rights organizations, Black businesses, the Black church, the Black middle class, and whatever else is relevant to an understanding of the issues. With his learned background, the author is wide-ranging, and can deftly call on endless sources, insights, and perspectives. There is no substitute for first-rate scholarship and erudition.

The infinite problems, struggles, setbacks, roadblocks, disappointments, frustrations, nightmares, heartaches, suffering, dehumanization, contradictions, and tragic negations of the Black experience in the New World have not been final, ultimate, and exhaustive. The mountain has had another side.

The deeper meaning and significance of this study of Black-college graduates is a compelling affirmation of progress, success, hope, dignity, self-help, resilience, pride, the work ethic, and the vitality, power, optimism, and residual "aliveness" and ultimately creative "activism" of the American Dream and the nobility and transcendent influence and inspiration of the promise of American life.

The inexhaustible love affair of Black people with education has paid off—handsomely. The daring and incredible faith and investment of Blacks in education have been more than justified and rewarded by dramatic achievements against formidable odds. They have outstripped all rational and empirical expectations, anticipations, and predictions. Education has produced not only survival but also advancement and great success.

Ultimately, this book is a heartwarming story of quiet eloquence and deep beauty about the glory and creative power of the human mind and spirit at their best. It is a great story of Black people and their faith, hard work, perseverance, determination, struggles, and triumphs. It is a great story of the American people in the flux and flow of the drama of history. This is characteristically a great story of America.

A critical example will illustrate the validity and deep beauty of this story of affirmation, hope, progress, pride, and success. First, the socio-economic status of offsprings in this study is much higher than that of their parents, which is atypical. "The socio-economic status achieved by the college-educated Blacks in our sample, on the whole, is far beyond the level that may have been rationally expected of them." Dr. Thompson goes on to say that "not only have most of the black college graduates in this study moved beyond their parents, but ... their success, overall, is indeed comparable to that of their White peers from much more affluent socio-economic backgrounds." This is quite an achievement!

"Despite the heavy odds against it, at least 82–85 percent of the college graduates in our study have received a higher level of education than either of their parents." This represents dramatic, remarkable progress and commitment.

In this extraordinarily magnificent story of progress, Black colleges, which have welcomed, nurtured, inspired, and motivated students from all socio-economic backgrounds and levels of academic preparation and achievement, have played a key, Godsent role. "Black colleges," Dr. Thompson asserts, "will continue to be the main, essential gateway through which Blacks from all social origins in the United States will enter and succeed in mainstream American society." Black colleges have performed miracles in terms of the American educational structure, process, and product. Black colleges for what? "Black colleges are still," Dr. Thompson observes, "the only truly reliable institutions fully dedicated to the education of Black students from all socio-economic areas in the Black community, and with varying kinds and levels of abilities and achievements."

Black colleges have prepared students from all kinds of backgrounds and walks of life not only to complete their collegiate education, but also to successfully attend the most prestigious graduate and professional schools in the country and compete successfully in the mainstream of American life and marketplace in terms of jobs and the professions. Blacks have no rational choice but to be competitive in our increasingly scientific, technological, and complex culture.

Dr. Thompson has a functional conception of the "Black elite." It is the leadership or middle class in Black America, committed to Black advancement and the democratization of American culture. Members of the elitist subgroup "are in the vanguard of those who are most effective in the advancement of Blacks toward equality in American society." The Black-college graduates who constitute the elitist subgroup "still believe that a good education, hard work, and excellent skills in racial diplomacy are the most effective means of getting ahead in American society. In this respect, they are quintessential Americans."

The emergence of a significant Black middle class, which is largely the product of Black colleges, is also a great sign of progress, success, hope, and pride.

Dr. Thompson's book is good news.

Samuel DuBois Cook
President
Dillard University

Preface

This volume is the product of a three-year study (1982–1985) of black college graduates. It is the first such study since Charles S. Johnson's, *The Negro College Graduate* (1938).

Unlike more recent studies of blacks in higher education, which have characteristically focused upon the academic, psychological, and social handicaps of black students, or the history and alleged shortcomings of black colleges, this study presents a comprehensive profile of black college graduates as a distinct, self-conscious segment in American society. This profile includes a systematic description and interpretation of their socio-economic origins, racial disadvantages, academic handicaps and successes, philosophies of human relations, levels and fields of post-baccalaureate education, career patterns, social class identities, community services, civil rights attitudes and activities, political persuasions, and leadership styles and achievements.

The central finding of this study is that graduates of the forty-two United Negro College Fund (UNCF)* member institutions constitute an integral, creative element within this nation's college-educated Black elite which deligently strives for personal success and racial advancement in American society.

Basic to the analyses and interpretations presented herein is the proposition that a degree from any fully accredited college tends to bestow upon the recipients certain privileges and opportunities ordinarily withheld from the non-college population. Therefore, the emphasis is not upon the

---

*There are now (1985) 43 UNCF member institutions. See Appendix A.

differences which may be found among black graduates of the colleges constituting the research sample, nor is it upon how their overall profile differs from that of black college graduates at large. Rather, emphasis is on black college graduates per se as members of a vital, rapidly expanding black middle class.

Information about the socio-economic status and activities of college graduates, particularly black college graduates, was painstakingly gleaned from a wide range of sources. Among the secondary sources drawn upon are newspapers, popular magazines, and scholarly writings which often present comprehensive profiles of black college graduates, especially those who seem to be successful. A valuable source regarding successful blacks in various walks of life is the well-researched volume *Who's Who among Black Americans, 1980–1981*.

A review of information regarding higher education in the United States, and specifically the higher education and career patterns of black college graduates, makes it possible to interpret the profile of career patterns, social status, community involvement, and values of the respondents in the context of the college educated in American society in general.

Information about the socio-economic status and achievements of the college graduates constituting the research sample was drawn from four main sources:

1. A lengthy questionnaire especially designed for this study was mailed to 8,342 alumni selected at random from a master list made up of alumni rosters submitted by the sample colleges. This questionnaire was completed and returned by 2,089, or 25 percent, of the research sample. There were responses from alumni representing all of the 42 UNCF member colleges. The range of responses was 32 from one college to 126 from another.

The data furnished by the respondents to the questionnaire have been carefully analyzed and interpreted and used as the ultimate validation for the conclusions in this study.

2. Focused interviews with forty representative graduates of the sample colleges, plus numerous informal interviews conducted throughout the research period. These interviewees represented the various age groups, occupations, socio-economic origins, college majors, levels and fields of graduate study, extent and kinds of social participation, styles of life, and leadership activities characteristic of graduates constituting the research sample.

3. Personal documents submitted by twenty-four of the respondents to the questionnaire provided valuable insights into the life and goals of the college-educated black middle class. Some submitted copies of their public speeches, newspaper clippings of their public activities, and scholarly works they had published. Others volunteered to write somewhat lengthy responses to questions raised in the formal questionnaire.

4. I have drawn extensively upon my forty years of observations and

experiences as a student, teacher, researcher, and administrator in UNCF member colleges and upon various rich experiences I have had in higher education in general.

The data presented and the conclusions reached in this volume should help to understand better the many complex problems, challenges, and coping strategies used by well-educated, ambitious, upwardly mobile blacks in our ponderously desegregating American society.

Acknowledgments

This study was cosponsored by Dillard University and the United Negro College Fund, Inc. (UNCF). Samuel DuBois Cook, President of Dillard University, has supported this study since its inception. He recommended sponsorship of the project, provided space for the research, and permitted me to use the facilities at Dillard during my three years of research and writing. Christopher F. Edley, Executive Director of the UNCF, helped to provide funding for the study, mailed the questionnaires, and encouraged the research department to extend assistance to the study.

I am indebted to Alan H. Kirschner, Director of Research, UNCF. He has been of invaluable assistance throughout the research period. He served as consultant and research associate from the earliest planning stages to the proofreading of the manuscript.

I want to express my appreciation to the foundations that contributed to the UNCF on behalf of this study. Prominent among them were the John D. and Catherine T. MacArthur Foundation, Alfred P. Sloan Foundation, the Lilly Foundation, Mobil Oil Co., and especially Robert Brocksbank, who encouraged the research project and recommended its funding.

I am especially obligated to the Dillard University librarians who went far beyond the call of duty to assist me in this research. I gratefully acknowledge the encouragement and cooperation I received from my esteemed colleagues and the staff of Dillard University.

My special thanks go to Sonia M. Wilson for the late evenings and weekends she spent patiently typing and retyping the final draft of my manuscript. I also appreciate the services of Helen R. Malin, Assistant Professor of English, Dillard University. She, likewise, gave up evenings and weekends to proofread my manuscript with technical precision and thoroughness.

I am grateful to my daughters, Danelle and Wilma Sarah, whose experiences in a UNCF college I was privileged to share.

Above all others I would like to express my gratitude and thanks to my wife, Barbara, Professor of Sociology, Dillard University, who served as a non-paid research associate throughout the various stages of this study and remained patient even when mountains of research materials necessitated the rearrangement of our household.

Finally, this report would not have been possible without the enthusiastic cooperation of the graduates of the UNCF member colleges who completed the lengthy questionnaire and willingly gave the necessary time for long and sometimes repeated interviews.

It is my fervent hope that the findings of this study will justify the confidence and time of all who made it possible.

A Black Elite

1 The Black Elite

Graduates of the forty-two colleges constituting the United Negro College Fund, Inc. (UNCF), may be regarded as quintessential representatives of the black college-educated in American society in general.[1] Thus while this study focuses upon graduates of UNCF-affiliated colleges, which constitute the research sample, basic or overall conclusions arrived at are very likely to be apropos to black college graduates at large. Consequently, data to be presented throughout this study should help to understand better the complex problems, challenges, and achievements of black higher education per se, and the struggles, accomplishments, and rewards of the black college-educated specifically.

On the basis of available information, it may be argued that college-educated blacks on the whole actually constitute what amounts to a separate, distinct, self-concious social class—even an elitist subgroup in the black community. Historically, black Americans have placed unusually strong faith (some say an almost blind confidence) in the efficacy of formal education.[2] The fact of having graduated from college functions to set individuals apart and to bestow upon them a number of special rights and opportunities that are ordinarily withheld from non-college individuals, especially non-college blacks.[3]

In this connection a recently vocal group of black "conservative" intellectuals tend to defend the proposition that college-educated blacks are beginning to constitute a sort of premium group insofar as corporate America is concerned. Thus, they hold, young black college graduates are somehow managing to transcend traditional, debilitating racism to the extent that their chances in the job market are about as good as, and in some instances even better than, those for white college graduates in the same age category. For instance, a highly respected black intellectual reports that "by 1973 college-educated black males aged 25–29 had earnings 9 percent greater than white college males in the same age category."[4]

There is some strong, persistent doubt that college-educated blacks have been able to transcend the negative pull of traditional racism to the extent the "black conservatives" claim, or that they constitute a sort of premium group favored by corporate America. However, a close examination of the careers of graduates of UNCF colleges does reveal that a surprisingly large number of them have had considerable success in overcoming some firmly established, stubborn racial barriers in a rather wide range of occupations in both the public and private sectors of the economic life of the United States.[5]

It is important to note that in the process of advancing their own individual careers, in the overall context of the civil rights movement, which spawned the basic concepts and nurtured the issue of "equal opportunity" and "equal employment," graduates of the sample colleges have functioned, wittingly and unwittingly, as effective pioneers in opening new occupational opportunities for other blacks. In this sense they have been always in the vanguard of those who engage in blacks' perennial, epic struggle for survival and advancement in a more or less racially hostile American society.

Further, as members of a relatively small, but well-educated, ambitious, articulate subgroup, black college graduates tend to function as significant pacesetters and leaders in just about all major areas of black life in the United States.[6] They are always in the forefront of those who constantly challenge various forms and patterns of racial traditions and barriers to occupational success and full citizenship, both in their local communities and throughout the nation. Characteristically, they belong to organizations and efforts which may be described as the cutting edge, so to speak, of the various programs which constitute the civil rights movement, and which are always deliberately designed to advance the status of black Americans in the narrow sense, and the cause of American democracy in the broader sense. Consequently, it may be said that

> In one way or another the egalitarian ideology so central to the civil rights movement, and primarily propagandized by Blacks, [has] infused non-Black movements...seeking to advance the citizenship and social status of other relatively powerless groups ...Women liberationists (ERA), the aged, labor, several ethnic groups, and especially students.[7]

On this point James E. Blackwell also observes that "all races derived direct or indirect benefits from many programs...and legislation spawned by the civil rights movement."[8]

Basically the black college graduates' persistent identification with the problem of black inequality in American society functions as a common thread which binds them together as a distinct people; a significant, social category. Their dedication to the survival and advancement of the race, as such, is due primarily to the fact that "no matter how well-educated or affluent individual blacks may become, the network of social forces stemming from racism reminds them that they share a common destiny with all other blacks, even the most economically disadvantaged."[9]

Gunnar Myrdal very perceptively referred to this black identification phenomenon a generation ago when he declared:

> The Negro genius is imprisoned in the Negro problem. ...He can grow to a degree of distinction but always as a representative of "his people". ...The pressure of this expectancy on the part of society conditions his personality and forces him willy-nilly, into the role of a Negro Champion.[10]

Not only does the Negro genius (the black college-educated in this context) tend to identify with the plight of blacks on all socio-economic levels, but as Myrdal observed, they have been prepared, even conditioned, by their black undergraduate colleges to be champions of the black cause. Therefore, a significant number of them, representing a variety of occupations, have emerged as worthy advocates and effective leaders who, as W.E.B. Du Bois eloquently pointed out eighty years ago, devote themselves to the uplift and progress of the less fortunate members of their race. Du Bois contended that "in the professions they are slowly but surely leavening the Negro church, are healing and preventing the devastations of disease, and beginning to furnish legal protection for the liberty and prosperity of the toiling masses."[11]

A generation after Du Bois' evaluation of the black college-educated, Charles S. Johnson, writing in the same vein, concluded after an extensive empirical, systematic study of black college graduates that "Negro College graduates are most likely to disturb the custom of social and racial matters and also most likely to contribute constructively to social adjustment. ... All in all, they are the ones who ...most frequently engage in elevating the stagnant masses of their own race."[12]

THE CONCEPT: "BLACK ELITE"

The concept "elite"[13] as applied in this study refers to the same distinct social category or social segment as did Du Bois' concept of the "Talented Tenth."[14] While Du Bois' formulation suggested that individuals constituting this select group would be recruited from the more affluent black families where they would be "well-bred" and "well-born," in this context the concept "elite" refers specifically to individuals of talents and achievements who may have come from all of the socio-economic levels and social classes in the black community from which UNCF-related colleges recruit their students.[15]

Essentially the concept "elite" as used here has about the same meaning as does Thomas Jefferson's concept of a "natural aristocracy." For instance, in a letter of 1813 to his fellow former president John Adams, Jefferson made a clear, precise, classical distinction between what he regarded as an "artificial," "pseudo," or "tinsel" aristocracy, which he described as being founded on wealth and birth (ascribed social status), but possessing neither virtue or talents, and a "natural aristocracy," which he described as especially characterized by virtue, talents, and personal achievements (achieved social status).[16]

Jefferson strongly criticized the "pseudo aristocracy," accusing them of "shallowness," and "snobbishness," and said that they constituted "a mischievous ingredient in government which has no worthy function in a democratic society."[17] By contrast he lauded the "natural aristocracy" as being composed of individuals of "inherent worth and genius" who set and maintain high standards of honesty, trust, industry, freedom, and progress.

Further, it is significant that Jefferson, despite his strong, avowed belief in equality and the democratic process, insisted that an elite social class—a "natural aristocracy'—is absolutely essential to the establishment and conduct of a free, progressive, humane democratic society. Consequently, he insisted that individuals of "worth" and "talent" should be consciously sought out from every social segment and from every socio-economic background and deliberately prepared by education for top positions of trust and leadership. This principle is reflected in the recruitment practices of UNCF colleges.

> Black colleges literally reversed a basic tradition of social class and academic exclusiveness which has been characteristic of higher education.... In the foreseeable future Black colleges must perforce continue to practice some form of "open enrollment" ...students will continue to reflect various levels of ability, attainment, and ambition.[18]

Therefore, the primary aim of this study is to ascertain and evaluate the success the sample colleges have had, insofar as their basic mission is concerned: the preparation of an elite class of individuals dedicated to the survival and advancement of blacks specifically and democracy and justice in a larger sense.

THE HISTORIC MISSION OF BLACK COLLEGES

To understand and appreciate the manifest worth and talents of graduates of the selected black colleges, it is necessary to recall that the movement to provide higher education for black Americans began during the
very politically turbulent, violent, racist-ridden decade following the Civil
War and the emancipation of slaves. Before then, attempts to provide higher
education for blacks had been at best sporadic and half-hearted. The fact
is that in most antebellum states blacks were legally prohibited from receiving formal schooling.[19] Consequently, at the close of the Civil War,
between 90 and 95 percent of the approximately 4,500,000 blacks in the
United States were functionally illiterate, and there were only twenty-eight
known black college graduates in the total population.[20] All concerned
observers, especially some influential northern church leaders and philanthropists, agreed that if black freedmen were to retain their uncertain,
tenuous freedom and meet the demands of citizenship necessary for survival and advancement in the white-dominated, politically hostile communities, they desperately needed schools to prepare them to compete for
the opportunities to fill key professional and leadership roles. In many
communities blacks had been legally and traditionally regarded as mere
chattel—having "no rights white people needed to respect."[21]

From the very beginning, then, private black colleges founded by northern church bodies and humane philanthropists defined and established as
the intrinsic, avowed dual mission of black higher education as that of
preparing students to pursue various careers and to function as effective,
humane leaders and advocates for the great disadvantaged, disesteemed,
and relatively powerless black masses. Blacks desperately needed to establish essential social institutions and to develop moral and ethical norms
designed specifically to facilitate their survival and advancement under the
peculiar circumstances thrust upon them. This need is still critical. Therefore, according to Samuel DuBois Cook, president of Dillard University, the
black college continues to be dedicated and committed to its historical
"dual socio-ethical" mission:

> [T]he black college has the same general mission as the white
> college, but, additionally the black college has a special unique
> purpose.... It is about human excellence, the superior education
> and training of tender minds, nourishment of the creative imag-
> ination, and reverence for learning; it is also about the devel-
> opment of moral character and the production of better men
> and women for a humane, decent and open world.[22]

While Cook emphasizes the conviction that "there is no substitute for
academic excellence," he also contends that "students at black colleges

...will acquire a set of values, a spirit of social service, social conscience, moral sensitivity, and sense of personal and social responsibility—principally with reference to social and racial justice—that will stay with them and motivate them after graduation.[23]

The central mission, then, of black colleges, such as represented in this study, is still essentially the same as it was in the beginning, just after the emancipation of slaves: to prepare students to make necessary and unique contributions to the survival and advancement of black Americans and to improve the overall social condition of the less-advantaged masses. They are dedicated to the proposition that "as long as social injustices exist, priority must be given to black concerns by preparing students who can right these wrongs."[24]

A careful reading of bulletins published by the colleges in this sample underscores the fact that these institutions have been committed to the teachings of democratic principles and evaluation. According to their formal curricula and informal programs, their students are taught that all men are created equal and have inherent worth and dignity.[25]

It is, therefore, in the general academic and leadership context described above that I use the concept "black elite." As employed here it is the very opposite of social exclusiveness, snobbishness, and pretentiousness so often associated with the concept "elite." These undemocratic characteristics were scathingly denounced by the great black sociologist, E. Franklin Frazier, who accused the "Black Bourgeoisie" of living in a "world of make-believe," and of deliberately and artificially isolating themselves from the basic concerns and struggles of the less fortunate black masses.[26]

The vast majority of black college graduates who constitute this research sample certainly do not fit into the superficial black society of Frazier's formulation. For the most part they strongly identify with the problems, concerns, and struggles of their fellow black Americans and manifest a compelling feeling of responsibility to set and maintain high moral and ethical standards and to serve as dedicated, effective leaders of institutions, efforts, and programs designed to advance the status and outlook of blacks.

NOTES

1. See for comparison, Alan H. Kirschner, Jacqueline Fleming, and Kathleen Payne, *UNCF 1985 Statistical Report* (New York: United Negro College Fund); National Advisory Committee on Black Higher Education and Black Colleges and Universities, *Equity for Black Americans*, vol. 1 (Washington, D.C.: U.S. Government Printing Office, 1980); Charles V. Willie and Arline S. McCord, *Black Students at White Colleges* (New York: Praeger, 1972); Alexander W. Astin, *Minorities in American Higher Education* (San Francisco: Jossey-Bass, 1982); Donald H. Smith, *Admission and Retention of Black Students at Seven Predominantly White Universities* (Washington, D.C.: U.S. Government Printing Office, December 1979); and especially Lorenzo

Morris, *Elusive Equality* (Washington, D.C.: Howard University Press, 1979). See also Charles V. Willie and Donald Cunnigen, "Black Students in Higher Education," *Annual Review of Sociology* 7 (1981): 177–198.

2. See Daniel C. Thompson, *Private Black Colleges at the Crossroads* (Westport, Conn.: Greenwood Press, 1973), pp. 10–11; and Henry A. Bullock, *A History of Negro Education in the South* (Cambridge, Mass.: Harvard University Press, 1967), p. 19–69.

3. Daniel C. Thompson, "Black College Faculty and Students: The Nature of Their Interaction" in Charles V. Willie and Ronald R. Edmonds, eds., *Black Colleges in America: Challenge, Development, Survival* (New York: Columbia University, Teachers College Press, 1978), pp. 181–194.

4. Martin Kilson "Black Social Classes and Intergenerational Poverty," *Public Interest* 64 (Summer 1981): 67. See also Thomas Sowell et al., *The Fairmont Papers*: Black Alternatives Conference (San Francisco: Institute for Contemporary Studies, 1980), pp. 39–45.

5. See also, for example, Maureen Burnley, ed., *The Significant Difference Black Colleges Make* (New York: United Negro College Fund, June 1982), p. 7.

6. Just 7 percent of blacks twenty-five years old and over had completed four or more years of college in 1978. This is far short of the "Talented Tenth" visualized by W. E. B. Du Bois more than fifty years ago: see U.S. Department of Commerce, Bureau of the Census, *The Social and Economic Status of the Black Population in the United States, 1970–1978*, series p–23, no. 80 (1978), p. 93.

7. Daniel C. Thompson, *Sociology of the Black Experience* (Westport, Conn.: Greenwood Press, 1974), p. 51.

8. James E. Blackwell, "The Crisis upon Us," *Social Problems* 29 (April, 1982): 333.

9. Thompson, *Sociology of the Black Experience*, p. 227.

10. Gunnar Myrdal, *An American Dilemma* (New York: Harper and Row, 1944; reprints, New York: Pantheon Books, 1975), p. 28.

11. W.E.B. Du Bois, *The Souls of Black Folk* (originally published 1903; reprinted, Nashville, Tenn.: Fisk University Press, 1979), p. 103.

12. Charles S. Johnson, *The Negro College Graduate* (Durham: University of North Carolina Press, 1938), p. 355.

13. For a comprehensive discussion of this concept, see Daniel C. Thompson, "The Black Elite," *Boulé Journal* 39 (Summer 1976): 10–18. This paper reports a study of 505 black college graduates located throughout the United States. All were recognized as community and/or national leaders. See also, W.E.B. Du Bois, "The Talented Tenth" in Booker T. Washington, et al., eds., *The Negro Problem* (reprinted, New York: Arno Press, 1969), p. 33; David McBride and Monroe H. Little, "The Afro-American Elite, 1930–1940: A Historical and Statistical Profile," *Phylon* XLII (June 1981): 105–119; and Charles P. Henry, "Ebony Elite: America's Most Influential Blacks," *Phylon* XLII (June 1981): 120–132.

14. Francis L. Broderick, *W.E.B. Du Bois* (Stanford, Calif.: Stanford University Press, 1959), pp. 50–54.

15. See, for instance, United Negro College Fund, *1985 Statistical Report*, pp. 12–14. Students in these colleges are recruited from all economic levels of the black community.

16. Correspondence, Jefferson to Adams, October 28, 1813, cited in Kenneth M.

Dolbeare, *American Political Thought* (Monterey, Calif.: Duxbury Press, 1981), pp. 192–193.

17. Ibid., p. 193.

18. Daniel C. Thompson, "Black Colleges: Continuing Challenges," *Phylon* 40 (Summer, 1979): 186.

19. John Hope Franklin, *From Slavery to Freedom* (New York: Vintage Books, 1969), pp. 202–203.

20. Johnson, *The Negro College Graduate*, pp. 7–8.

21. Dred Scott v. Sanford, 19 Howard 393 (1857).

22. Samuel DuBois Cook, "The Socio-Ethical Role and Responsibility of the Black College Graduate" in Willie and Edmonds, eds., *Black Colleges in America*, p. 55.

23. Ibid., p. 54.

24. Lorene Barnes Holmes, "Black Colleges—Miracle Workers," *Journal of Black Academia* 1, no. 1 (November 1980): 3.

25. Thompson, *Private Black Colleges at the Crossroads*, pp. 14–15.

26. E. Franklin Frazier, *Black Bourgeoisie* (New York: Collier Books, 1962), pp. 166–172.

2 Equality

The most basic and sacred principle inherent in the American Creed is that "all men [persons] are created equal," and that ipso facto government should guarantee every citizen equal rights, equal opportunities, and equal dignity.

Historically, Americans' profound belief in the essential equality of all persons has functioned as a cardinal principle impacting every established pattern of social interaction in American society and especially the structure and function of government on all levels. Historian John Hope Franklin argues that "every generation of Americans, from the very first handful in the seventeenth century, has sought to create a social order in which equity and justice, as they understood it, would prevail."[1] Indeed, the belief in equality is deeply rooted in the American mentality. It is the fountainhead of the more or less commonly shared American Dream, that any qualified, ambitious American can logically expect to ascend to the top without artificial, legal, or traditional incumbencies. Accordingly, the rags-to-riches Horatio Alger legend is still alive and widely regarded as a valid and cherished success model in American society.

So central and precious is the belief in equality that Americans on all socio-economic levels tend, characteristically, to cling tenaciously to it despite centuries of persistent, convincing, ubiquitous evidence of inveterate inequalities, and deeply entrenched and institutionalized racism.

Ironically, since equality of all persons is the cardinal principle inherent in our national culture, unwittingly the status and rights accorded black citizens have been the ultimate test of the degree to which this nation actually measures up to the lofty standards of democracy and human rights to which it is ideologically and constitutionally committed and for which it has sacrificed so much. Thus in spite of glaring contemporary contradictions, such as slavery, "Jim Crow," decades of unpunished lynchings, and unmitigated economic discrimination in both the public and private sectors, Americans of all races and socio-economic classes still tend to be steadfastly committed to the proposition that equality of all citizens is the basic value in our national culture. It is certainly the primary value this nation emphasizes when it claims the legitimate right to "leadership of the free world."

CONCEPTIONS OF EQUALITY

A PREVALENT "WHITE" CONCEPTION OF EQUALITY

John Hope Franklin calls attention to a kind of legerdemain, or mental strategy, characteristic of some whites who attempt to hold onto the principle of "equality for all," while reconciling it with crass examples of racial discrimination. Franklin maintains that such advocates generally insist that the concept "equality" be divided so that it has different meanings for whites vis–à–vis blacks. He says that "for the entire life of this nation an effort has been made to divide equality—to create a social order in which equality was enjoyed by some on the basis of race and denied to others because they did not belong to that race."[2]

This myopic, over-simplified, distorted conception of equality is based upon a mean, biracial principle whereby American society is perceived to be composed of two extended primary groups—one white and the other black. Accordingly, the rights and privileges enjoyed by individuals are determined by personal preferences, traditions, and esoteric standards of equity. Thus formal codes and objective standards of merit may be categorically rejected as vexing intrusions upon sacred, primary group values and the traditional social order.

Gunnar Myrdal, too, recognized the racially discriminatory function of this primary group conception of equality, where "white equality" is clearly distinguished from "black equality." He insisted that according to norms among whites, the "Negro genius," regardless of his preparation or the authenticity of his credentials, is "imprisoned in the Negro problem."[3] The primary group conception of equality alluded to by both Franklin and Myrdal gives rise to an in-group versus out-group principle of justice and equity which functions to frustrate and penalize ambitious, highly qualified blacks who would be on their way up in some otherwise "open" bureaucratic organizations or corporations. That is, according to basic primary group values it may be only fair, and certainly expected, that one should give preference "to his own" over those classified as outsiders. Unfortunately, this esoterically divided conception of equality may function to exclude blacks from key jobs in a variety of positions for which they qualify.

For instance, even in the most formal bureaucratic corporations, where appropriate credentials are demanded for initial employment and promotions, there may be a network of primary groups or buddy systems which have sufficient power to modify or compromise established, objective criteria of equal access and equal career mobility. As a result, a rather small number of white employees, representing various occupational ranks within a given enterprise, may systematically prevent blacks (who would naturally represent the out-group) from achieving anything like equity in the organization.

According to information provided by some of the college graduates in our study, primary or small, intimate friendship groups are prevalent in some of the corporations in which they are employed. These cliques tend to be difficult to penetrate, even by white newcomers. They are usually closed altogether to blacks who are the perennial newcomers in staff and managerial positions, and who also may be classified as outsiders simply because they are blacks—regardless of tenure, talents, and other positive qualities they might have. Several of our respondents concur with one who wrote:

> The most frustrating thing I encounter on my job is the fact that some small cliques of on-the-make white guys seem to have all of the inside information about what is or will be going on in the firm before anyone else. They know what jobs will be open or closed, and even what is going to happen to me before I do. Sometimes I feel left out and helpless.

This primary group structure within bureaucracies frustrates blacks who are pioneering in erstwhile totally white positions in large public establishments, such as the police and fire departments in cities throughout the United States, especially in the South.

In most urban places blacks constitute a much larger proportion of the total population than they do of the public service employees, or for that matter, of the staff and management in private corporations. New Orleans, Detroit, and Boston are typical examples. In these cities the proportion of blacks in the total population has been larger than their proportion employed by police and fire departments. To achieve some measure of equity, blacks are challenging these cities to take a definite, unequivocal position on the principle of affirmative action insofar as the employment and promotion of police and firemen are concerned.

The discrimination against blacks in public service employment is only a mirrored image of discrimination characteristic of various corporations in the private sector. In both public and private sectors blacks have usually held a more or less equal proportion of the menial, dead-end jobs but few of the top staff and administrative positions which require a college education or jobs which have the most promising career ladders.

While there is a tendency for disadvantages suffered by upwardly mobile blacks to accumulate, so that several factors may be cited as causes for their relatively slow and ponderous advancement in some key bureaucracies, one important cause should be emphasized here: the influence of primary groups are held together by commonly shared esoteric values. Such indigenous primary groups may become quite influential in the hiring, promotion, and salary practices in otherwise rational institutions or corporations.[4]

Frequently, primary groups within certain occupations may extend quite beyond the specific occupations in question to include a network of selected families and potential members (future employees) in the community at large, who more or less literally inherit jobs in certain public services, especially police and fire departments.

In many instances various interlocking occupational primary groups develop a sort of subculture where their strongly held esoteric values are often suspected of mitigating against the public interest when they happen to conflict with the in-group interests of fellow members. An example of this is the perennially disquieting problem of police brutality against blacks which, despite some efforts to control it, is apparently still rampant. Some doubt that the police can effectively police themselves.

The primary groups in rational bureaucracies may be instrumental in the accumulation, analysis, and distribution of information about the workings of their particular enterprises which could give their friends distinct occupational advantages insofar as initial appointments and promotions are concerned.

When blacks demand an equal proportion of available jobs on various levels of a given bureaucratic structure, they almost invariably encounter stiff, deeply entrenched resistance from white indigenous primary groups, who insist that there are whites available who have greater seniority and more acceptable credentials than the black aspirants.

Since blacks are, in fact, usually the last hired, white employees are indeed very likely to have a monopoly on positions, or ranks, where seniority is required. Consequently, just about all efforts, so far, to achieve racial equity in most large bureaucracies have had to contend with the problem of seniority on the part of whites vis-à-vis blacks.

The key problem is this: To achieve racial equity in formerly all-white, or predominantly white, establishments, it is, of course, absolutely necessary to employ and promote a larger proportion of blacks than whites. Yet when such action is taken there is always a loud cry protesting favoritism or preferential treatment of blacks. Frequently, concerned groups or individuals have formally charged would-be equal opportunity employers with reverse racial discrimination. Such charges are indeed serious because on their face they appear to be flagrant violations of the very principle of equal opportunity which black leaders, institutions, and the civil rights movement per se have been always determined to secure. As I shall point out in another connection, even black leaders in all walks of life tend to shy away from outright advocacy of preferential efforts to achieve racial equity. Furthermore, in some notable instances the charge of reverse racial discrimination has been tested in courts on all levels of the judiciary, and black litigants have generally lost.[5]

So far, despite two decades or more of persistent efforts to solve the problem of black equity in erstwhile segregated enterprises, this nation still does not have an established procedure whereby blacks may routinely expect to achieve that goal.

In commenting on the racial discrimination suit brought by black policemen in New Orleans, which has been before the courts for about ten years, Benjamin Hooks, president of the National Association for the Advancement of Colored People (NAACP), called attention to the frustrations blacks encounter in attempts to achieve equity in American society. He said that "for hundreds of years we have had a system of racism. Blacks could not apply for the police department in New Orleans. That's a historical fact; you can't hide it. You can't disguise it." Then paraphrasing a U.S. Supreme Court Justice's opinion in the Bakke case, Hooks concluded: "It may be that in order to arrive at a color-blind society that has exercised color as a law for years and years, we have to have a period where you look at color before we arrive at the ultimate solution."[6]

There will be occasions to point out later in this report that black college graduates are especially frustrated by the double meaning of equality as applied in various areas of employment. Too often, they complain, their success is measured by norms set by the less successful blacks rather than by their more successful white fellow employees. This may imply, for instance, that "as a black person, you are doing well" in terms of equal status or salary: white versus black.

The strategies black college graduates tend to employ in dealing with inequities inherent in their work situations will be of major concern throughout this report.

THE CIVIL RIGHTS CONCEPT OF "EQUALITY"

No one has defined the concept "equality" in more vivid and unequivocal terms than did Dr. Martin Luther King, Jr. In his memorable address before the great throng of perhaps 250,000 civil rights supporters in the famous March on Washington, on August 28, 1963, King spelled out a concept of equality which, he insisted, is the indispensable basis for this nation's

greatness. Essentially, to him, "equality" and "democracy" are synony-
omous concepts, or at least equality is intrinsically related to democracy.

He expressed a dream which, in retrospect, has always been at the heart
of the black civil rights movement. "One day this nation," he prophesied,
"will rise up and live out the true meaning of its creed, 'we hold these
truths to be self-evident, that all men are created equal.'...And if America
is to be a great nation this must come true."[7]

The main strategy that King and other effective black leaders have traditionally relied upon to stimulate and chide this nation toward the establishment of equality for blacks has been to point out how far the United
States actually deviates from its most cherished egalitarian norms insofar
as its black citizens are concerned. They have constantly emphasized the
idea that since this nation is in a crucial life-and-death struggle with com-
munism—the Soviet Union in particular—for the minds and loyalty of men,
it cannot afford to allow racial discrimination to tarnish its image and
undermine its role as leader of the free world.

Indeed, in a study of black leadership during the 1960s, I was struck with
the fact that "at all times Negro leaders have considered it their most
important duty to keep reminding their followers and the nation at large
of the basic democratic principles inherent in our American Creed.... 'The
New Negro leadership sounds more Jeffersonian than did Jefferson.' "[8]

The fact is, all recognized black intellectuals and spokespersons for black
organizations have generally emphasized how far this nation deviates from
its own greatly celebrated, basic norms of equality and justice for all.
Because King's dramatic interpretation of equality voiced not only blacks'
cry for equality but articulated an image of this nation of which all Americans are singularly proud, it quickly became a classic.[9]

OTHER CONCEPTIONS OF EQUALITY

In attempts to reconcile the embarrassing interrelationship of what this
nation ought to do to ensure the equality of all persons under its auspices,
and the critical degree to which it, in fact, tolerates flagrant deviations
from the avowed norms of equity inherent in the American Creed, and the
involved individuals' own sense of justice—white Americans characteristically become defensive. They are likely to assume one of the following
ethical stances:

1. Where employment policies and practices are concerned, some employers and responsible public officials simply ignore or otherwise deny
deeply entrenched racism and glaring anomalies which are categorical
contradictions of the principle of equity. This denial of racism and discrimination may be done by employers who openly or tacitly (depending
upon the reality of affirmative action agreements) set aside certain top
jobs for "whites only" for purely arbitrary reasons with little or no obvious

consideration given to the fairness or even the logic of such unequal racial distribution of economic opportunities.

2. Throughout the centuries this nation supported slavery, various forms of servitude, and Jim Crow practices. Yet there have been always prestigious white intellectuals and leaders who have literally dedicated themselves to the task of developing and defending sometimes quite elaborate pseudo-plausible, very damaging systems of apologetics especially designed to explain and justify critical ideological and practical contradictions in this nation's (and often their own) avowed commitment to the principle of equality and fairness on the one hand and obvious racial discrimination on the other. These explanations have varied all the way from the now thoroughly discredited theory of inherent white supremacy to the inane conclusion that it is "God's will" that blacks should be accorded the mudsill economic status in American society: the proverbial "hewers of wood and drawers of water."

Meritocracy

Certainly the most rational, sophisticated, and modern approach to the problem of equal opportunity is the merit system.[10] Essentially this approach is corollary to the belief that occupational hierarchies in the United States, as well as the social class structure per se, are open and that all individuals of talents and ambition are free to move up the socio-economic ladder at will, and the strong implication is that those who do not reach the top simply do not deserve to do so. As Leonard Reissman observed, "Americans of all classes have held to this belief [in unhampered social mobility] and made it a legend.... The rags to riches legend continues to remain alive and real to the cynics as to the patriots."[11] The belief in the normalcy of social mobility as an integral aspect of equality makes it logical, or ideologically sound, to view certain patterns of racial inequalities as anticipated consequences or necessary outcomes of the democratic process, rather than as discordant, contradictory aberrations from the principle of equality inherent in the American Creed.

It is, therefore, to be expected that the stubborn belief in the reality of an open social class system as characteristic of American society, where social mobility is unimpeded by sex, race, creed, color, or "previous condition of servitude," has functioned to justify certain of the most damaging patterns of racial inequalities. This is especially true when such inequalities seem to be the result of certain well-established so-called merit examinations which are purported to be fairly and scientifically designed.

During recent years, for instance, some patterns of crass racism in education and employment have been under persistent attack from several quarters, especially from some federal agencies set up to monitor equal opportunity federal contracts. Thus race as such, some insist, has been declining as the obvious cause for continuing discrimination against blacks in these areas.[12] Today, however, some of the most discriminatory racial patterns are justified in terms of the relatively poor performance of blacks on various types of standardized tests. Ironically, such tests too often provide acceptable bases and alleged scientific legitimation for maintaining patterns of racial discrimination which were originally based solely on the now discredited doctrine of white supremacy. Consequently, even now, blacks who would ordinarily be on their way up, so to speak, say that they feel challenged to prove that they actually merit the opportunity to move from one rung to the next on the career ladder. They generally agree that in the predominantly white bureaucratic structures in which some are employed, to receive promotions to top positions they feel that they must be twice as good as their white competitors.

This constant challenge to be better than their white competitors, whether real or imagined, was expressed by a significant number of our respondents who hold relatively high positions in a variety of occupations. Also, this challenge was publicly voiced by certain black journalists who are employed by white-owned newspapers.[13] One journalist, Robert Newberry, expressed the general opinion of his black colleagues in similar situations. "I have always felt that blacks had to prove themselves daily and give 110%, or be regarded as lazy, though a white colleague is not."[14] Another black journalist concluded that "white males are often promoted on the basis of potential, but minorities and women need proven ability."[15]

There seems to be at least one basic explanation for the perceived double standard of expectations where blacks are concerned. Whenever blacks are appointed to erstwhile all-white job categories, whites who aspire for these positions always raise the question of fairness, or they suspect reverse racial discrimination. Their protests may become charges which must be answered in boardrooms and in the courts. The supervisors who recommend the initial employment and/or promotion must be prepared to give sound, acceptable reasons for their actions. This might result in over-cautious hiring and promotions of blacks unless they have proven superior ability. Such practices would indeed give credence to the complaint some black observers often make that white employers, in most segments of our national economy, are primarily looking for "super," "blue chip" blacks—the legendary John Henry.

Standardized Tests

Despite the persistent contention on the part of some black scholars and spokespersons that current standardized tests are significantly weighted in favor of the white experience, as opposed to the black experience, the apparent consensus among some of the most influential white intellectuals and personnel experts seems to be that such tests should be continued because so far there is no satisfactory substitute for them in our highly developed, complex, meritocratic, industrial/post-industrial society.[16]

Therefore, a variety of standardized tests will undoubtedly continue to be used to define and modify the meaning and practice of equality, insofar as educational and occupational opportunities are concerned.

Black college graduates are keenly aware of the nature and demands of our meritocratic society, where great, deterministic emphasis is placed upon "credentials . . . in which certification of achievement through the college degree, the professional examination, the license—becomes a condition for higher employment."[17]

Thus the colleges in our sample deliberately attempt to prepare their students to compete successfully with all other students and college graduates for access to and advancement in graduate and professional schools and for available jobs in American society. The competition for which they are prepared is not conditioned by a divided meaning of the concept "equality," but the concept as understood in mainstream American society, where there is one acceptable standard of merit: color-blind excellence.

On this point Franklin concludes with an admonition:

> More than anything else, however, Americans of every race, creed, economic rank, and social position need to recognize that equality is indeed indivisible. . . . On the basis of our experiences we are now faced with the grim choice of declaring that we shall adhere to a position that equality has no place in our society and sink to a state of general degradation . . . or concede that equality is a principle so essential to . . . any civilized community that we must adhere to the principle of sharing it.[18]

The respondents in this study generally concur that they would much prefer to compete for jobs according to a single standard of merit or equality, even when they might stand to benefit immediately by a double standard which allows for preferential considerations.

Some so-called black militants, during the turbulent black civil rights struggle of the 1960s and 1970s, contended that black Americans should be accorded special privileges and assistance to compete in the economic life of the United States. Even the great black leader and diplomat, Whitney M. Young, former executive director of the National Urban League (NUL), called for a sort of "Domestic Marshall Plan" for blacks, such as the United States established to hasten the recovery of devastated western Europe after World War II. However, black leadership per se and black college graduates specifically have generally insisted that they do not want special privileges or special assistance but equal opportunities to enter and succeed or fail in all educational and economic aspects of American life.[19]

One of the respondents in this study echoed an opinion frequently expressed less directly by others:

As I see it, black people must always insist that success should result from being well-qualified and having won in competition with others. White people have had special privileges too long. Some seem to believe that they actually deserve special favors and special honors. Our young blacks must be taught to stand on their own two feet and demand respect for their rights.

SOCIAL MOBILITY

As pointed out above, even when blacks as a racial group have been ill-prepared to compete as equals in mainstream American life, college-educated black leaders or spokespersons have been most reluctant to advocate special, compensatory or preferential considerations. Generally speaking, they have taken the position that in the long run the American Creed and their own particular interests would be better served by a definite, honest shift from a system of ascription, where some individuals automatically inherit certain rights and opportunities because of their race or social class, to merited achievement, where all individuals, regardless of race or social class, are unequivocally guaranteed equal rights and equal opportunities to succeed or fail in all areas of American life. They reaffirm their position as follows:

> Since its inception, the civil rights movement, and the influential Black leaders who identified with it, have placed major emphasis on the attainment of two interdependent and logically insepar-able goals: the elimination of legal and traditional barriers to full and equal citizenship of Blacks, and Black self-improvement.[20]

Throughout the epic history of blacks in this nation, their most trusted and frequently used approach to social mobility has been formal education. Somehow, even during the darkest period of slavery, when this country was deeply involved in the slave trade, blacks became convinced that education was a pivotal, key catalyst insofar as genuine self-esteem and social mobility are concerned.

Blacks' profound faith in the efficacy of education may imply two very basic assumptions. First, they reject the label of inherent racial inferiority which was once generally propounded by whites. They always seemed convinced that once they had acquired a good education, on the level of the better educated whites, they would discredit the insulting theory of black inferiority. Second, they have maintained a naive belief that if they were well educated, they would be treated more humanely and with greater respect.[21]

Throughout blacks' long struggle for full citizenship, this faith in education as the most effective way to achieve black liberation and equal economic participation in American society has come to be an obsession on the part of black parents. From the earliest days of emancipation, when schooling for black freedmen was in its embryonic stage, to the present, blacks have been steadfast in their belief that self-improvement through education will eventually lead to equality of citizenship.

BLACK COLLEGES

The rapid growth and stability of black colleges, despite constant criticism, meager financial support, and the many unique handicaps suffered by their students, can be attributed to the faith blacks place in a good education. Black parents on the whole have manifested a willingness to make almost any sacrifice to assure their children a college education. Even during the early days of black colleges this was true. James E. Blackwell puts it this way: "So great was the value placed upon educational achievements that black mothers and fathers labored at low wages for white people in order to send their children to college and professional schools."[22]

Black colleges, then, actually symbolize blacks' (even this nation's) continuing belief in the efficacy of education as the most reliable basis for achieving the equality and democracy at the heart of the American Dream. To blacks, a good education is the ultimate equalizer. Certainly the career patterns of the college graduates in our sample reflect this conviction.

NOTES

1. John Hope Franklin, *Racial Equality in America* (Chicago: University of Chicago Press, 1976), pp. 3–4.

2. Ibid., pp. 107–108.

3. Gunnar Myrdal, *An American Dilemma*, (New York: Harper and Row, 1944; reprint, New York: Pantheon Books, 1975), p. 28. The frustrations blacks encounter when they attempt to transcend the limited range expected of the "race man" will be discussed in connection with "integrated" black leaders.

4. On the ways primary groups manage to influence the policies and practices of bureaucracies, see Fritz J. Roethlisberger and William J. Dickson, *Management and the Workers* (Cambridge, Mass.: Harvard University Press, 1959), and George C. Homans, *The Human Group* (New York: Harcourt, Brace, 1950).

5. New Orleans is an excellent example. Larry Williams et al. v. City of New Orleans. Civil Action No. 72–629 (1982).

6. "Civil Rights Heads Differ on N.O. Police Settlement," *Louisiana Weekly* newspaper (January 15, 1983): 1, 13.

7. Quoted in Flip Schulke, ed., *Martin Luther King, Jr.* (New York: W. W. Norton and Co., 1976), p. 218.

8. Daniel C. Thompson, *The Negro Leadership Class* (Englewood Cliffs, N.J.: Prentice–Hall, 1963), p. 19.

9. For an in-depth discussion, see Daniel Yankelovitch, "Who Gets Ahead in America?" in Ian Robertson, ed., *The Social World* (New York: Worth Publishers, 1981), pp. 173–179.

10. See Daniel Bell, "Meritocracy and Equality," *Public Interest* 29 (Fall 1972): 29.

11. Leonard Reissman, *Class in American Society* (New York: Free Press of Glencoe, 1959), pp. 293–294.

12. See an extensive analysis of this in William Julius Wilson, *The Declining Significance of Race* (Chicago: University of Chicago Press, 1980), pp. 167–175.

13. William A. Henry, II., "Double Jeopardy in the Newsroom," *Time Magazine*, (November 29, 1982): 59.

14. ibid.

15. ibid, 60.

16. For an in-depth discussion of this, see Charles S. Farrell, "NCAA's New Academic Standards," *Chronicle of Higher Education*, XXV, no. 20 (January 26, 1983): 1, 17–19.

17. See analytical discussion of meritocracy in Daniel Bell, *The Coming of Post-Industrial Society* (New York: Basic Books, 1973), pp. 414–436; Christopher Jencks and David Reisman, *The Academic Revolution* (Garden City, N.Y.: Doubleday and Co., 1968), pp. 121–136, 425–432; Christopher Jencks, et al., *Inequality: A Reassessment of the Effects of Family and Schooling in America* (New York: Basic Books, 1972), pp. 62–84; K. Patricia Cross, *Beyond the Open Door* (San Francisco: Jossey-Bass, 1974), pp. 117–125; and Thomas Sowell, *Black Education: Myths and Tragedies* (New York: David McKay Company, 1972), pp. 171–185.

18. Franklin, *Racial Equality in America*, pp. 107–108.

19. For a discussion of this, see Daniel C. Thompson, *Sociology of the Black Experience*, (Westport, Conn.: Greenwood Press, 1974) pp. 13–18. See also Daniel C. Thompson, "The Black Elite," *Boulé Journal* 39 (Summer 1976): 16–17.

20. Thompson, *Sociology of the Black Experience*, p. 13.

21. Henry A. Bullock, *A History of Negro Education in the South*, (Cambridge, Mass.: Harvard University Press, 1967), pp. 24–35.

22. James E. Blackwell, *The Black Community: Diversity and Unity* (New York: Dodd, Mead & Co., 1975), pp. 71–72.

3 Social Origins

The great majority of black college graduates have come from rather non-descript, humble homes in the South where their parents have received a high school education or less and either have been or presently are employed in low-status, blue-collar jobs, with below-average wages.[1] The significant amount of social mobility on the part of the alumni of black colleges, such as that represented in our sample, can be attributed directly to the formal education they have acquired. In most instances, as will be discussed in another context, they are the first members of their families who have made it to middle-class socio-economic status and above.

Because blacks, as a race, have espoused education as absolutely essential to their individual and group survival and advancement, it has been always a sort of "holy crusade" which has attracted an unusually large core of furiously dedicated and highly competent teachers. Thus despite relatively low salaries and often substandard working conditions, these colleges have been able to attract and retain such renowned teachers as W.E.B. Du Bois, Booker T. Washington, Thurgood Marshall, E. Franklin Frazier, Charles S. Johnson, George Washington Carver, Frederick D. Hall, Benjamin E. Mays, Willa B. Player, Joseph Dennis, and a host of other truly great teachers, many of whom are still on the faculties of these colleges.

The most effective teachers on the faculties of black colleges perform at least two closely related functions. First, they set and maintain excellent academic standards. They consciously attempt to prepare their students to compete as equals to graduates of the most affluent, prestigious colleges. Second, they present themselves as models of "how to make it" as a black in an often hostile, inherently racist American society. Actually, the most prevalent characteristic of effective black college teachers is that they inspire their students to believe that they have the ability and knowledge to transcend the racial barriers they are likely to encounter as they move toward the mainstream of our complex, demanding, meritocratic society.[2]

Generally speaking, the black college graduates in this study regard their education as basically serving two fundamental purposes. First, it is a means whereby they are personally prepared to compete for educational and career advancement. Second, they tend to link their own desire and efforts for personal advancement with blacks' overall struggle for respect and equality. For instance, a young physician in our sample was among the first blacks to be accorded a high position on the staff of an affluent white hospital. In expressing his opinion of his new pioneering role, he confided:

> I tried very hard to fit into the activities of the hospital. I knew that some top people in the profession were watching me. I felt that some of them expected me to fail. Others wanted me to be a perfect showcase black. In either case I felt that if I did well I would be opening doors for other blacks, if I didn't I would be closing doors which were just beginning to open for us.

He validates Gunnar Myrdal's observation that a primary function of black college graduates as a group is that of opening doors for other blacks by proving to skeptical white officials and employers that if blacks are given equal opportunity they can compete successfully with the so-called better classes of whites.[3]

Blacks' strongly felt need to prove their personal and racial equality is a creative response to the numerous negative black stereotypes inherent in American lore. In spite of the tenuousness of these stereotypes, they still persist, embarrass, and frustrate blacks' efforts to gain the respect and equality they deserve in various areas of American life.

Well-educated, upwardly mobile blacks tend to reject the representative racial role often thrust upon them, because it is theoretically unsound and particularly burdensome. They are, however, frequently forced willy-nilly to accept it. As more or less reluctant black representatives, they have in fact helped to discredit or unmask some very damaging stereotypes which have functioned to explain or justify widespread discrimination in some major occupations.[4]

PLACE OF BIRTH

Respondents to our mailed questionnaire were born and reared in just about all states in this nation, with 1 percent to 2 percent coming from foreign countries. However, the vast majority, or 80 percent, were born and reared in the South, the former slave states. Although today there is a trend toward an increase in the proportion of students from states outside the South, still more than two-thirds, or 64.6 percent of the students in the UNCF colleges are native southerners.[5]

Any valid interpretation of the academic and career patterns of the college-educated blacks in this study must take special account of the fact that most of them were born in states where throughout their histories white social power figures, lily-white institutions, and various indigenous white supremist organizations (the Ku Klux Klan, the White Citizens Council, etc.) have traditionally conspired to prevent, at all costs, any significant social mobility of blacks. As a result of anti-black forces, it is a notorious fact that the general status of blacks in the South, especially before the late 1960s when just about all of our respondents were born, represented the most serious contradiction to the principle of freedom and equality to which this nation is dedicated. The total culture of the South was organized along racial lines meticulously drawn to accord by customs, mores, and laws all white people to the upper or superior status, and to relegate all blacks, regardless of their talents or achievements, to the lower or inferior status.

The essentially unjust and punitive nature of the white supremacy tradition, which was long regarded as a sacred principle to be adhered to in absolutely all areas of race relations, and which still remains viable, at least as a sub-rosa principle, was given a classic definition and interpretation by Henry W. Grady of Georgia.

Grady, who was certainly the most influential and eloquent spokesman for the celebrated "New South" concept around the turn of the century, insisted that the New South, which he envisioned as a leader in industrial development, cultural affairs, and prosperity, with great national political power, would have to be a Solid South based upon the unshakable principle of white supremacy. Grady stated the proposition this way: "the supremacy of the white race must be maintained forever. ...southern whites have agreed everywhere to sink their differences on moral and economic issues and present solid and unbroken ranks to this alien and dangerous element."[6]

Lerone Bennett Jr.'s perceptive summary of Grady's position on the issue of white supremacy calls special attention to five major points made by Grady in numerous speeches throughout the United States:

1. White people in the North and South must unite on a common racial platform: white supremacy.

2. There must be no agitation on the race question.

3. The Negro must remain in his "ordained place," for "what God hath separated let no man join together."

4. The Negro must abandon politics and accept the clear and unmistakable domination of the white man.

5. Negro leadership must accept, support, and sustain the racial policies of the white power structure.[7]

The rigid patterns of racial segregation and discrimination characteristic of the South in which most of our respondents were socialized definitely fostered the development of some invidious stereotypes which, as Myrdal observed, pictured blacks "as stupid, immoral, diseased, incompetent, and dangerous—dangerous to the white man's values and total control of the social order."[8]

These widely propagandized black stereotypes usually went unchallenged, with little or no systematic rebuttal from the few black intellectuals of that time (1865–1930). Actually, it was not until the 1930s that the number of black intellectuals was large enough to deal effectively with the many stereotypes fabricated by anti-black southern spokesmen. Scholars in black colleges, led by such sound social science researchers as W.E.B. Du Bois, Charles S. Johnson, and E. Franklin Frazier, began writing and publishing scholarly papers, graduate theses, and dissertations which served to unmask some of the ancient myths and damaging stereotypes which, in the minds of white supremists, justified the existing "caste system" that was deliberately designed to victimize blacks and severely restrict their educational and occupational mobility.[9]

THE COMPENSATORY ROLE OF BLACK COLLEGES

The colleges represented in this study have always openly dealt with the unique socio-economic handicaps their students and graduates face because of their race. For example, they have developed, at relatively great expense, compensatory (remedial) academic courses and programs carefully designed to provide their students with the level of college preparatory knowledge they should have received in segregated public schools but did not. Studies reveal that

> from half to three-fourths or more of the freshmen students in these colleges require some significant amount of remedial instruction if they are expected to achieve according to national norms....Extensive data underscore the fact that most Black children have been victimized by tragically inadequate, criminally inferior education—from kindergarten through high school.[10]

All of the UNCF colleges have, in one way or another, adopted as one of their central objectives, and an inherent aspect of their mission, that of providing their students with special preparation (e.g., beyond ordinary academic experiences) intended to help them deal effectively with the unique problems associated with being black in the United States, and especially in the South. In other words, students in these colleges are prepared to cope with racism, as well as with the disciplined academic information expected of all college graduates. The mission statements of Dillard University and Morehouse College well express the official race relations stance of the forty-three UNCF colleges. Dillard University states that it "seeks to aid students.... In meeting with understanding and decision, the acute problems which they currently face by virtue of their racial identity, and in developing a perspective of race relations in America and in the world."[11] Morehouse College's mission statement also reflects a central concern with racism and the special preparation its students will need to cope with it as they move toward graduate education and employment. Objective number 4 is a key statement of the college's race relations posture: "Acquainting students with the history, culture, and problems of black people and developing leaders qualified to make intelligent approaches to the problems of black people at the local, state, regional, national, and world levels."[12]

The continuing need of black colleges to prepare their students to deal effectively with the problems stemming from white racism is succinctly reflected in a speech Samuel DuBois Cook made before the Dillard community shortly after he accepted the presidency of Dillard University. He proclaimed that "the first and foremost goal...is academic excellence at Dillard.... Blackness is not enough; we must be good! Indeed, we must be commandingly competent precisely because we are black."[13] Ideally, then, students in UNCF colleges are consciously prepared to transcend racial handicaps by being "commandingly competent" insofar as understanding the nature of racism and by developing excellent, competitive academic and occupational skills. It is in this context that the achievements of the college graduates in this study should be interpreted. The respondents in this study have been consciously prepared to deal intelligently, even creatively, with certain debilitating, derogatory racial stereotypes, and with the complex, unique demands and frustrations associated with blacks' social mobility efforts, especially in the South where the racial handicaps have come to focus. Truly, any significant degree of upward social mobility for the majority of southern-born, college-educated blacks has been no easy task. In some instances, especially until a decade or so ago, blacks' struggle for self-improvement and socio-economic advancement has been a social example of what it means to "make bricks without straw," a frustrating and unrewarding experience.

BLACK MIGRATION

As pointed out above, about 80 percent of the college graduates in our sample were born and reared in the South. It is, therefore, significant that despite family ties and the large number of white-collar and professional positions in black institutions, businesses, and other areas, only 61 percent of the college educated still reside in the South. This bears out an important factor: a significant number of the college-educated blacks, like the poor, unskilled black masses, have sought to advance their overall socio-economic status by migrating to large cities outside the South. They, too, have regarded the North or West as the land of greater opportunities for blacks.

Since the dramatic beginning of blacks' Great Migration from farms, towns, and cities of the South in the wake of World War I, the trend to move North has been sustained, although at an uneven rate. While approximately 90 percent of all black Americans lived in the South in 1910, today only about 52 percent live in the South. During a three-decade period (1940–1970), at least 1.5 million blacks migrated from the South.[14]

It is a fact that some blacks who migrated North did find it to be a "land of promise" and greater opportunities. Some of them greatly improved their economic and social status and found better schools for their children. There were many others, however, who simply did not make it. Some actually encountered the same degree and kinds of discrimination and job ceilings they had experienced in the South.[15]

Actually, the great majority of black migrants after World War I were concentrated in the least desirable jobs, resided in the poorest and most isolated neighborhoods, and possessed little or no social power to improve their lot. Though they escaped from the legally supported system of segregation of the South, they encountered new forms of discrimination and disesteem in the North. Ironically, the overall status of the great masses of black migrants in large northern ghettos between World War I and World War II may have represented the ultimate nadir in blacks' long, frustrating struggle to survive and to achieve a significant level of security and social power in American society.

In some basic respects the more or less anomic conditions experienced by the economically poor, unskilled, inadequately schooled, largely unorganized blacks in large northern ghettos between World Wars I and II, were strikingly similar to conditions faced by their ancestors in the South immediately following the Civil War and the emancipation of slaves. Only this time the leaders of the twentieth-century "Black Reconstruction" were not white humanitarians and northern church bodies, but college-educated black leaders who founded much-needed relevant black churches, social agencies, newspapers, businesses, and social or service societies, all specifically designed to bring a significant degree of unity and purpose to the black community. These organizations became the foundation of a "New Negro," which clearly and boldly articulated a new, militant, aggressive, creative black identity.[16]

It is, indeed, interesting to note that some of the more influential of the black preachers, teachers, and other intellectuals who came North in the

Table 1
Education of Parents

Level of Education	Father	Mother
Less than high school	61%	50%
High school	24%	32%
Baccalaureate degree	8%	12%
Graduate/professional degree	7%	6%

wake of the Great Migration became the parents and grandparents of some of today's very class-conscious black elite, who represent the most successful blacks in American society.[17]

FAMILY BACKGROUND

The most valid measure of upward social mobility in any given society is the degree to which the status of adult children is superior to the status of their parents. In this connection I shall employ three basic criteria as key indicators of social status: level of schooling, rank and prestige of occupation, and annual income.

Just about all experts in the behavioral sciences concur that parents' educational attainments significantly influence the educational and occupational achievements of their children.[18] Simply put, the basic hypothesis is that the greater the educational and occupational level of the parents, the greater will be the educational and occupational achievements of their children. Stated another way, children from economically poor homes where the parents have received below-average schooling have relatively limited chances of educational and occupational success as adults.

Of course, the hypothesis above is over-simplified and exaggerated by such popular cliches as "the apple does not fall far from the tree" and "the child is the father of the man." However, while the numerous hypotheses and analyses of data regarding the relationship of parents' socio-economic status vis-à-vis the attainments of their children are complex and many-sided, the essential conclusion is generally the same. Children, especially black children, of parents with little formal schooling and employed in blue-collar jobs will be severely disadvantaged in competition with their peers from well-educated, affluent backgrounds.

Despite the heavy odds against it, at least 82–85 percent of the college graduates in our study have received a higher level of education than either of their parents.[19] Actually, some of the most successful of the black college graduates came from homes where both parents had only an elementary school education or less (see Table 1), and were employed in marginal

Table 2
Occupation of Parents

Occupations	Father	Mother
Blue collar	57%	28%
White collar, professional and business not specified	18%	22%
Retired, housewife, etc.	25%	50%

Table 3
Annual Family Income of Parents When Subjects Entered College

Under $10,000	67%
$10,000–19,999	22%
$20,000–29,999	7%
$30,000–50,000	3%
$50,000 and over	1%

blue-collar jobs (see Table 2) with annual wages often below the poverty level as set by federal agencies.

The majority of respondents in this study entered college during the late 1950s and early 1960s. At that time, more than two-thirds of them (at least 67 percent), came from homes where their parents were employed in low-status jobs and where the median family income was considerably below $10,000 annually (see Table 3). The recruitment policies of the sample colleges seem to remain the same, and the vast majority of their students still come from economically disadvantaged homes. Thus, the median family income of the 1984 freshman class in these colleges was still only $16,200 or just over half the $30,400 median for freshmen nationally.[20]

Further, only 4 percent of the respondents came from families with an annual income of $30,000 and over. And even recently, with the average national income considerably inflated, only 22 percent of the 1984 freshman class came from families with annual incomes of $30,000 and over. While half of the students in UNCF colleges come from homes where the total annual income is below $16,200, at least half of the students in American colleges at large come from homes where the annual income is almost twice that, or $30,400, and fully 51 percent of the students in American colleges come from homes with incomes of $30,000 and over.[21]

SIGNIFICANCE OF SOCIAL ORIGIN

The colleges represented in this study have traditionally recruited students from all socio-economic classes in the black community. Because they have been always committed to the task of providing higher education for academically and economically disadvantaged blacks, the great majority of their students have come from lower socio-economic class homes. Many of them graduated from the lowest-ranking high schools in their respective communities, and often grew up in some more or less isolated, under-organized, politically powerless black neighborhoods where the day-by-day way of life was likely to differ in some important respects from the ideal white middle-class or mainstream American culture.[22]

According to our findings, at least 60 percent of the graduates of the sample colleges were reared in homes where their parents were under-employed in low-status, blue-collar jobs and had acquired considerably less than a high school education; only 15 percent of the fathers and 18 percent of the mothers had graduated from college.

Even in 1982, when the majority of all college students in the United States came from homes where the median annual income was $26,800 and more than 43 percent came from homes in the $30,000-and-over range, the great majority of students in UNCF colleges came from homes where the median annual income was about half the national average, or $13,700, and a mere 16 percent came from homes in the $30,000-and-over range.[23]

According to research findings, the parents of approximately 80 percent of our respondents a generation ago were much too poor and too academically limited to be expected to encourage their children to place high value on formal education and sufficiently motivate them to make almost any sacrifice to do well in school. Certainly they would not be expected to prepare their children to go on to graduate or professional schools and finally to compete successfully for some high-status occupation with challenging career opportunities. Yet as we shall see subsequently, this is precisely the academic and career scenario characteristic of the graduates of UNCF colleges.

Furthermore, several systematic studies of the academic and career aspirations of college-bound and beginning college students have found that the aspirations of black college students, even those from the poorest homes, are often impressively higher than the aspirations of their white peers from affluent homes.[24]

The high academic and occupational aspirations and achievements of the black college graduates in our sample are certainly in sharp contradiction to social mobility expectations based upon some prevalent research findings. For instance, after an exhaustive analysis of traditional patterns of social mobility in the United States, Stephan Therstrom concluded:

The mere fact of being born into a middle-class or working-class home still profoundly influences the life chances of every American—his prospects of obtaining a college education, finding a good job, living in decent housing, even the prospects of enjoying mental and physical health and living to an advanced age.[25]

Therstrom finally concluded that very few children of working-class parents ever rose very far up the occupational and social scale, even during the period of very rapid industrial expansion in the United States.

A number of other prominent sociologists have reaffirmed the general conclusion that the socio-economic status of adult offspring in the United States is seldom much higher than that of their parents. An extensive review of research findings concerning career patterns of fathers and sons concluded that "more important in evaluating the 'rags to riches' myth is the fact that while many sons experience *some* mobility, very few experience *much*. They move, but not far....Most sons work at either the same occupational level or one immediately adjacent to that of their fathers."[26]

The central, most significant finding of this study is quite clear: the socio-economic status achieved by the college-educated blacks in our sample, on the whole, is far beyond the level that may have been rationally expected of them. The fact is, the considerable academic and occupational success attained by the representative respondents in our sample is a diametrical contradiction to the basic findings of sound social research that children are not likely to move far from the academic or occupational level of their parents. Nevertheless, not only have most of the black college graduates in this study moved far beyond their parents, but as will be discussed later, their overall success is indeed comparable to that of their white peers from much more affluent socio-economic backgrounds.

THE BASIC QUESTION

How can we account for the fact that, contrary to some expert observations and predictions that American children seldom move far above the socio-economic level of their parents, the vast majority of our sample of college graduates have been able to transcend the many negative social forces inherent in their backgrounds to the extent that they have been able to compete as equals in mainstream American society and have achieved a socio-economic status much higher than that of their parents? The answer to this question is indeed complex and must ultimately take into account the nature and development of the black subculture in the United States.

Essentially, blacks' unique thirst for formal education and the efficacy they have traditionally placed in it, as well as their surprisingly high level of occupational aspirations, stem from their perennial need to struggle for survival and dignity against great odds. The uniqueness of blacks' epic struggle "to be somebody" is due mainly to the cultural setting in which they have been required to prove their worth over and over again, and to reaffirm their humanity according to firmly established white norms, where the culture fosters deep-seated skepticism about blacks' inherent ability as individuals and as a group.

Their urgent, persistent need to prove themselves, according to the late professor Henry A. Bullock, began during the earliest days of slavery when the newly transplanted Africans had their initial interracial experiences in America with wealthy, educated white families. Bullock surmised that the captive Africans must have suffered, to an exaggerated degree, the confusion and feeling of utter inadequacy common to strangers in a foreign land, where they are unable to communicate effectively with the natives. This feeling would, of course, be greatly exacerbated by the fact that the slaves were owned by these strangers who literally had the power of life and death over them. It is logical then that their top-priority survival strategy would be to learn to speak and read the language of their captors. Furthermore, Bullock believes that in some important respects the slaves actually admired some of the qualities of the master class, such as their learning, manners, and self-confidence. The "house-slaves," at least, often came to identify with the wealthy, better-educated white masters and sincerely wanted to be like them. Bullock surmised:

> In many instances psychological identification with the master class and its high-toned ways was firmly internalized by those slaves who had access to these experiences.... They thought that being able to read and write made them quality people, and they used all opportunities to become literate and informed that the system afforded them.[27]

Bullock later concluded, "By the time of their emancipation, almost all of them had come to believe that those qualities of white people which they admired so much and tried so hard to emulate had resulted from formal education and that they too could acquire them if they once got the necessary schooling."[28]

The compelling need felt by black slaves to develop and emulate certain qualities characteristic of powerful, special-privileged whites has tended to persist to some degree among blacks ever since. Its persistence results from powerful social forces inherent in a Jim Crow–dominated American society which conspired to preserve certain white qualities and to make them a condition for blacks' survival and advancement. Even now some upwardly mobile blacks apparently feel challenged to be culturally whiter than whites, in response to unspoken, sub-rosa racial prescriptions which they perceive as nevertheless real insofar as their own socio-economic aspirations are concerned.

Consequently, some blacks, such as those in our sample, have strong aspirations and strive to succeed not only far beyond the level attained by their parents but also beyond the level expected of their more affluent white peers. This, then, is a creative response deeply implanted in the black subculture and is deliberately and vigorously nurtured and enhanced by the UNCF colleges constituting our sample.

Basically, since several other avenues of social mobility and advancement open to whites such as the acquisition of substantial wealth, acquiring effective political power, and the shrewd manipulation of social class opportunities and prerogatives have been traditionally closed or severely limited for blacks, they have had no reliable avenue of advancement except through education.

Fortunately, formal education, whose basic values are intrinsic in the American Creed, has worked for blacks. It has certainly proven to be blacks' most consistently reliable means of survival and advancement. Since blacks as a race have been conditioned by unique historical circumstances to be a pragmatic people, it is logical to expect that they will continue to rely primarily upon formal education as a means of achieving the long-sought-after equal socio-economic status in American society. Black colleges, therefore, will continue to be the main, essential gateway through which blacks from all social origins in the United States will enter and succeed in mainstream American society.

NOTES

1. United Negro College Fund, *1985 Statistical Report*, p. 5.

2. For a systematic discussion of this, see Daniel C. Thompson, "Black College Faculty and Students: The Nature of Their Interaction," in Charles V. Willie and Ronald R. Edmonds, eds., *Black Colleges in America* (New York: Columbia University, Teachers College Press, 1978), pp. 181–184.

3. Gunnar Myrdal, *An American Dilemma* (New York: Harper and Row, 1944; reprint; New York: Pantheon Books, 1975), p. 879.

4. A truly classic example of this is the case of Jackie Robinson's desegregation of big-league baseball during the 1940s. His impressive demonstration that talented blacks could make it in big-league sports opened the door so that today sports is perhaps the most integrated institution in America.

5. United Negro College Fund, *1985 Statistical Report*, p. 5.

6. Henry W. Grady, *The New South and Other Addresses* (New York: Robert Bonner and Sons, 1890), pp. 104, 242–243.

7. Lerone Bennett, Jr., *Confrontation: Black and White* (Chicago: Johnson Publishing Co. 1968), pp. 87–88.

8. Myrdal, *An American Dilemma*, pp. 100–101.

9. St. Clair Drake, "The Social and Economic Status of the Negro in the United

States" in Talcott Parsons and Kenneth B. Clark, eds., *The American Negro* (Boston: Houghton Mifflin, 1966), pp. 3–5.

10. Daniel C. Thompson, *Private Black Colleges at the Crossroads* (Westport, Conn.: Greenwood Press, 1973), pp. 198–199.

11. Dillard University, *Bulletin*, 1982–1984, p. 17; see also, previous *Bulletins*, "objective 8."

12. Morehouse College, *Catalog*, 1983–1985, p. 3, "objective 4."

13. Samuel DuBois Cook, *Promises To Keep* (New Orleans: Dillard University, 1974), p. 2.

14. U.S. Department of Commerce, Bureau of the Census, *The Social and Economic Status of the Black Population in the United States, 1970–1978*, series p–23, no. 80, p. 7.

15. St. Clair Drake and Horace R. Cayton, *Black Metropolis* (New York: Harper and Row, 1945), pp. 112, 223–228; William Julius Wilson, *The Declining Significance of Race*, (Chicago: University of Chicago Press, 1980), pp. 65–76; and Daniel C. Thompson, *Sociology of the Black Experience* (Westport, Conn.: Greenwood Press, 1974), pp. 139–156. See especially Kenneth B. Clark, *Dark Ghetto* (New York: Harper and Row, 1965), pp. 21–26, and Barbara Guillory Thompson, "The Black Family: A Case for Change and Survival in America," Ph.D. diss., Tulane University, New Orleans, 1974.

16. For a comprehensive examination of the "New Negro,'" see Melvin Drimmer, *Black History* (Garden City, N.Y.: Anchor Books, 1969), pp. 410–421.

17. See, for example, Alice Randall and Stanley Tretick, "Washington's Other Elite," *Washingtonian*, May 1982, 111–119; Cathy L. Connors and John Bowen, "New York's Black Elite," *Town and Country*, September 1982, 222–229, 295–306; Lawrence Wright, "Easy Street; Houston's Black Elite," *Texas Monthly*, November 1982, 174–181, 285–292; and Marylouise Oates, "Black Society in Los Angeles," *Los Angeles Times*, June 27, 1982, 1, 12–13.

18. For a systematic summary of research findings regarding this topic, see Frederick Mosteller and Daniel P. Moynihan, eds., *On Equality of Educational Opportunity* (New York: Random House, 1972), pp. 254–269.

19. The considerable odds against this have been analyzed by William G. Goode, "Family and Mobility" in Reinhard Bendix and Seymour Martin Lipset, eds., *Class, Status, and Power* (New York: Free Press, 1966), p. 591; see especially Horace Mann Bond, *Black American Scholars* (Detroit: Belamp, 1972), pp. 32–56.

20. United Negro College Fund, *1985 Statistical Report*, p. 12.

21. Ibid.

22. For a vivid description of the black Ghetto subculture, see St. Clair Drake, "Social and Economic Status of the Negro in the United States," *Daedalus* 94 (Fall 1965): 777–778. See also Daniel C. Thompson, "Teaching the Culturally Disadvantaged," *Speaking about Teaching* (New York: College Entrance Examination Board, 1967), pp. 51–74.

23. United Negro College Fund, *1982 Statistical Report*, pp. 11–12.

24. For an extensive examination of this phenomenon, see Mosteller and Moynihan, eds., *On Equality of Educational Opportunity*, pp. 25–27. See also United Negro College Fund, *1985 Statistical Report*, p. 3.

25. Stephan Therstrom, "Class Mobility in a Nineteenth Century City," in Bendix and Lipset, eds., *Class, Status, and Power*, p. 614.

26. Kimball Young and Raymond Mack, *Sociology and Social Life* (New York: American Book Co., 1965), pp. 186–187. See also Bond, *Black American Scholars*, pp. 32–56. In this study Bond insists that black children tend to inherit the social class advantages and disadvantages of their parents: "The apple does not fall far from the tree."

27. Henry Allen Bullock, *A History of Negro Education in the South*, Cambridge: Harvard University Press, 1970), pp. 9–10.

28. Ibid, p. 169.

4 Education

The very familiar and challenging slogan of the UNCF is "A mind is a terrible thing to waste." This slogan reflects two basic, interrelated realities which have shaped and guided much of the black experience in the United States: First, blacks' profound and abiding faith in the efficacy of formal education, the systematic cultivation of the mind, as the most estimable means of achieving racial survival and advancement in American society. Second, blacks' perennial fear that their children will be denied the amount and quality of education they will need vis-à-vis the complex racial handicaps they face in their struggle for equality in mainstream American society.

The UNCF slogan, therefore, brings to dramatic focus a primary concern of all effective black leaders—that the intellectual potential and talents of far too many blacks will remain undiscovered, underdeveloped, and wasted because of undereducation and miseducation.

This central concern was clearly and forcefully enunciated by the towering black intellectual, W.E.B. Du Bois, on several memorable occasions during his long and fruitful career as a scholar and social activist. Some indication of Du Bois' deep concern about the amount and quality of education provided black children and his well-founded conviction that they were not getting the education they deserved, and of which they were capable, is expressed in the following litany:

> My brothers and dark sisters; educate your children. Give them the broadest and highest education possible; train them to the limit of their ability.... Never forget that if we ever compel the world's respect, it will be by virtue of our heads and not our

heels.... Train them so that in the day of sundered bonds they can take their place beside their fellows and not be held back then by ignorance as they are now by prejudice.[1]

After eloquently admonishing black parents to make almost any sacrifice to see that their children received the very best education of which they were capable, Du Bois then expressed the corollary fear that white-controlled public school systems were not providing the kinds and quality of education black children must have in order to overcome the generations of personal and racial restrictions and disesteem to which they have been brutally subjected. He protested that "as a race we are still kept in ignorance far below the average standard of this nation, and of the present age, and the ideals set before our children in most cases are far below their possibilities and reasonable promise."[2]

At the same time that Du Bois gave us a brilliant insight into blacks' profound faith in the efficacy of formal education as a means of achieving equality and respect, he quickly called attention to the fact that the education of far too many black children was woefully neglected. He therefore articulated both aspects of the perennial concern expressed by the UNCF slogan that the minds and special talents of black children and ultimately their potential services to their race and age will be wasted unless special efforts are made to discover and develop them.

Unfortunately, Du Bois' scathing criticism of the relatively low quality of public education provided black children seven decades ago is still amazingly apropos today. Despite the fact that a sound, broad education is increasingly essential to any significant level of predictable success in our complex, rapidly changing technological society, Bernard Watson's well-informed evaluation is that even today public schools throughout this nation are still allowing the precious potential of the great majority of black children to lie fallow, underdeveloped, and too often totally wasted. He puts it this way: "The quality of education provided black children is nothing short of a national scandal, an absolute disgrace.... High school graduates unable to read, write or perform mathematical functions at the sixth grade level.... Truancy is epidemic, psychological or physical dropping-out commonplace."[3]

In evaluating the quality of public school education generally provided black children, especially those in inner-city schools, a respondent in this study, who is a top official in a large city public school system, categorically concluded that

Black children in "all black" and "predominantly black" public schools are wittingly or unwittingly programmed for mediocrity. They are too often regarded as uneducable by their teachers and are seldom challenged to perform on high levels of schol-

arship. It is a frustrating situation: Children who need the very
best education are getting the worst.

Again, the critical assessments of the relatively poor, inadequate quality
of public school education traditionally provided black children is strongly
supported by the research findings of M. Lee Montgomery. He points out
that 60 percent of black students who graduate from inner-city high schools
are functionally illiterate. He carefully examined the several reasons teachers and school administrators usually give to explain this nationally embarrassing phenomenon. Generally they are defensive, in the sense that
they tend to insist that their schools are already doing everything professionally possible to discover and cultivate the minds of black children, but
they argue that most of the students seem to be too socially and culturally
disadvantaged to respond positively.

Montgomery concludes that the low quality of education provided for
far too many black children is due to the fact that they are not expected
to perform on high academic levels; they are seldom challenged to achieve
to the highest levels of their abilities. "Every black child," he insists, "has
a constant battle to keep from being shunted aside as incapable of learning."[4]

The gloomy picture of the quality of education provided black youth as
presented above is validated and underscored by the authoritative report
published by the National Commission on Excellence in Education. According to this report, "our greatest resource—and the greatest resource
of any nation—is the education of its people." At the same time, "more
and more young people emerge from high school ready neither for college
nor for work. This predicament becomes more acute as the knowledge
base continues its rapid expansion, the number of jobs shrinks, and new
jobs demand greater sophistication and preparation." It is obvious that "a
high level of shared education is essential to a free, democratic society
and to the fostering of a common culture." It is, therefore, a "national risk"
that "the educational foundations of our society are presently being eroded
by a rising tide of mediocrity that threatens our very future as a nation
and a people." Thus, for example, "about 13 percent of all 17-year-olds in
the United States can be considered functionally illiterate. Functional il-
literacy among minority youth may run as high as 40 percent."[5]

The report just quoted confirms and emphasizes the urgency of the UNCF
slogan that "a mind is a terrible thing to waste." Not only does a low quality
of education have negative consequences for the life chances of the individuals involved, but it endangers the nation in a much larger, far-reaching sense. Far too many of this nation's children, especially black children,
are simply not getting the knowledge, the skills, and the values which made
this nation great in the first place and which are essential to its continuing
strength and greatness.

THE SOCIAL ROLE OF UNCF-AFFILIATED COLLEGES

The essential social role of the colleges represented in this study, like any group of colleges, is complex. The central role or ultimate mission of all institutions of higher learning is to enhance, enrich, and communicate, directly and indirectly, all aspects of knowledge of the society of which they are a part. This is done primarily by preparing individuals to perform the various jobs which must be done in a modern civilized society, and by preserving, enriching, and extending cultural continuity.

In addition to the general social role or mission shared with all institutions of higher learning, black colleges have always had a special, unique mission thrust upon them by blacks' peculiar status in American society. Unlike some comparable white private colleges, "black colleges have never enjoyed the luxury of admitting only those students adjudged to be middle class or middle class oriented.... The very opposite is more often true: The great majority of students enrolled in the sample colleges come from the 'wrong side of the track.'"[6] Thus, a primary social role of black colleges has been always to seek out and cultivate the minds of black youths from all areas of society, especially those whose talents might be otherwise wasted. Consequently, any truly valid interpretation of the colleges studied herein must take into account their unique social role in higher education.

All too often students enrolled in black colleges have been recipients or victims of inferior, inadequate schooling on some or all levels from the first through the twelfth grades. Characteristically, they will have experienced a well-documented common scenario. They received careless, uninspiring, often inferior training in the early elementary grades which successively triggered a series of relatively low academic performances throughout later grades. Thus, there resulted a measurable, cumulative negative effect. The longer they remained in school the farther they fell behind grade norms. That is, some who entered first grade, for example, had performance levels three or four months below their grade level and often fell progressively below academic norms so that by the time they completed the twelfth grade they were able to perform only on the eighth- or ninth-grade level—three to four years below the level of academic expectations.

There are certainly several reasons why black colleges may have been compelled to practice what often amounts to a modified form of open enrollment.[7] The fundamental, abiding reason, however, has always been the critical need to make these colleges accessible to poor, often inadequately trained, black high school graduates whose minds and talents might be otherwise wasted. Therefore, a major social role of the sample colleges has been that of creative intervention in the intellectual development of a cross section of black students, especially those from disadvantaged back-

Table 4
Racial Composition of High Schools Attended by Respondents

All black	79%
Predominantly black	4%
Predominantly white	13%
Regarded as racially balanced	4%

grounds, to prevent an inevitable, disastrous waste of this nation's human resources.

GRADUATES OF UNCF MEMBER COLLEGES

It is important to remember that the median age of the respondents in our sample is forty-three. A majority of them were in public school during the late 1940s and 1950s when racial segregation in the South was mandated by laws and traditions and was a more or less de facto reality throughout the United States. The pattern of this biracial system of education is reflected in Table 4.

As may also be seen in Table 4, 79 percent of the respondents in the sample attended all-black high schools, with 4 percent coming from predominantly black high schools. The vast majority, 81 percent, of those in these two categories attended high schools in the South, when there was no serious effort underway to make black schools equal to white schools. A segregated black grade school in the 1940s and 1950s was likely to be inferior to the segregated white schools in the same community or region.[8] As a rule, especially in the South, schools designated for black children were notoriously inferior to schools designated for white children. The overall inferior quality of black schools is so well-documented that it has been seldom denied, even by white officials bent upon preserving them. The goal of "separate but equal" was never seriously attempted. It was always a mocking cliche, a tantalizing myth.

Legally segregated black public schools lacking the financial and social support needed to provide a high quality of education, or at least a quality of education comparable to that provided for white children, always functioned as a badge of black inferiority. The myth of inherent black inferiority was supported by a well-knit system of stereotypes (discussed in Chapter 3), the cardinal one being that blacks are mentally inferior. This myth was effectively used to rationalize inferior schools for blacks, because it implied that blacks could not learn on the same level as whites.

The function of the black inferiority myth in the maintenance of inferior schools for black children, was insightfully interpreted by Robert K. Merton, of Columbia University, in the context of "self-fulfilling prophecy." He pointed out:

> If the dominant in-group believes that Negroes are inferior, and
> sees to it that funds for education are not "wasted on these
> incompetents" and then proclaims as final evidence of this in-
> feriority that Negroes have proportionately "only" one-fifth as
> many college graduates as whites, one can scarcely be amazed
> by this transparent bit of social legerdemain.[9]

Therefore, as long as black and white children attended separate schools, prejudiced whites could conveniently hold onto the racial inferiority myth by claiming that black students in segregated schools were not required to achieve at the same level as white students.[10] This did, in fact, develop into a vicious self-fulfilling prophecy which tainted every aspect of blacks' academic, economic, and social life. It was used, for example, as a rationale for classifying certain of the most desirable jobs as "white jobs," and the most undesirable, low-paying, dead-end jobs as "black jobs." This classi- fication of jobs was supported and perpetuated by segregated schools and all-white colleges which protected whites from competition with their black peers.

In a sense, then, segregated black schools have functioned as an effective deterrent to ambitious, able blacks who would enter mainstream American society. After a careful examination of the cumulative negative effects of segregated black schools, Professor Franklin concluded that "there can be no doubt that separate schools have been one of the strongest supports of the concept of white supremacy in the South."[11] Although knowing full well that historically public schools have not usually challenged black students to achieve excellence, black colleges have always vigorously re- cruited students from all types of accredited high schools with varying overall academic standards. However, the colleges constituting the sample for this study evidently carefully screen individual high school graduates. They have definitely preferred those with records of superior academic achievements: 63 percent of the respondents made mostly "A" and "B" grades in high school, and 52 percent graduated from high school with honors.

A larger proportion of those graduating from all-black high schools (68 percent) had mostly "A" and "B" grades than did those (42 percent) grad- uating from predominantly white high schools. This difference may mean that there is a tendency to screen graduates from all-black high schools more carefully than is true of those from predominantly white high schools, because it is suspected that the former might be more likely to inflate grades; or that top black graduates of predominantly white high schools are more often recruited by predominantly white colleges, leaving a smaller

Table 5
Respondents' Ratings of Their High Schools

Excellent	30%
Good	42%
Fair	21%
Poor	7%

proportion of the best black students available to black colleges. This is, indeed, an important aspect of the black "brain drain" which some black college officials have noted with considerable alarm.

In any case, the sample colleges have a history of searching out fertile minds in all socio-economic areas of the black community and from all types of high schools and providing them with the inspiration and relevant training and guidance they must have to develop their fullest potential. In this respect they conform to the definition of academic excellence as propounded by the National Commission on Excellence in Education in *A Nation at Risk*: "Excellence characterizes a school or college that sets high expectations and goals for all learners, then tries in every way possible to help students reach them."[12]

HIGH SCHOOL PREPARATION

When respondents were asked how well they felt their high school had prepared them for college, 47 percent indicated that they were well prepared, and 53 percent acknowledged that their high school education was somewhat or quite inadequate (see Table 5). However, when they were asked to rate their high schools, per se, 72 percent rated them as excellent or good, and only 28 percent rated them as fair or poor.

While there was little difference in the ratings of the high schools in terms of their various geographic locations or racial characteristics, two exceptions should be noted:

1. The largest proportion of respondents (51 percent) who rated their high schools as "excellent" were referring to schools in middle-sized cities (population 100,000–250,000) outside the South. Just 5 percent of these particular respondents rated their high schools as "poor."

2. Only 21 percent of the respondents who graduated from high schools in small towns and rural areas of the South rated them as "excellent," with 10 percent rating them as "poor."

It must be understood that the respondents' ratings were purely subjective, and may or may not make a definitive statement about the actual or objective merit or rating of the high schools from which they graduated. However, their subjective evaluations do help us to understand something about the respondents' interpretations of their own academic achievements. Some were token black students in the initial desegregation of white schools, and others were observers, at least, of the more or less stormy school desegregation crises when the alleged merits and demerits of black and white schools were accorded center-stage concern and loudly debated throughout the United States. To some extent they may have consciously or subconsciously rated their high schools in terms of some hypothetical black-versus-white standard. Yet in the context clearly suggested by the question, they most likely rated their high schools in terms of the degree to which they were personally prepared academically to gain admission to and succeed in college.

The fact that almost half (47 percent) of the respondents, including some graduates of substandard high schools feel that they were well prepared for college may speak more to the point of the quality of their undergraduate colleges than to the quality of their high schools per se. That is, all of the sample colleges have put in place very carefully designed special curricula or enrichment programs, expert counseling, and a number of extracurricular experiences especially intended to facilitate a smooth, even creative, transition of students from various types and qualities of high schools to their more academically rigorous and intellectually demanding college programs. Actually, just about every promising effort is made to prevent what would certainly be for some a damaging academic and cultural shock.[13]

During the last twenty years or so black colleges have led the way in instituting bold, imaginative, innovative efforts aimed at breaking what actually amounts to a vicious cycle, or a predictable scenario according to which the academic disadvantages of many black children have tended to cumulate from the elementary grades through their educational experiences. Consequently, the colleges in this study have been able to take a significant proportion of rather unpromising students from some high schools with questionable academic standards and transform them into "urbane, self-confident, competent black college graduates."[14]

Significantly, teachers in all of the UNCF colleges can cite notable examples of some of their graduates who came from socio-economically disadvantaged backgrounds and nondescript high schools, where their intellectual potentials and special talents had been neglected at best, and often brutalized, yet they managed, with various kinds of help from these teachers, to achieve significant academic and subsequently occupational success.

Incidentally, these are precisely the academically handicapped students who are generally rejected by the "better" white colleges. Yet the awesome challenge to admit a large proportion of such ill-prepared high school graduates and develop their potentials to the fullest extent possible has been always a cardinal mission, the raison d'être, of black colleges.

Table 6
Undergraduate College Education: Grades in High School and College

Grades	High School	College
Mostly A's and B's	63%	39%
Mostly B's	17%	23%
Mostly B's and C's	17%	34%
Mostly C's	3%	4%

It should be noted at this point that teachers in the euphemistic "enrichment programs" in UNCF colleges often report that they have taken certain high school graduates whose reading, writing, and occupational performance levels were at the seventh or eighth grade and had them performing at the eleventh- or twelfth-grade level by the end of their freshman year. This is only an example of how the sample colleges have somehow managed to achieve a high degree of success in the education of disadvantaged students from substandard high schools. Their overall success in this endeavor is, without doubt, unmatched by any other group of colleges in the history of higher education.

It is indeed intriguing to speculate about the nature and extent of success these colleges might have in educating economically poor and disadvantaged students if their promising, innovative teaching ideas were given the same level of respectability and financial support extended promising research ideas in the great universities of this nation. In addition to literally salvaging much of the otherwise wasted or underdeveloped potentials of many disadvantaged black American youths, they might also develop methods and strategies which would be useful in freeing and developing the minds of youths throughout the third world nations, who want so desperately to latch onto and participate in today's advanced, rapidly changing, complex technological civilization.

It is interesting to note that while 63 percent of the respondents made mostly "A" and "B" grades in high school (see Table 6), only 52 percent graduated with honors. Also, while 39 percent of them made mostly "A" and "B" grades in college, just 23 percent qualified with honors. Table 7 shows the distribution of honors among this select group of graduates.

As a rule, high school and college honors are intended to reflect students' total academic record. Thus a student may earn mostly "A" and "B" grades while earning a number of low grades, including some failing grades. Such an overall record would prevent honors recognition.

There are three very important items of note in this particular context. First, even though all of the respondents in this study are college graduates—from various socio-economic and academic backgrounds—only 3 or

Table 7
College Honors According to Sex

Types of Honors	Male	Female
Cum laude	32%	68%
Magna cum laude	23%	77%
Summa cum laude	50%	50%

4 percent achieved the mere "gentleman's/lady's" proverbial "C"; almost two-thirds (62 percent) earned mostly "A's" and "B's" in college. This suggests something about the character of the respondents. They evidently took their college work seriously and did not simply work to "get by" or "go through the motions" of study, as some critics contend.

Second, while about half of the respondents are male (51 percent), a significantly larger proportion of those receiving high honors are female: Only on the level of the highest honors (summa cum laude), which is ordinarily attained by a few of the most able, conscientious, well-rounded students, do we have an even proportion of male and female respondents. (Just 58 of the 2,089 respondents who answered this question, or .028 percent, were summa cum laude college graduates.)

Third, not reflected in the data is the fact that despite these colleges' herculean efforts to perform near academic miracles (fully developing the minds and talents of all of their students), up to half of the high school graduates admitted as freshmen are likely to drop out, for one reason or another, before graduating.

These colleges are terribly concerned about their high student attrition rates because they not only indicate a definite waste of intellectual and occupational potential, but student dropouts also exacerbate the already critical financial situation faced by these colleges. Each student enrolled represents a substantial investment which these colleges can hardly afford to lose. Therefore, all of them make special efforts to reduce their student attrition rates. Some have instituted elaborate innovative academic and academically related counseling and advisement programs involving all faculty members and some of their most successful students in efforts to substantially reduce their overall dropout rates.

It should be properly noted here that the flexible admissions standards adhered to by UNCF colleges as a group, whereby students are recruited from various types and qualities of accredited high schools, is rather effectively compensated for by the generally higher academic standards maintained by the individual colleges. While these colleges are usually willing to accept graduates from almost any accredited high school on the basis of their potential, as well as proven abilities, they tend to require uniformly high academic standards for degrees. Consequently, many students take more than the normal four years to complete requirements for their degree. The colleges' generally flexible admissions standards are thereby balanced by their carefully designed selection process according to which all students are challenged, assisted, and expected to achieve academic excellence, as measured by their individual abilities. Admission is not a guarantee of graduation.

In this respect, the sample colleges certainly do not fit into the simplistic, generalized pattern presented by Christopher Jencks: "In many institutions admission has become a virtual guarantee of graduation, at least for students who are willing to go through the required motions."[15]

Much more appropriately, Samuel DuBois Cook, president of Dillard University, has given a personalized definition of "academic excellence" which seems to be inherent in UNCF colleges' selection processes:

> Everyone cannot be an A student, but everyone should strive to be an A student.... Personal academic excellence is within the grasp as well as the reach of us all. We, all of us, can do our best with what we have.... That is all that is and can be required of us.... The giving of our best is the ultimate form of self-liberation and self-fulfillment.... He who does his best but is a C student is more worthy ... than the student who makes all A's but who has not done his best.[16]

The overall effectiveness of these colleges' selection process is affirmed by some unpromising high school graduates who managed to graduate from UNCF colleges and have gone on to receive advanced degrees from some of the top-ranking, most prestigious universities in the world. And as we shall point out subsequently, an impressive proportion of them have achieved distinction in their chosen occupations in open competition with other graduates of top-flight white colleges.

COLLEGE MAJORS

College students are expected to select some definite range of academic disciplines in which to major or invest special emphasis. Students are usually required to select a major by the end of their sophomore year. However, in many instances students will have chosen a probable college major even before graduating from high school.[17] I have observed that the pre-college selection of majors is especially characteristic of students from economically poor homes. They often tend to be unusually pragmatic, and too often their primary or singular interest in seeking a college degree is that they expect it to be a valuable, necessary credential for securing a better-than-average job.[18] In most instances choosing a college major is tantamount to choosing a career and reflects an interplay of academic, economic, and social forces, or realities, which may not be as well thought out or as balanced as they might be.

The fact is that some academic counselors in the sample colleges report that the high school graduates they admit have too often made career decisions without benefit of either proper parental or high school counseling. They are prone to select careers or academic majors into which blacks have gone traditionally. There is a strong tendency for many black college students to make career choices from a very narrow range of "safe," estimable occupational role models. Since their intersocial class and interoccupational contacts are generally quite limited, the great majority of them usually select occupations most common to their restricted socioeconomic environments: teaching, medicine, nursing, social services, and the ministry.

As a result of their limited interclass experiences, high school graduates from poor black families are not very likely to visualize themselves as becoming scientists, engineers, business managers or entrepreneurs, political leaders, or otherwise influential intellectuals. Occupational horizons, however, broaden quickly after students are admitted to college. For instance, somewhat more than 20 percent of our respondents changed their original choice of a college major by the end of their freshman year in college.

Unfortunately, according to some respondents, it was often quite difficult to change to a more desirable college major. Usually this was due to the necessary academic prerequisites in high school. For example, some of the most promising careers, such as medicine, engineering, computer science, accounting, and those stemming from the natural sciences, presuppose above-average competency in mathematics, which a large proportion of black high school graduates do not possess. Therefore, some students find themselves stuck in majors they are better prepared for, rather than choosing majors they actually desire but for which they were inadequately prepared in high school (see Table 8).

As we noted earlier, black colleges have always had to deal with the very real, urgent problem of liberal arts versus vocational education. It was first thrust upon them by circumstances surrounding the emancipation of slaves. The black freedmen desperately needed to prepare for available jobs and the basic professions, plus the general need to prove that their intellectual abilities were equal to those of their white peers. The various nuances of this issue came to dramatic focus during the early years of the twentieth century when the two most outstanding black intellectuals, W.E.B. Du Bois and Booker T. Washington, debated both sides of the issue.[19]

At least one thing both of these intellectual protagonists made clear. Black colleges simply could not afford to deal gingerly with the issue of liberal arts versus vocational education as some of the more affluent white colleges were doing. Some of the most prestigious white colleges were

Table 8
College Majors According to Sex

Majors	Male	Female
Business/Accounting	7%	9%
Education	21%	42%
Engineering	5%	1%
Humanities	4%	4%
Natural Sciences	18%	8%
Nursing/Health Services	1%	8%
Religion/Philosophy	1%	0%
Social Sciences	10%	9%
Social Work	3%	2%
Others	30%	17%

greatly influenced by the very elitist European model which regarded higher education as the privilege of young men from affluent families. The early European universities were dedicated to the training of the head, not the hands. Some European universities and their American counterparts once seemed to agree with Aristotle, who regarded any paid employment as vulgar and degrading. He insisted that a liberal arts education was suitable for free men of thought and that a vocational education was designed for slaves.[20]

Obviously, the nature of Western civilization and the basic concept of work have changed greatly since Aristotle's time. However, today as in the ancient past, the argument in one form or another continues. Basically, the case for the liberal arts or the humanities is about the same as it has been for centuries: if people of different races and cultures are to live together creatively in a rapidly changing, civilized society such as ours, they must preserve historical ties and consciousness; share common basic values; appreciate and enhance the beautiful; continue to reinterpret and redefine the nature and function of basic institutions; maintain a lively interest in and relationship to the wellsprings of ideas and inspirations that flow from religion; develop and interpret a common conception of the good; promote genuine concern for the human condition; nurture and dignify humane and humanistic habits; and prepare intelligent, dedicated, moral leaders who are capable of charting the course of social institutions and nations according to the richest, most effective, rational store of accumulated knowledge available.

The very idealistic mission of a liberal education as presented above has had to be modified, of course, by the fact that black Americans have been always in desperate need to prepare for available jobs. Therefore, the old adage "education for the sake of knowing" is essentially elitist. Youths from poor black families can hardly afford to spend four or more years in college, training the mind, and end up with no salable skill. They have always felt the urgent need to prepare for remunerative work as soon as possible in order to escape chronic unemployment or underemployment and the vicious cycle of welfare which have been often the perennial lot of their parents and grandparents. Consequently, as higher education becomes increasingly available to black youths from poor families, we can expect increasing pressure for black colleges to extend vocational and vocationally related training.

Traditionally, the black colleges in this study have met the pressure for vocational training by offering a number of job-oriented majors within the overall liberal arts framework. Accordingly, students have been expected to spend the equivalent of two academic years in general education or liberal arts courses and two academic years during which most or all of their courses would be in or related to their major field of study.

Until a decade or so ago the range of professional opportunities available to black college graduates was relatively narrow when compared with that of white college graduates. The fact is, the vast majority of all black professionals were teachers and preachers. Teaching was the principal black profession.[21] Thus with the number and proportion of black children in school ages 5–13 increasing from less than a third (31 percent) in 1960 to more than 98 percent today, the need for additional black teachers has been more or less constant.[22] In some southern states there existed a chronic shortage of qualified black teachers until a few years ago, so much so that it was common to fill teaching vacancies in black schools by employing teachers who did not have a college degree. Therefore, college-trained black teachers usually had no difficulty in finding immediate employment. There was always a teacher shortage.

The immediacy of certain employment and job security, plus the relatively high social status of teachers in the black community, accounted for the fact that until the 1970s education was always the most popular major in black colleges. Actually, a large proportion of the respondents who listed the natural sciences, the social sciences, and the humanities as their college major, really majored in secondary education where they prepared to teach these subjects on the high school level.

The younger graduates in this study, those who received their degrees after 1970, were much more likely to have selected as their major business administration, accounting, engineering, pre-law, pre-medicine, allied health, nursing, communications, urban studies, computer science, or some new combination of disciplines where vocational preparation is definitely the primary, obvious concern. Some of the new majors are subsumed under the "other" category (see Table 8), in which 30 percent of the male respondents and 17 percent of the female respondents specified their college major.

Table 9
Would You Choose the Same Major Now?

Yes	48%
Uncertain	13%
No	39%

Incidentally, just about all of the comments made by those who listed their major in the "other" category strongly suggest that they feel that their undergraduate colleges might have offered them a wider range of vocational or vocationally related majors from which to choose.

The respondents were asked, "If you could relive your undergraduate college life, would you still major in the same field of subjects?" Their replies are listed in Table 9.

Those who indicated that they would now choose some other major gave various reasons why they would not now choose their original major. These reasons vary from such considerations as a change in personal interest, the narrow range of majors from which they could choose at the time when they were in college, to basic changes in American society. However, at least 67 percent of them indicated that they would now choose some other major which would likely lead to a more desirable or lucrative career than has the major they chose.

Only about 8 percent of the respondents majored in business. Prior to 1970 when the great majority (67 percent) graduated from college, relatively few jobs in business administration and accounting were available to blacks. Since 1970 the number and range of such jobs available to black college graduates have increased significantly. In 1981 the National Urban League (NUL) reported that "the largest increase in Black employment (42%) occurred among Blacks going into managerial and administrative jobs—which rose by 120,000, or from 287,000 (in 1975) to 407,000 (in 1980)."[23]

The rapid increase in job opportunities for college-educated blacks who were qualified in business administration and accounting was immediately reflected in students' choices of college majors. Thus in the UNCF's *1985 Statistical Report* (p. 9), we find that almost one-third (31 percent) of all 1984 graduates of UNCF colleges took degrees in business. The business major is the most popular on these campuses since corporate employment opportunities for black college graduates have improved.

There is, then, a clear and positive relationship between students' choices of academic majors and their perceptions of available job opportunities in specific areas of the economy. As career opportunities for college-educated blacks expand, we can expect to have increasing pressure from students to broaden the range of job-related majors. This will certainly put greater economic strains on black colleges which, in effect, will be forced into ever-increasing, direct competition with more affluent white colleges for the most promising black students. Actually, the pressure of this black-white college competition is being felt already. For instance, some of the UNCF colleges have instituted a major in engineering. Not having the necessary faculty or facilities to offer an excellent major in engineering themselves, a few of these colleges have entered into promising, imaginative consortia with some strong complementary engineering schools. This is only a salient example of how the sample colleges contribute to the strength of this nation by developing the minds and talents of black students. In so doing they help to increase this nation's pool of qualified engineers who would not otherwise have had the opportunity to become such.

Again, providing opportunities for socio-economically disadvantaged black youth to become valuable, productive, contributing citizens is certainly in keeping with the standard of academic excellence as defined by the National Commission on Excellence in Education: "Excellence characterizes a school or college that sets high expectations and goals for all learners, then tries in every way possible to help students reach them."[24] These colleges increase the amount and quality of this nation's intellectual capital.

UNDERGRADUATE COLLEGE EVALUATED

The representative sample of college graduates participating in this study were asked, "If you were entering college now would you still choose the college from which you graduated?"

The preponderance of extant survey data shows that most blacks, particularly the more vocal black college educated, are generally committed to the desegregation of American society. It is certainly true of those constituting the sample for this study. This ultimate goal has been sanctioned by an overwhelming majority of bona fide black leaders and organizations and underscored by numerous legal acts initiated by blacks throughout the past one hundred or more years. Yet in spite of persistent negative evaluations of black colleges per se by some influential educators and lay analysts, plus the widespread, pragmatic myth that graduates of traditionally white colleges usually have a distinct advantage over graduates of traditionally black colleges when it comes to selecting prestigious graduate and professional schools and to entering the more promising occupations in mainstream American society, more than two-thirds (67 percent) of our respondents would still choose to attend the UNCF colleges from which they graduated (see Table 10). The proportion who would still prefer their alma mater varies very little according to sex, age, social status, or the amount and kind of post-graduate study they have done.

Another consideration is that college-educated black parents are, without doubt, among the most ambitious parents in regards to the academic

Table 10
Would or Would Not Again Choose Alma Mater

	Male	Female
Yes (definitely)	69%	65%
Uncertain	16%	20%
No	15%	15%

Table 11
Childrens' Desire to Follow in Parental Careers

Yes, definitely	46%
Yes, probably	29%
Uncertain	22%
No	3%

and occupational success of their children. This fact is reflected in many statements made by our respondents, whose parents made great sacrifices to send them to school. Like their ancestors, they seem willing to make almost any sacrifice to see that their own children receive the very best education available to them. Their answers to the following question, then, are quite revealing: "If you have/had children, would you want them to attend your undergraduate college, or some similar black college?"

At least one clear statement emerges from the data in Table 11: graduates of the sample colleges (from about a half to three-fourths) are more or less convinced that the colleges from which they graduated serve the best purposes for them and would be the best choice for their children. They confirm this conclusion by personal statements to be presented in another section of this study.

A close examination of the data above reveals that even among those who are uncertain, or certain that they would not prefer their children to attend their undergraduate college, 38 percent would choose another UNCF college; 16 percent would choose some public black college, and the remaining 46 percent would choose among a variety of colleges ranging all the way from local community colleges (7 percent) to the most prestigious Ivy League colleges (46 percent). Generally speaking, they seem to suggest that the kind or rank of the particular college is not important as long as their children receive a college degree—the credential per se.

Some Reasons Why They Would Still Choose to Attend Their
Undergraduate College

When asked why they would still choose to attend the college from which they graduated—despite ever-increasing opportunities to attend other colleges—the respondents cited many reasons which may be subsumed under twelve general categories. However, the reason most often given (20 percent) was that they would simply prefer a black college where they feel that they would constitute an integral part of the total life of the campus, "a feeling," as stated by several, "that this is my college, that I am not regarded as an outsider, I belong."

Others cited the "good academic reputation" of their alma mater; it was/ is relatively small and provides each student a considerable amount of personalized attention; it is a part of their family tradition; it is located in a convenient or culturally rich geographic area; it has an excellent, caring faculty; it is definitely committed to the preservation and enhancement of black cultural heritage; it has successful, proud alumni; it produces competent, dedicated black leaders; it is concerned about producing competent graduates who will succeed in various careers, and a few would still choose to attend their undergraduate college because it offers strong remedial or enrichment programs. It is interesting that only about 2 percent cited the relatively low cost of tuition and fees as a major attraction.

At first glance it may be surprising that so few of the respondents cited the relatively low cost of attending UNCF colleges as a predisposing reason for choosing again to attend one. Upon close analysis, however, this should be understood: the vast majority (up to 90 percent) of our respondents could not have attended college at all without very substantial financial assistance from sources outside their families. As late as 1985 "approximately 90% of the students enrolled in UNCF institutions received some type of financial assistance ... the median expected parental contribution toward the college education of the prospective UNCF freshman was $0, compared to $1,650 for prospective freshmen nationally."[25] Since practically all of the respondents, as well as students presently enrolled in these colleges, had to depend heavily upon financial assistance from their colleges and other outside sources for college expenses, the actual cost of attending a particular college would not be deterministically significant since it would be covered primarily by student aid anyway.

WORK-STUDY PROGRAM

It must not be assumed that the respondents simply sat back and passively passed the cost of their college education onto the student aid programs in their respective colleges. This is definitely not the case. Fully 68 percent of the respondents worked their way through college, in the sense that they held various kinds of jobs to supplement whatever amount of student aid they may have received.

Further, 74 percent of the respondents held full-time or part-time jobs before enrolling in college to absorb some of their anticipated college expenses. A large number, 82 percent of them, held various types of jobs simultaneously with their full-time college enrollment. Some 18 percent of these held semi-professional or assistantship jobs on their college campuses, and a few (4 percent) earned substantial incomes from apprenticeship types of jobs related to their major academic interests.

Finally, more than 7 percent of the respondents actually held full-time jobs while enrolled as full-time students. Some held what they described as part-time jobs while they were in college, yet they often worked forty or more hours a week, which included weekends, holidays, and frequent overtime.

Full-time or nearly full-time employment was especially prevalent among the respondents who graduated from college prior to 1960. Among these, 26 percent claimed that they earned all or practically all of their college expenses by working on campus, at special jobs off campus, and during vacations or recess periods. Just about all of these who graduated before 1960 (93 percent) had some significant amount of work experience during their college years. They seem to be very proud of their work experiences and eagerly recount them whenever they have the opportunity to do so. The work ethic is obviously very real among the black college educated. Some, however, are prone to speculate, with some degree of envy, about how much better they might have done in their college studies if they, like many college students today, had received substantial student-aid packages which would have made it possible for them to have spent more time studying. One wrote, "If I had had the time to study my science courses as I wanted to do, I would perhaps be a doctor (physician) today instead of a junior high school teacher of mathematics." Another wrote, "I had to spend a fifth year in college, and hardly graduated even then. I had to spend far too much time working on various jobs to pay my expenses. I am what some call a 'self-made' man. The kids today don't know how lucky they are." All in all, the great majority of the respondents would again choose to attend the undergraduate colleges from which they graduated. They believe that they would still have a feeling of "belonging" that they would hardly have at some other black college or at a white college. Also they feel that their particular college experiences helped them to develop greater self-respect and personal worth during a very key period in their lives. Further, they are generally proud to be identified with the alumni of their alma mater.

Some Reasons Why Some Respondents Would Not Now Prefer to Attend Their Undergraduate Colleges

Those who would not now prefer to attend the colleges from which they graduated gave negative reasons which are generally the direct opposite of the positive reasons cited by the great majority. Some were critical of their particular college's lack of a strong academic reputation, relatively small student body, inconvenient geographic location, "weak" emphasis placed upon vocational preparation, relatively "weak faculty," and a few (6 percent) were critical of black colleges per se. They contended that black colleges are now anachronous and have no legitimate place in a desegregating American society. One respondent summarized this point of view in this way: "It is a contradiction, and hypocritical to demand the desegregation of white colleges and at the same time stress the need for support of black colleges."

On the whole, the various attitudes expressed by our respondents in the evaluation of their undergraduate colleges, and black colleges at large, suggest at least three basic conclusions: 1. Black colleges are still the only truly reliable institutions fully dedicated to the education of black students from all socio-economic areas in the black community and with varying kinds and levels of abilities and achievements; 2. UNCF colleges are sincerely devoted to the discovery and tempering of effective black leadership. This was dramatically expressed, for instance, by Samuel DuBois Cook, a graduate of a UNCF college (Morehouse) and president of Dillard University. He insisted:

> It is hardly an accident that Martin Luther King, Jr., was an alumnus of Morehouse College rather than of Harvard College and that the overwhelming majority of the leaders of the civil rights movement—nationally and locally—are graduates of black colleges.... Unlike white colleges, black colleges can hardly foster a love of, and a passion for, the status quo.[26]

The great majority of our respondents tend to agree that despite some shortcomings, black colleges, particularly the ones from which they graduated, are essential for black advancement; 3. Black colleges per se constitute a valuable national resource because they make significant contributions to our national strength and greatness by discovering and developing much of the vast intellectual potentials, some of which would be otherwise wasted.

GRADUATE STUDIES

There have been many attempts to rank institutions of higher education. Various standards of measurement have been used: the alleged quality of their students, the quality of their academic programs, the amount and quality of published research by their faculties, and the number of their graduates who go on to do graduate/professional study. All of these criteria of merit were considered by Martin Trow in his extensive analysis of data gathered by the Carnegie Commission on Higher Education. He divided all institutions into universities, four-year colleges, and junior colleges. He

Table 12
Advanced Study of Respondents

Hold advanced degree(s)	54%
Still in graduate/professional school	9%
Some graduate study (no degree)	14%
Never attended graduate/professional school	23%

Table 13
Graduate/Professional Schools Awarding Advanced Degrees

Types of Schools	Masters	Ph.D., Ed.D.	M.D., D.D.S.	Law	Others
Black universities	34%	8%	61%	16%	61%
Southern white universities	22%	18%	13%	40%	13%
Other white universities	44%	74%	26%	44%	26%

then divided each type of institution into three subcategories, or ranks: "High," "Medium," and "Low."[27]

According to Trow, and others, a major measure of the quality of an undergraduate college is the proportion and success of its graduates who go on to graduate and professional schools. Using that criterion, the colleges included in this study rank very high. This can be seen in Tables 12 and 13.

The respondents constituting this research sample manifest the same high level of post-baccalaureate aspirations as have been documented time and again.[28] In all instances the proportion of black students who aspire to go on to graduate or professional schools is considerably higher than is the case with their non-black peers. Therefore, we find that despite socio-economic, academic, and racial handicaps, fully 77 percent of those in this sample have had some graduate or professional training, with 54 percent having received some post-bachelor's degree.

The data in Tables 12 and 13 suggest certain significant conclusions:

1. The sample colleges are indeed reliable stepping-stones to all kinds of universities and professional schools. Obviously, graduates of these colleges have had little or no difficulty in satisfying the credentials demanded of graduate schools on all levels or ranks. While there has been a tendency for most of them to receive the first post-baccalaureate from black and white institutions in the South, the vast majority (74 percent) of those with academic doctorates received them from prestigious uni-

versities outside the South; with at least 6 percent of their advanced degrees being awarded by the most prestigious Ivy League universities.

2. To understand why the great majority of the respondents with doctorates earned them from universities outside the South, it is necessary to recall that half of them were enrolled in graduate schools prior to 1960. Until the 1960s, with few notable exceptions, southern white universities excluded black students, and except in a few limited academic areas, black universities did not have doctoral programs. Consequently, it was necessary for blacks to seek doctorates from universities outside the South. This, of course, made graduate education for blacks, on the whole, much more costly than it was for their southern white peers who were privileged to choose among universities in their native states, and even in their own cities.

The necessity to attend universities outside the South, where most respondents then resided, functioned to limit the number of doctorates earned by blacks, and it enhanced the social and professional status of the black recipients.

3. The unusually high aspiration for advanced degrees on the part of our respondents may indicate some significant amount of insecurity related to the fact that they are black. That is, they generally reflect an intuitive conviction that if they would succeed in competition with their white peers, they must, in fact, be much better prepared than they. Research shows that the academic goals of black youths are uniformly higher than for whites from high school through college.[29]

4. Almost a fourth (23 percent) of the respondents are still attempting to complete requirements for some post-baccalaureate degree. Some are full-time teachers in schools and colleges who attend graduate school during summers or on occasional scholarships during regular sessions to complete requirements for some advanced degree required by their employers. The "All But Dissertation" teachers ("ABDs") are quite common on all-black college and high school faculties. An apparently large number of teachers continue to study for advanced academic credits in order to qualify for promotions within their particular colleges or school systems.

Though there seems to be no concrete information available at this time, during the last decade or so an apparently significant number of college-educated blacks who are employed in relatively low-income white-collar jobs have been seeking to upgrade their employment by pursuing advanced degrees.

For whatever reasons, then, the college graduates in this study have been outstanding in their efforts and success in the pursuit of post-baccalaureate degrees. The majority (61 percent) went on to graduate/professional school almost immediately upon graduating from college. The others tended to postpone graduate studies until after beginning their careers.

Graduates of UNCF colleges convincingly validate the fact that blacks, on the whole, still have great faith in the efficacy of formal education in their continuing, epic struggle for equality in American society. Therefore, despite tremendous odds against it, an increasing number of black youths from all socio-economic classes are seeking higher education (the number of black college students in 1982 was 1,101,500; see the UNCF, *1985 Statistical Report*, p. ii). They have been inspired by examples of others from similar circumstances who have made it. They have known other black youths from unpromising backgrounds who have qualified themselves to compete successfully with their white peers from much more affluent social backgrounds, for admission to prestigious white colleges, and who went on to careers in mainstream American society.

Finally, the black college graduates of primary concern in this study symbolize a basic faith, a fundamental principle, an enduring hope which is the ethos of the black subculture and which has sustained blacks' attempts to acquire the best education available to them. For a disesteemed racial minority, education has both an individual and social dimension. On the individual level they know that the better educated they or their children become, the better chances in life they will have. On the social or racial level, education of a substantial proportion of black youths is regarded as essential for racial survival, respect, and advancement. One respondent wrote:

> Every time a black person succeeds, it makes it better for all of us. We still need blacks with know-how to help other blacks who had to drop out of school. Also we still need to prove to ourselves and to the white man that we can perform on all levels as well or better than any other people.

The idea of an inherently dual mission of education (personal and racial) was put in a national context by the prestigious and very influential National Commission on Excellence in Education, which emphasized the following proposition:

> Learning is the indispensable investment required for success in the "information age" we are entering ... a high level of shared education is essential to a free, democratic society and to the fostering of a common culture, especially in a country that prides itself on pluralism and individual freedom.[30]

The black colleges in question and the commission agree that education has two inherent dimensions—that is, education at its best serves two interrelated purposes: it develops and frees the minds and abilities of the learners, and by so doing it contributes to national, and in this context, racial strength and progress.

Fundamentally, this dual purpose or function of education was always the rationale behind the founding and support of black colleges. It is the main reason why blacks, who have had to struggle constantly for survival and advancement, have made formal education a sacred endeavor, a cardinal value in their subculture. It is also the primary reason why black students, even those from the most socio-economically disadvantaged backgrounds, often manifest such a strong predisposition to make great sacrifices to get an excellent education.[31]

Finally, respondents in this study, who came from just about every socio-economic class in the black community and graduated from all types and ranks of high schools, have, on the whole, eagerly grasped the opportunities for learning and for social mobility their undergraduate colleges provided them and have gone on to acquire about the best education this nation offers in their respective fields of interest. They have certainly cultivated their individual minds and talents, and are thereby contributing to this nation's strength and greatness. Their "minds" would have been indeed "a terrible thing to waste."

In an attempt to account for blacks' propensity to set and attain high academic goals, Merton introduces an interesting, intriguing theory of "natural selection" which may be apropos in this connection. He points out that "apparently, the Negroes who are hardy enough to scale the high walls of discrimination represent an even more highly selected group than the run-of-the-mill-high-school white population."[32]

The natural selection process of Merton's formulation may have, indeed, resulted in winnowing out all but a relatively small proportion of the most able, ambitious, determined black students who stubbornly challenged and overcame great odds in the pursuit of an excellent education. The great tragedy is that so many others who might have been equally capable were lost to the process, their potential abilities, their fertile minds wasted. The reclamation and maximum development of the minds of black youths, which are even now being wasted, is the constant, haunting challenge of UNCF-related colleges.

NOTES

1. Henry Lee Moon, *The Emergent Thought of W.E.B. Du Bois* (New York: Simon and Schuster, 1972), pp. 122–123.

2. Ibid., p. 123.

3. Bernard Watson, "Education: A Matter of Grave Concern," in *The State of Black America, 1980* (New York: National Urban League, 1980), pp. 68–69.

4. M. Lee Montgomery, "The Education of Black Children" in Nathan Wright, ed., *What Black Educators Are Saying* (New York: Hawthorn Books, 1970), pp. 49–51.

5. National Commission on Excellence in Education, *A Nation at Risk*: The Im-

perative for Educational Reform (Washington, D.C.: U.S. Department of Education, April 1983), pp. 5–12.

6. Daniel C. Thompson, *Private Black Colleges at the Crossroads*, (Westport, Conn.: Greenwood Press, 1973), p. 65.

7. See Charles V. Willie, "Black Students in Higher Education," *American Sociological Review* 7 (1981): 182, 187–190. See also the Dillard University, *Bulletin* 31, no. 3 (February 1965): 1, on the original role of UNCF colleges.

8. See Kenneth B. Clark, "Educational Stimulation of Racially Disadvantaged Children" in A. Harry Passow, ed., *Education in Depressed Areas* (New York: Columbia University, Teachers College Press, 1963), pp. 142–148.

9. Robert K. Merton, *Social Theory and Social Structure* (New York: Free Press, 1968), p. 481.

10. Daniel C. Thompson, "Social Class Factors in Public School Education as Related to Desegregation," *American Journal of Orthopsychiatry* 26 (July 1956): 449–452.

11. Franklin, *From Slavery to Freedom*, p. 549.

12. National Commission on Excellence in Education, *A Nation at Risk*, p. 12.

13. See, for example, Shirley M. McBay, "Black Students in the Sciences: A Look at Spelman College" in Charles V. Willie and Ronald R. Edmonds, eds., *Black Colleges in America: Challenge, Development, Survival* (New York: Columbia University, Teachers College Press, 1978), pp. 217–221.

14. Daniel C. Thompson, "Black College Faculty and Students: The Nature of Their Interaction" in Willie and Edmonds, eds., *Black Colleges in America*, p. 194.

15. Jencks et al., *Inequality: A Reassessment of the Effects of Family and Schooling in America* (New York: Basic Books, 1972), p. 144.

16. Samuel DuBois Cook, quoted in Dillard University, *Academic Orientation* (New Orleans, La., 1977), pp. 14–15.

17. For a systematic study of this, see Charles S. Johnson, *The Negro College Graduate* (Durham: University of North Carolina Press, 1938), pp. 181–194. See also United Negro College Fund, *1985 Statistical Report*, p. 4.

18. Thompson, *Private Black Colleges at the Crossroads*, pp. 80–82.

19. W.E.B. Du Bois, *Dusk of Dawn* (New York: Harcourt, Brace, 1940), pp. 68–95.

20. Robert Maynard Hutchins, ed., "Aristotle's Politics," in *Great Books of the Western World*, vol. 2 (Chicago: William Benton, 1952), pp. 387–389.

21. For a discussion of this, see Gunnar Myrdal, *An American Dilemma* (New York: Harper and Row, 1944; reprint, New York: Pantheon Books, 1975), pp. 318–322; and Johnson, *The Negro College Graduate*, pp. 92–105.

22. U.S. Department of Commerce, Bureau of the Census, *The Social and Economic Status of the Black Population in the United States, 1970–1978*, p. 89.

23. National Urban League, *The State of Black America 1981*, p. 22.

24. National Commission on Excellence in Education, *A Nation at Risk*, p. 12.

25. United Negro College Fund, *1985 Statistical Report*, p. 12.

26. Samuel DuBois Cook, "The Socio-Ethical Role and Responsibility of the Black College Graduate," in Charles V. Willie and Ronald R. Edmonds, eds., *Black Colleges in America: Challenge, Development, Survival*, p. 54.

27. Martin Trow, *Teachers and Students* (New York: McGraw-Hill Book Co., 1975), pp. 1–38. See especially David S. Webster, "America's Highest Ranked Graduate Schools, 1925–1982," *Change Magazine*, May/June 1983, 15–24.

28. Trow, *Teachers and Students*, p. 147.

29. Frederick Mosteller and Daniel P. Moynihan, eds., *On Equality of Educational Opportunity* (New York: Random House, 1972) pp. 25–27.

30. National Commission on Excellence in Education, *A Nation at Risk*, p. 7.

31. See a confirmation of their high academic aspirational level in the United Negro College Fund, *1985 Statistical Report*, p. 3. Here the aspirational level of prospective UNCF college freshmen was noticeably higher than for prospective freshmen at large.

32. Merton, *Social Theory and Social Structure*, p. 481.

5 Occupations

In his monumental study of race relations in the United States, Gunnar Myrdal constructed a classic schema depicting "The Rank Order of Discrimination" to which southern whites characteristically adhere in their private and public relations with black Americans. Accordingly, whites tend to rank six major types of racial discrimination in a consistent hierarchy. Certain types are thus ranked above or below certain other types according to their perceived importance in the preservation of the traditional biracial status quo. This means, in essence, the preservation of a system of race relations whereby blacks are arbitrarily assigned the inferior, or mudsill, status in all areas of the system, and whites are recognized as having the higher, privileged status.

He listed the rank order of discrimination as follows:

1. The bar against interracial sex relations and intermarriage involving white women
2. Formal etiquette in all black-white relations, which is designed to deny blacks social equality or to depict racial inequality
3. Segregation and discrimination in the use of public facilities such as schools, churches, public conveyances, and so forth
4. Political disenfranchisement
5. Discrimination in courts of law and by all public servants
6. Discrimination in employment or earning a living[1]

According to Myrdal's schema, southern whites regard the bar against interracial sex relations and intermarriage involving white women as the most essential or sacred of all patterns of racial discrimination and the pattern to be the most strenuously supported. Myrdal's expert observations in this instance square with those of numerous other scholars and lay observers when he concludes that white southerners seem to have an "'instinctive' repugnance in thinking of 'intermarriage.'...It takes precedence before everything else."[2] It is the most forbidden of all things.

At the bottom of the white man's hierarchy of racial discrimination, Myrdal listed the bar against equal employment or equal economic opportunity. He insisted that the bar against equal employment was the most flexible of the types of discrimination. Presumably, then, we should expect that blacks would meet with the least resistance when they attempt to achieve equal economic opportunities and the greatest resistance when they attempt to transcend the bar to interracial sex relations and intermarriage involving white women.

Myrdal very perceptively pointed out that blacks have their own rank order of race relations, which is "just about parallel, but inverse to that of the white man's".[3] Consequently, whites tend to place the greatest value upon discrimination against blacks where interracial sex and intermarriage involving white women are concerned; blacks manifest the least interest in removing this form of discrimination. Conversely, where whites seem to be the least concerned about preserving economic or job discrimination against blacks, blacks themselves have always placed the achievement of equal economic or employment opportunities at the very top of their hierarchy of goals to be attained. Characteristically, blacks rank the achievement of equal economic opportunity, especially equality of employment, above everything else—including justice in the courts, or even the right to vote. In this context, education, so highly valued by blacks, is strongly regarded as the most estimable means of acquiring a good job.

While Myrdal's rank order of discrimination may be challenged from the point of view of constant validity—as values and situations change, the rank order of discrimination is likely to experience corresponding changes— at the same time, it does contribute to our understanding of the nature of race relations in the United States, especially racial dynamics and conflict in the economic arena.

To fully appreciate the very high value blacks place upon a good job, it is necessary to recall that throughout the history of this nation blacks have been a central focus of economic interests. They themselves have been always a key economic issue. During the earliest decades of this republic, blacks' indentured-servant status rapidly degenerated into slavery, which received statutory confirmation in 1661. As slaves they were legally regarded as chattel or property, with no economic rights as persons.

From the end of slavery until recently, with some notable exceptions, blacks have been more or less restricted to the most difficult, low-paying, dead-end jobs in the communities where they have resided. Thus despite

Myrdal's schema, which places economic discrimination at the bottom of whites' priorities, blacks have, in fact, always encountered formidable resistance from whites when they have attempted to secure traditionally white jobs. This resistance seems to stem from at least two major conditions. First, white workers and professionals seem to have a pathological fear of competition with blacks for the more desirable jobs, especially those in mainstream American society. This may result from a prevalent myth that all black economic gains must be made at the expense of white economic security. Therefore, whites have usually fought bitterly to maintain a monopoly of the better jobs on every level of the occupational hierarchy. In the struggle for job monopoly, they have employed just about every available method, ranging from the crass political or regulatory exclusiveness of labor unions, to the more polite yet equally effective qualifications ploy, characteristic of white faculties in some major institutions of higher education. Thus, despite black student protestors and affirmative action requirements to employ black teachers, only about 1 percent of the total full-time instructional faculty in traditionally white institutions is black.[4]

Second, the most widely regarded symbol of social status in American society is the occupation of the individual. Therefore, whites who consciously or unconsciously support the notion of white supremacy, or who would protect the social class implications inherent in certain occupations, may tend to resist the inclusion of blacks, who are widely regarded as a disesteemed people. Despite the very careful, systematic research by some reputable scholars, who have generally concluded that race has declined as a deterministic consideration in the employment of blacks, there is still some very convincing evidence that being black may be a great deal more deterministic than some data indicate. Race in American society is still an important factor in a complex syndrome which includes a variety of personality quirks, stereotypes, and some emotionally charged concepts such as "merit," "fair play," "friendship," "belonging," "tradition," and so forth. Any one or all of these factors may come into play when a given employer has to make a decision about the employment of blacks for erstwhile white jobs.

Certainly, the great majority of upwardly mobile black college graduates in this study have had to regard race as an important factor in their own bid for occupational success. Thus, they report, while being black may not now impose the rigid job ceiling it once did, it still may have some significant deleterious effects on employers when it comes to the hiring of blacks in competition with white applicants. This seems to be especially true of positions where black incumbents would be expected to supervise white employees.

According to data gathered for this study, it would be misleading to assume that black persons, no matter how well they may be qualified, can afford to regard the acquisition of high-level jobs in mainstream American society as a routine happening. They are still hard to come by. Actually, blacks who hold such jobs are likely to regard them as more than simply a means of earning a measure of economic security. Such jobs also symbolize a long-sought-after goal of racial freedom and first-class citizenship. They indicate a sort of public recognition of personal worth. Basically, a top-level job in mainstream American economic life functions to debunk some damaging racial myths about blacks' alleged inferiority. Consequently, when blacks acquire top jobs or get significant promotions in competition with white peers, other blacks tend to regard their success as a vindication of the race's claim of equal ability. This is especially true of blacks who become the first of their race to fill certain top-level jobs. As a rule, the honor and acclaim showered upon the first black in a highly competitive, erstwhile white job is far in excess of that accorded comparable white incumbents by the white community.

EMPLOYMENT OF RESPONDENTS

When evaluated strictly from an employment point of view, the college graduates constituting the sample for this study epitomize the degree to which blacks have overcome racial barriers and related obstacles in their movement toward equality and respect in the United States. They are, as a highly selected, representative group, among the most successful citizens in the black community. Although the number or proportion of blacks employed in the more desirable, top jobs is still far short of equity, enough have acquired such positions and succeeded in them to validate blacks' persistent contention that members of their race are quite capable of succeeding in any position available, in direct competition with white peers.

UNEMPLOYMENT RATE

At the time when the questionnaire used in this study was mailed to the respondents (August 1982), the official unemployment rate in the United States was hovering around 9 percent, and the unemployment rate for blacks was usually more than twice as high as that for Americans generally, or about 18 percent. At that time the unemployment rate for the respondents was somewhat less than 6 percent. Even so, a close examination reveals that 63 percent of the unemployed respondents were young college graduates (under thirty) waiting for their first regular career job and young married women perhaps trying to find a job, as one put it, "that will allow me to perform my duties as a wife and mother." Therefore, essentially, only about 3 or 4 percent of the respondents would be classified as unemployed according to established official national procedures, and some of these described their situation as "between jobs." Actually, only about

Table 14
Time Elapsed between Graduation and Career Employment

Immediate Employment	57%
A few months	23%
About a year	8%
More than a year	10%
Still unemployed	2%

Table 15
How First Career Job Was Acquired

Key Job Contact	
College university placement	12%
Former teachers	6%
Personal efforts	55%
Parents, relatives, or friends	21%
Former employer	5%
Self-employed	1%

2 percent regarded themselves as unemployed in the ordinary sense of that concept.

The range of unemployment among them was from 2.2 percent of those in the fifty–fifty-nine age category to 13.2 percent among those who are in the under-thirty category. The overall unemployment rate for the male respondents was just 3 percent, and for the female respondents it was 7.4 percent. There was a noticeable difference between the unemployment rates of those who hold some post-baccalaureate degree and those who do not: the rate for the former was only 2.9 percent; for the latter it was 10.5 percent. Again, for those who attended graduate school but did not receive a degree, the unemployment rate was 6.3 percent.

Clearly, the rate of unemployment in the black community tends to vary according to the amount of education received by individuals, with age and sex functioning as constant intervening variables. On the whole, however, the employment status of black college graduates is a great deal more favorable than it is for blacks who have not attended college.

FIRST CAREER EMPLOYMENT

As can be seen in Tables 14 and 15, the college graduates in our sample had various experiences in their attempts to get started in their chosen careers.

More than half (57 percent) of the respondents literally found jobs waiting for them upon graduation from college (see Table 14). This is about as true of those who graduated before 1960 (54 percent) as it is of those who graduated from college after 1960 (59 percent). A close examination of those who compose this most fortunate group of college seniors reveals that most of them (78 percent) accepted jobs as public school teachers, nurses, welfare workers, athletes, and as entrance-level managers or technicians in business and service corporations. These were jobs for which they were systematically prepared in college.

Respondents who majored in traditional liberal arts disciplines usually had to wait somewhat longer before entering their first career jobs. For instance, only about a fourth (24 percent) got jobs immediately. However, 70 percent of those who waited a year or more for their first career employment were among those who deferred immediate employment in order to engage in graduate or professional studies.

At least two things stand out in the data regarding how the respondents got their first career jobs (see Table 15). First, 12 percent got jobs through their college or university's placement office. This was especially true of those who graduated during the 1970s. It was then that some large business corporations began or intensified their recruitment efforts on black college campuses.[5] A quintessential example of recruiters for big corporations is Robert W. Brocksbank, manager of college relations and college recruiting for Mobil Oil Corporation. He has not only placed a significant number of black college graduates in challenging jobs on the management ladder, but he has greatly enhanced students' knowledge about the corporate culture and how to pursue careers in the world of work. He has been widely recognized and honored by several black college faculties and administrators for his distinguished contributions.

Brocksbank challenges the general philosophy of the sample colleges when he insists that they should

> give students *options* through business-oriented electives, through early career-counseling, and through faculties who have been led to recognize the value of education for the world of work.... That bomb [the fear of not finding a job after college] will be replaced with confidence and high expectations, and their chances of finding work that satisfies and fulfills them will be vastly increased.[6]

Then he admonished college administrators, "Remember that your placement office is the real development office for your college. The best endowment you will ever have is a group of successful and affluent alumni."[7]

Not only have certain recruiters representing large corporations worked closely with black colleges' placement offices in finding career employment for a significant number of their graduates, but they have passed on their expert knowledge to other students who were not directly recruited for their particular corporations. Thus, 72 percent of the respondents who have found various types of employment since 1970 cited their colleges' placement offices as directly or indirectly helpful in that respect. UNCF colleges obviously take a serious interest in the job placement of their graduates.

Second, the majority of our respondents (55 percent) assumed the primary responsibility of getting their first career job. Some used every available means of seeking employment: personally developing and distributing their curriculum vitae or resumes to a considerable number of probable employers, along with supporting recommendations from teachers and other reputable persons. Some followed up on contacts with corporate representatives they had made through their colleges' placement offices.

One respondent put her efforts to find a career job in these words, which illustrate Brocksbank's concept of "The Bomb in their Desks":

> When I got to my senior year in college, like most of my class-mates, I became frantic about getting a job in the field I had prepared for. I constantly looked for job leads, and sent my resume to every promising employer. My teachers were understanding and helped me to develop my resume and prepare for interviews.

When senior students in the sample colleges receive promising career job offers, or are awarded lucrative fellowships to attend prestigious universities, they are usually given wide recognition and honor on their campuses and also in the larger communities in which the colleges are located. If such upcoming appointments represent some sort of racial breakthrough, the recipients may receive special attention in the news media, especially the black press.

TYPES OF EMPLOYMENT

In response to the question "If you are employed, what is your current main occupation?," the respondents named a wide variety of occupations, and numerous specific jobs. However, upon close inspection, the many different jobs in which they are engaged may be functionally classified into four traditional categories, plus one general or residual category. For this analysis these categories are operationally defined in terms of the amount and kind of formal education expected of incumbents.

Blue-Collar Jobs

Ordinarily, jobs in this category require little or no formal education in the traditional sense. Even top-level blue-collar jobs may be filled by workers with only an elementary education, plus what the given employer might regard as appropriate apprenticeship experiences. There is, however, a diminishing number of blue-collar jobs, and even now the great majority of such jobs are restricted to workers with at least functional literacy, and some already require a certificate attesting formal vocational training.

Only about 3 percent of our respondents indicated that they were employed in such blue-collar jobs as waiters, maids, cooks, taxi drivers, construction workers, farmers, and so forth. However, it should be noted that just about all of these (98 percent) regarded their current blue-collar jobs as temporary, that they were seeking better jobs, or that they regarded themselves as over-prepared for their current jobs. They did not regard such jobs as careers.

White-Collar Jobs

Usually jobs in this very broad category are held by individuals with at least a high school education. Often, such jobs are held by upwardly mobile college graduates who have set more prestigious professional goals.

Generally, blacks, even the college educated, have been greatly underrepresented in white-collar jobs.[8] For instance, in 1960 only 16.1 percent of employed blacks held white-collar jobs, compared with 46.6 percent of whites employed. By 1972, the proportion of black workers in white-collar jobs had increased to 29.8 percent. At the same time, the proportion of white workers in such jobs had increased to 50 percent.

Fully 8 percent of the college graduates in this study hold white-collar jobs. Among these are salespersons, secretaries, office managers, policemen, firemen, clerks, inspectors, and a variety of jobs subsumed under the general rubric "staff member."

The vast majority (81 percent) of our respondents who are engaged in white-collar jobs regard them as temporary or interim positions, their ultimate goal being some professional position in their present career to which they aspire through promotions or some professional position in another career.

As an example of the former, a young respondent, a patrolman in a large city police department, said that he is definitely planning and preparing himself to become chief of police or police commissioner within ten years through promotions based upon qualifying examinations and exemplary performances. An example of the latter is a secretary who attends law school in the evenings obviously aspiring to become a lawyer.

The status of "staff member," which may include various forms of assistantships, has been used as a dependable stepping-stone to professional and managerial positions by black college graduates. One of the most valuable serendipitous functions of the federally funded human services programs, which were part of the short-lived "war on poverty" efforts during the 1960s and 1970s, was to provide opportunities for experiences as professionals and managers to black college graduates who otherwise would not have had such opportunities in some of the racially segregated communities where they resided.

For instance, when several large-scale human services programs were begun in the South during the 1960s and 1970s, blacks were almost completely excluded from professional and managerial positions in the mainstream economic life of the South and generally encountered low, discriminatory job ceilings throughout the United States. This very pertinent point was made by a respondent who holds the powerful position as director of personnel in a medium-sized city in Georgia. In that city historical racial segregation and discrimination permeated and contaminated every aspect of the social system. There blacks were, in fact, relegated to the lowest-level jobs. This respondent explained in an interview how his work, first as a staff member, and eventually as director of a local federally funded agency, provided him the opportunity to discover, develop, and manifest his excellent managerial abilities. Especially significant has been his ability to pinpoint key interracial problems and suggest effective ways of dealing with them. According to his account, he has been a racial diplomat par excellence. Therefore, some powerful white citizens in his city recommended him to fill the very powerful and prestigious position as director of city personnel, in direct competition with a number of white applicants.

About 10 percent of the college graduates in this study, who now hold responsible professional and managerial positions in both the public and private sectors, received valuable informal or apprenticeship training in various federally sponsored human services programs and agencies, such as the Manpower Development Training Act (MDTA) and its successor, the Comprehensive Employment Training ACT (CETA). Some of them point out that their present level of occupational success—especially in mainstream jobs in the South, which traditionally excluded blacks—is due directly to the learning experiences they received in federal programs that required equal opportunity employment for minorities. In this way, they were able to escape or transcend a vicious trap so frustrating to many blacks who attempt to secure top-level jobs. They lack the experience necessary because they have not had the opportunity to secure the necessary experiences in less demanding jobs.

Professional and Managerial Jobs

Jobs in this category usually require a college degree plus specialized professional or technical training. Where medicine, dentistry, pharmacy, nursing, law, and most recently, teaching are concerned, state laws require the passing of a rigid formal examination as part of the licensing process.

A central mission of the sample colleges has been always that of encouraging and preparing their students to become professionals and managers. This mission seems to be well understood and accepted by their students. Consequently, after varying time lapses, the vast majority of the graduates of these colleges do, in fact, achieve that goal.

Among our respondents 89 percent held professional jobs at the time of the study. Just about all of the others held what they regarded as temporary blue-collar jobs or white-collar jobs while waiting for some professional or managerial job to become available. The fact is, fully 97 percent of the respondents regarded themselves as qualified professionals, even if they were actually employed in non-professional work or unemployed altogether.

To understand why just about all of the respondents regard themselves as professionals, even when they are not so employed, it is necessary to understand that they generally regard their undergraduate education as basic preparation, even without specialized graduate or professional training.

An example of how these colleges realistically prepare students for alternative professions, while also giving them basic pre-professional training for some other first-choice profession, is that of a physician in the sample. As a college student he carried a major course of studies designed to prepare him for medical school. However, inherent in his program of pre-medical studies was a core of courses the state board of education required for teachers of biology on the secondary school level. While preparing to become a physician, he was simultaneously preparing to become a high school teacher as a second or alternative choice, if the first-choice goal had not worked out.

The option of a first choice plus an alternative pre-professional choice is often formally instituted by the practice of double majors in college. The first-choice pre-professional major is designed so that the student may take a second major which will prepare him or her to enter some profession immediately, without the post-baccalaureate training and the several academic hurdles and expenses involved in the pursuit of the first-choice profession.

A typical example of the double major approach to a professional career is a successful journalist in the sample. He said that even as a high school student he wanted to become a journalist on some big-city newspaper. He was advised that it would be first necessary to graduate from college and then secure a professional degree from some recognized school of journalism. However, he was not at all sure that he would be able to go on to graduate school immediately after college because he might be called upon to help pay for the schooling of younger siblings. He was advised to select a double major in college, communications, which was regarded as a pre-journalism major, and accounting, a profession for which he could technically qualify in college. As an accountant he would have an opportunity to meet required economic responsibilities while waiting for an opportunity to continue the pursuit of a career in journalism.

Still another approach college students or graduates often take to insure professional careers is that of deliberately preparing for two occupations at different times. The reasoning is that if for some reason one cannot find satisfactory employment in one, he or she is prepared to accept a position in the other.

An example of this reasoning is a respondent whose ambition it was to become a lawyer. He enrolled in college during the 1940s, when judiciaries were lily-white throughout the South, and there were naturally very few black lawyers. In the large southern city where the respondent lived and attended college, there was only one black lawyer, and he actually earned a living as a businessman, not as a practicing lawyer per se. It was indeed doubtful whether a black lawyer would be accorded the respect and authority necessary to earn a living in an otherwise lily-white judiciary. Therefore, the respondent majored in sociology in college and went on to earn a graduate degree in sociology to prepare for college teaching. After receiving a graduate degree in sociology, he then went on to law school. Today he is a very successful, wealthy lawyer and judge.

The career pattern of the would-be college instructor/lawyer just noted is another indication of the strong sense of pragmatism many blacks have developed in response to chronic economic insecurity. It is a characteristic survival strategy. That is, in order to achieve ordinary occupational success in what they perceive to be a hostile, anti-black environment, some blacks evidently feel that they really must be twice as good as their white competitors, or have the added insurance of an alternative profession. They manifest a strong doubt that "the system" can be depended upon to work for them as effectively as it works for their white competitors.

Teaching as an Alternative or Second-Choice Profession

Many students in black colleges seem to regard teaching as the most estimable, quintessential alternative or second-choice profession. Some of the respondents who definitely planned to enter other professions, such as medicine, law, the ministry, sports, entertainment, and business, took an alternative college major in education. They apparently did this for one or two reasons: first, some evidently doubted their ability to complete a degree in their first-choice college major at an academic level high enough to ensure their acceptance at an appropriate graduate or professional school. Second, some doubted that they would be able to find a satisfactory position in their first-choice occupation, even when the required formal preparation was completed.

This latter doubt was expressed by a respondent who would have prepared for a career in the U.S. foreign service. He did not do so because he believed that his chances of securing such a position were too limited. Therefore, he took his college degree in political science, and at the time of the study he was planning to get an advanced degree in political science in preparation for college teaching.

The question of why so many black college students or graduates are likely to choose education as the most preferred second-choice profession is a difficult one to answer, yet the preponderance of information gathered for this study suggests that it is due primarily to the fact that teaching has been much more open to blacks than any of the other traditional professions. For instance, while blacks constitute about 12 percent of the total population of the United States, they constitute only about 3 to 5 percent of the overall professional or managerial class. This glaring inequity would be even more pronounced were it not for the fact that insofar as the teaching profession is concerned, blacks are approaching equity. Approximately 10 percent of all teachers in the United States are black.[9] Consequently, teaching does in fact offer blacks the best opportunity of becoming professionals.

Furthermore, as we have noted, a little more than a hundred years ago when the first black colleges were founded, the vast majority of blacks in the United States (probably 95 percent) were functionally illiterate. Education was regarded as the most urgent, top priority if blacks were to hold onto their strongly contested freedom. This meant that teachers of black children were badly needed. Thus the central mission of the first black colleges was that of training urgently needed teachers. The great need for teachers, plus the very short supply of blacks qualified to teach, functioned to ensure teachers a very high status in the black community. Next to the black preacher, the black teacher seems to have enjoyed the most respected position in black society during the first decades after slavery.

To some very significant degree, the crisis in black education has stubbornly persisted throughout the decades. Even now we are reminded that perhaps 40 percent of young black Americans who should be finishing high school are still functionally illiterate.[10] If older miseducated or undereducated black adults are counted, it may be that more than half of the blacks in the labor market are inadequately prepared to compete as equals with their white peers for jobs in our highly developed technological society. Thus, while the urgent need for black teachers one hundred years ago emphasized the small supply per se, today the emphasis is upon the need for a larger number of excellent, dedicated teachers. In both instances a complex of circumstances make teaching an essential, dignified, highly respected, relatively secure (though low-paying) profession which is still attractive to a large proportion of black college students as either a first or a second-choice profession.

Table 16
Types of Employment

Employment	Male	Female	Total
Public service (federal, state, local)	24%	20%	21%
Business corporations	22%	12%	15%
Grade school education	17%	44%	34%
College/university education	12%	11%	11%
Medicine (physicians and dentists)	3%	1%	3%
Nursing	0%	2%	1%
The ministry	5%	0%	3%
Law (government)	2%	1%	2%
Self-employed	12%	3%	6%
Others	3%	6%	4%

Careers Chosen by Respondents

The largest proportion of black college graduates still choose some level of education as a profession. This is true of 29 percent of our male respondents, and 55 percent of our female respondents.

As suggested in Table 16, most respondents who did not choose education as a career tended to choose other traditional occupations such as in public service or government agencies, medicine, law, and the ministry, with 6 percent self-employed. Those who are counted as self-employed are engaged as entrepreneurs or heads of insurance agencies, undertaking establishments, certified public accountants (CPA) firms, medical clinics, law firms, real estate agencies, retail stores, banks, other financial agencies, and so forth.

Those listed in the "other" category hold several types of professional or managerial positions in tourist agencies, advertising, public relations, and promotions or consulting firms. A few (less than 1 percent) hold positions of leadership in black voluntary organizations as their main occupation.

Insofar as occupations in mainstream American society are concerned, despite some very impressive gains blacks still fall far short of equity, no matter how it is measured. Generally speaking, the most prestigious, highest-paying positions in all major careers are still reserved for white males.[11] However, enough blacks have succeeded in such positions to prove their unquestioned capability for top job performances when such opportunities are available.

Location of Present Job

While 95 of the 105 historically black colleges, and 41 of the 43 UNCF-member colleges, are located in the South, their graduates are pursuing careers throughout the United States and abroad (See Table 17).

Table 17
Location of Present Employment*

Large city, North	21%
Small city, North	9%
Rural, North	2%
Large city, South	33%
Small city, South	24%
Rural, South	10%
Outside U.S.A.	1%

*The "South" has been operationally defined in several ways. The term as used in this context refers to the eleven states which seceded from the Federal Union during the Civil War period of the early 1860s: South Carolina, North Carolina, Georgia, Alabama, Mississippi, Florida, Arkansas, Texas, Tennessee, Louisiana, and Virginia.

The "North" as used here is a residual concept which refers to all states not classified as in the "South."

From the point of view of the history of blacks in the United States, there has been a very significant difference between the South and other regions. The South, or the black belt, has always symbolized for blacks the ultimate in racial oppression—slavery, Jim Crow, lynching, and limited job opportunities. The North has been frequently romantically perceived by many blacks in sharp contrast to the South. It has been too often regarded as a symbol of blacks' freedom and a land of great opportunities in which blacks could develop and advance.

Of course, the distinctions many blacks have drawn between the North and South have not been always clear or accurate. Racism has been a manifest, inherent part of the culture and society of both regions, though varied to some extent according to particular times, places, and situations. Nevertheless, because of the strong perceptions that many blacks have had of these regions, the "South" and the "North" concepts have tended to become a significant theme in blacks' subculture, and indeed, in American culture at large. In a number of ways, the North and the South have been regarded as having separate and very different ways of life. Usually the North comes off as more democratic, a land of greater opportunity and more culturally developed than the South.

It is not surprising, therefore, that while fully 83 percent of our respondents were born and reared in the South, only 67 percent still work in the South. Actually, throughout the decades since World War I, college-educated blacks, along with the great black masses, have migrated North in search of better jobs and a generally better life for their families.

This process of moving from the South to the North has amounted to a sort of brain drain. However, this type of migration seems to be diminishing as more and more college-educated blacks remain in the South and acquire professional and managerial jobs traditionally filled by white persons.

Table 18
Racial Mix in the Workplace

All black	5%
Predominantly black	22%
Balance of black and non-black	21%
Predominantly white	47%
The only black	5%

Where our respondents are concerned, those employed in the South tend to report about the same degree of satisfaction or dissatisfaction with their careers as those employed in the North. The median annual income of the northern respondents is about $1,100 more than that of the southern respondents. However, this difference may be modified by the fact that the overall cost of living in the North is higher than in the South. This is particularly significant when we realize that about a third (34 percent) of the respondents work in small towns and rural areas of the South where the cost of living is considerably lower than it is in large cities where 54 percent of the respondents are employed.

Another fact that might help to account for the higher median annual income of the northern respondents is that fully 80 percent of all the respondents who hold professional and managerial positions in mainstream corporations are employed in the North. These are among the highest-income jobs reported by the respondents. Thus, generally speaking, the white South still seems quite reluctant to accord blacks well-paying professional and managerial positions in the corporate world.

THE MATTER OF RACE

About 95 percent of our respondents are employed in interracial situations. The racial mix varies from 5 percent with all-black fellow workers to another 5 percent who are the only blacks employed in their particular workplaces (see Table 18). Fully 47 percent have fellow workers who are predominantly white, and 43 percent are employed in various interracial configurations.

Eighty-seven percent of the respondents who are self-employed as physicians, dentists, lawyers, and entrepreneurs have interracial patients, clients, or customers (see Table 19). The range is from 13 percent who have all-black clientele to the 2 percent who have all-white clientele. Some of our respondents, especially among those who are achieving success in mainstream careers, insist that well-qualified blacks who are ambitious, persistent, willing to work hard and take risks can make it in mainstream American society on their individual merits, virtually unimpeded by the

Table 19
Racial Mix among Clientele of the Self-Employed

All black	13%
Predominantly black	32%
Balance of black and non-black	27%
Predominantly white	26%
All white	2%

matter of race. However, when asked to indicate the extent of interracial contacts they have in their workplace as well as the percentage of their black and non-black clientele, their answers indicated that the theory of unlimited progress for well-educated, ambitious, dedicated blacks is seriously questioned. The great majority of our respondents, along with other prominent black spokespersons, reject the theory outright. They call attention to examples of blacks in a wide variety of occupations, from sports to corporate management, where they were or are eminently qualified for top-level positions, yet they have been passed over again and again when such positions were available. For instance, astronaut Guin Bluford is now regarded as an exemplary folk hero because of his participation in the U.S. Space Agency's September 6, 1983, Challenger mission. Guin Bluford was the first black American to be chosen for a space flight—after twenty-two years of U.S. manned-flight missions.

According to some expert observers, the U.S. Space Agency deliberately disallowed blacks from space flights until 1983, despite the fact that some were well prepared as astronauts and could have been on previous missions. The exclusion of blacks, they insist, "had nothing to do with qualifications. It had to do with choice."[12]

The "First" Blacks

Blacks who are employed as professionals or managers in erstwhile all-white positions or who have stable interracial clientele are truly in the vanguard of those who are changing the essential nature of a long-established, deeply rooted, biracial socio-economic system. In this system black professionals and entrepreneurs have been forced to compete with their white counterparts for black clientele, while their white counterparts were immune from competition with them for white clientele. Until recently, whites have been forbidden by law or custom to seek the services of black professionals and entrepreneurs. It was a highly sanctioned taboo. The well-established "etiquette of race relations" required whites at large to seek professional services from whites only. The reverse was true for blacks. They have been always expected to seek professional services from white professionals and to patronize white businesses. Actually, there is a commonly held suspicion that, generally speaking, many blacks tend to prefer to deal with white professionals and businesspeople rather than black professionals and businesspeople. Whether this is true is not conclusive, yet there is some compelling evidence that it is often so. Black professionals and entrepreneurs often insist that fellow blacks are prone to prefer such services from whites, giving various alleged non-racist rationales for doing so. For example, whites are deemed to be better prepared than blacks or otherwise better able to deliver top-quality services.

This situation was insightfully described by Myrdal about forty years ago (1944). He pointed out that "Negro preachers, teachers, professionals, and businessmen have had to build their whole economic and social existence on the basis of the segregation of their people, in response to the dictates of the white society."[13]

The fact that a significant number of the professionals and entrepreneurs in our sample are among the first to hold certain positions or to serve white clientele is evidence that they are not as "imprisoned in the Negro problem" as was true when Myrdal made his classic observations. Yet some respondents commented at length upon the perception of their role as the first black. They all seem to take their pioneering role quite seriously. Responding consciously or unconsciously to the ancient stereotype that "all blacks are alike, inferior," they tend to feel that their success in the role of "first" will have immediate and even long-range consequences for other blacks. If they do well, they reason, they will open the way for other blacks. If they fail, they will provide concrete evidence of inferiority for white racists who would like to cite them as reasons for not employing other blacks in similar positions. Thus, an added burden placed upon the first black is that of proving that blacks per se are capable of excellent performances in erstwhile white jobs. This is true whether we consider the expectations of black athletes (the black football quarterback, for instance) or the black physician in a white hospital. Both are likely to be quite conscious that they are being closely observed and evaluated by their white clientele as well as by their black and white peers. Therefore, without exception, all of the first blacks to hold significant positions in mainstream American society with whom I've talked, especially those in our sample, report feeling and in some ways responding to the pressure of having to prove their abilities to what they perceive to be skeptical observers. Also, they feel that their success or failure would redound to blacks' struggle for equality in American society. For example, a respondent who was the first black to integrate one of the top-flight universities in the South, reported that she had to prove her superior academic ability before she was "accepted" by the faculty and students. She said, "After they got to know me as an 'A' student I became accepted on a limited social basis....Since I did well, I wonder why there are still only a few black students there after 20 years."[14]

This feeling that they are regarded as a representative of the black race is not unfounded. Many whites do, in fact, regard the black race as a sort of monolith, the basis for stereotypes. Thus, the success or failure of certain key blacks is often interpreted as due to inherent characteristics of the race and may, in fact, open or close doors of opportunity for other blacks.

Black Power Wielders

An important quasi-profession which black college graduates are beginning to enter in significant numbers is that of decision makers in mainstream American society. One key area of power brokerage is corporate board membership. While the number is very small (less than 0.5 percent of our respondents), they represent a significant breakthrough. They symbolize a change in the so-called power structure which has historically excluded blacks and made them a proverbial powerless people, to a situation where a few corporations with great social power have included at least a token number of blacks as wielders of socio-economic power.[15]

Politics and Government

Blacks in positions of power wielders are most obvious in politics and government. Yet while politics per se is an ancient profession, it was virtually closed to black Americans until the enactment of the 1965 Voting Rights Act. This Act guarantees the right to register and vote to millions of hitherto legally and de facto disenfranchised blacks throughout the southern states.

Since 1965, blacks have entered the profession of politics in ever-increasing numbers. The increasing number of black political candidates is due directly to the rapidly expanding black electorate. Not only are more black political aspirants getting elected to a variety of public positions on all levels of government, but many others are also receiving prestigious,well-paying political appointments which were traditionally filled by whites only.

In 1984 over 5,000 blacks held elective public positions, and among these were 286 or more city mayors. Also, an even larger number of blacks have been appointed to managerial and professional positions in local and state governments. Peter Eisenger, political scientist at the University of Wisconsin, did a study of black political appointments in forty cities. He found that in eight of the cities run by black mayors between 1978 and 1980, black municipal employment had increased by 16 percent with an increase of 20 percent in managerial positions and 18 percent in professional jobs.[16]

The number of black mayors increased from 48 in 1973 to 286 in 1984. It is evident that blacks are organizing and employing their newfound voting potential to secure responsible jobs which were closed to them before 1965. And though the number of blacks in the profession of politics is still very small (less than 1 percent of the 590,800 public officials in the nation in 1984), with only 1.6 percent of our respondents so employed, from an occupational point of view, politics seems to be the most rapidly expanding profession where college-educated blacks are concerned. The fact may well be that the number of blacks appointed to politically related professional or managerial positions in cities with black and white mayors will continue to increase at approximately the same rate as does the black electorate. This will happen because black voters are making specific job demands upon all candidates for public office and a strong, solid black voting bloc gives teeth to their employment demands, which are made as trade-offs for their political support.

One far-reaching demand black middle-class representatives are beginning to make of elected officials is that they support the development and expansion of black-owned business enterprises. Black mayors, for instance, generally insist that large corporations doing business in their jurisdictions set aside some significant proportion of their subcontracts for black-owned businesses. This procedure is beginning to stimulate black businesses as never before. Some are becoming major employers of blacks in a number of occupations, especially on the level of management. For example, Birmingham's black mayor, Richard Arrington, once pointed out that his administration has secured more business for minority (black) businesses than Birmingham had done in all of its 112-year history. The same can be said to some extent about all cities with black mayors.[17]

The black college educated are certainly in the vanguard of those who are pressing hard to enhance and organize blacks' newly acquired political power. This is especially evident now (1985). Spurred on by what many blacks perceive as an anti-civil rights, anti-poor stance of President Ronald Reagan and his administration, blacks in all walks of life are becoming significantly involved in the political process. Even such venerable civil rights organizations as the NAACP and the NUL have actively entered the political arena to an unprecedented degree in attempts to make politicians and government on all levels more responsive to blacks' economic needs and specific demands. The extent to which they are successful in this endeavor will be the extent to which politics and government will continue to open up what actually amounts to new professional and managerial careers for black college graduates.

Corporate Positions

Another important indication of blacks' occupational advancement during the last two decades, which has been pioneered by the college educated, is the 15 percent of our respondents who hold professional or management positions in the corporate world. These positions are, for the most part, on career ladders where regular promotions are just beginning to open for

blacks in any significant number. For instance, 87 percent of the respondents with promising careers in the corporate world are less than fifty years
of age.

In explaining how they were able to break the color barrier in their
particular corporations, the respondents listed several different strategies
and techniques they have found to be effective. Essentially, however, at
least three basic conditions have contributed to their success:

1. Federal affirmative action policies and programs, especially those written into contracts between private corporations and the federal government after the 1964 Civil Rights Act. As a result, some corporations, for
the first time, began active recruitment on black college campuses.

2. Enlightened self-interest on the part of some corporations. A few
corporations seem convinced that the employment of well-educated, ambitious, available blacks in high, visible positions is good for business. This
is particularly apropos of corporations where black consumers constitute
a significant proportion of their market.

3. Successful blacks in professional and managerial positions in mainstream corporations tend to be highly skilled in interracial diplomacy. By
and large blacks seem to accept the primary responsibility, or burden, of
establishing and maintaining creative racial harmony in the interracial
situations in which they are employed. Some are convinced that their
employers and supervisors fully expect them to be superb racial diplomats
and that their overall job rating may be greatly influenced by their ability
to establish and maintain a positive working relationship with even their
most bigoted white racist fellow workers.

In short, after centuries of struggle for economic recognition and advancement on the part of black Americans, and as a result of favorable
federal action and enlightened self-interest on the part of some large corporations, much of the uncertainty once attached to the employment of
blacks in traditionally designated white jobs has been removed. Consequently, black college graduates are now employed, even though often in
small, token numbers, in just about all basic white-collar and professional
jobs in American society. Some are achieving outstanding success in these
positions.

The respondents were asked to select what they regarded as the most
reliable means of achieving success in American society. Their responses
are summarized in Table 20.

The fact that 65 percent of the respondents believe that hard work and
a good education are still the best means of achieving success in American
society is an indication of their unswerving faith in the continuing efficacy
of the basic work ethic which has been the foundation of this nation's
industrial greatness. Thus while some acknowledge that such things as
personal contacts, family background, and luck do often play an important

Table 20
The Most Reliable Means of Achieving Success in the United States

Method	Male	Female	Total
Hard work and sacrifice	30%	24%	26%
A good education	38%	39%	39%
Knowing the right people	24%	28%	27%
Family background	2%	2%	2%
Luck	2%	2%	2%
Uncertain	4%	5%	4%

part in one's success, by and large they believe in the validity of the traditional American success formula: sound preparation and hard work.

When asked "Have you ever found your racial identity (being black) to be a factor in getting a particular job?" the respondents replied as follows:

Yes, a positive factor	36%
Yes, a negative factor	41%
Uncertain	23%
	100%

The great majority of the respondents (77 percent) feel that their racial identity has been a significant factor in their careers. Some (36 percent) believe that they secured certain jobs because they are black. Fully 84 percent of those who feel that being black has been a positive factor are employed in all-black or predominantly black situations: public school teachers, pastors of black churches, and managers of black-owned businesses. There are also a few who feel that being black has been a positive factor because they were employed by agencies or firms in response to Affirmative Action mandates, or conscious voluntary efforts on the part of some corporations. The largest group of respondents (41 percent) believe that being black has prevented them from getting some type(s) of employment, and 46 percent also indicated that being black had hindered what would have been normal promotions they might have received during their careers. Consequently, no matter how successful our respondents might have been in their particular careers, they still recognize race as an important reality to be dealt with. Only about a fourth (23 percent) are uncertain about the influence of race as a factor in their careers.

It is interesting that about two-thirds (62 percent) of those who are uncertain about the extent to which being black has influenced their careers are young (under forty years of age). Some have very high career expectations where they are now, and will continue to be, in direct competition with white peers. They have planned their careers very carefully and are supersensitive about factors which interfere with their progress.

Again, almost half (48 percent) of those who constitute the "uncertain" category indicated that they may have secured their present positions, or previous promotions, because of federal Affirmative Action agreements. Interviews with a few articulate individuals in this category reveal that they are characteristically embarrassed and frustrated because there may be reasons to believe that their success is due to factors other than genuine accomplishments and a superior quality of work. They generally resent the concepts of "tokenism" and "quotas" because they denigrate one's sense of personal achievement and worth.

In their determined thrust for upward occupational mobility, a considerable number of black college graduates have managed to transcend or otherwise successfully cope with a variety of complex, deeply rooted racial problems impeding their progress. Those who are succeeding in mainstream American society tend to attribute their success to an excellent education, which included basic occupational skills, plus a broad knowledge of race relations, high ambition, and a willingness to work hard and make necessary personal sacrifices.

One of our respondents, who is a highly paid vice president of a large corporation, volunteered an explanation of his considerable occupational success. He wrote:

> I have had some success. I was well-trained in a small black college where my teachers prepared me for the *real world*. I know how to get along with my white and black subordinates as well as my superiors. I work hard. I get results. I make my boss look good. I get promotions when my turn comes.

This respondent's formula for success is the one generally followed by other successful black corporate managers. In essence, it is the formula the Dickenses elaborated upon in their comprehensive study of black managers in various corporations throughout the United States.[18] Their respondents catalogued an impressive list of "do's and don'ts" on the "how-to's" of success-oriented first-generation black managers in mainstream corporations.They conclude that it is essential that black managers

> Learn those skills and techniques that are unique to the survival, adjustment, and planned growth of the corporation. [Also] learn how to interact with others who possess suppressed racism as well as those who display overt racism.... Learn to think like a racist. Try to see things as a racist would by using the concept "Behold! The other side of the coin."[19]

Based upon the informed discussion of the Dickenses, we may conclude that for black professionals and managers to succeed in mainstream corporations—where the culture articulates white middle-class, industrial values—they must be technically competent, possess a thorough knowledge of the norms and values which prevail generally in the corporate world as well as in their particular corporation, and be superbly skilled in the art of race relations with special emphasis upon racial diplomacy. The added burden of racial diplomacy, allegedly built into the job expectations of black professionals and managers in mainstream occupations in American society, may be the reason they often concur with the bitter cliche that "in order for blacks to succeed they must be twice as good as their white competitors."

When we take into account the wide range and peculiar combinations of technical and race relations skills characteristically expected of black professionals or managers in mainstream occupations, where they must first pass the "merit" hurdle and then compete with white peers, we are led to recognize the value of an education in historically black colleges. In these colleges students are especially provided formal and informal opportunities to receive expert training in race relations, as an integral, realistic aspect of their pre-professional education.

Insofar as our respondents are concerned, certainly much of their overall occupational and leadership success is due to their developed ability to cope with covert and overt forms of personal and institutionalized racism.

SOME MEASURES OF OCCUPATIONAL SUCCESS

There are several different measures of occupational success[20] from the point of view of individual workers. These measures are given various degrees of sanction by the particular culture of which the designated occupation is an inherent part. These measures range all the way from purely selfish goals to be attained, to the rendering of altruistic services to one's fellowmen. However, for our analysis we may consider five broad areas of measurement or goals to be attained, as cited by the respondents: the amount of income; a feeling of occupational adequacy; job security; a feeling of self-fulfillment that what one does for a living is important also to the welfare of others in his or her primary reference group, even the society at large—and respect from one's occupational peers.

Income

Income is certainly one of the most commonly used measures of success in American society. With few exceptions, such as in regard to individuals in our armed forces, the ministry, and teaching, persons with the highest salaries are generally regarded as the most successful and ranked above others with lower salaries.

Table 21
Respondents' and Spouses' Incomes from Main Occupations

Annual Income	Respondents	Male	Female	Spouses
Under $15,000	24%	19%	27%	21%
$15,000–$19,999	22%	15%	26%	20%
$20,000–$24,999	21%	14%	25%	25%
$25,000–$29,999	15%	18%	13%	15%
$30,000–$34,999	7%	10%	5%	9%
$35,000–$50,000	8%	16%	3%	7%
Over $50,000	3%	8%	1%	3%
Median	$22,000	$26,000	$18,000	$22,000

Table 22
Annual Family Income of Respondents

Under $15,000	12%
$15,000–$19,999	9%
$20,000–$29,999	11%
$30,000–$34,999	10%
$35,000–$50,000	29%
Over $50,000	18%
Median	$32,000

In addition to income received from their main occupations (see Table 21), almost a third (32 percent) of the respondents received some income from other sources: part-time second jobs, speaking engagements, consultant's fees, real estate, interest on investments, and so forth. About 70 percent of those with "other" incomes received less than $10,000 annually, and only 5 percent received as much as $25,000 annually from other sources. On the average, then, the actual annual family income of the respondents was between $32,000 and $35,000 (see Table 22).

To fully appreciate the economic success of our respondents, it is necessary to compare their income with those of other meaningful reference groups. Therefore, it is apropos to compare their income with other black workers and families, white workers and families, and with their white peers in similar positions.

Comparable Incomes

When we use constant dollars based upon the 1980 incomes of various comparable groups in American society, we find that the black college graduates in this study have been eminently successful as a group.[21]

The median annual salary in 1980 of black male workers in the United States generally was $13,321. The median annual salary of our male respondents was $26,000, or almost double that of black male workers at large. The contrast between the median income of the families of the respondents and other families generally was even more pronounced. The median annual income of all families in the United States (1980) was $21,023; for white families it was $21,904, and for black families it was just $12,674. The median income of black families headed by college graduates was $23,282, and for white families headed by college graduates, it was $30,321. Thus, the median income of the families represented in this study was at least $32,000. When income from other sources was added to salary, their median annual family income was about $35,000.

Furthermore, while approximately 40 percent of all black workers earned less than $10,000 when this study was done, less than 10 percent of our respondents (9.3 percent) had salaries below $10,000. Also, while just 8 percent of all black families may be classified as "affluent"—having an annual income of $35,000 and over—at least 47 percent of our respondents reported annual family incomes of $35,000 and over.

Not only does the proportion of affluent families among the black college-educated greatly exceed the (8 percent) proportion among black families on the whole, but the proportion is more than double the 21 percent among white families on the whole, whose annual income was $35,000 and over.

Salaries Compared with Those of White Peers

Although reliable data necessary to compare the annual salaries of our respondents with those earned by white peers in the same or similar positions are not available, some important light is thrown upon this problem by David H. Swinton. He estimates that on the average, black workers earn about 20 percent less than their white peers. While the salaries of professionally trained black females are consistently lower than those of their male peers, they are generally about equal to those of their white female peers. In a few top occupations highly trained black females have larger median salaries than do their white female peers.[22]

From evidence available, we may conclude that the salaries of black workers, on the whole, continue to lag significantly behind those of their white peers, who generally earn from 20 percent to 30 percent more. However, that traditional gap is slowly narrowing. The salaries of black college graduates are usually from 85 percent to 98 percent as much as those received by their white peers.

Where the black college educated are concerned, the main problem is not so much differential salaries for the positions they hold, as it is the fact that they have unusual difficulties in securing an equitable number of the better-paying positions in their chosen occupations.

Our respondents were asked "To what extent are you satisfied with your present salary?" They answered as follows:

Very satisfied	12%
Satisfied	40%
Not satisfied	38%
Very dissatisfied	10%
	100%

While almost half (48 percent) indicated that they were not satisfied with their present salary, 49 percent reported that they expected some salary increase. This was equally true of those who indicated satisfaction and dissatisfaction.

In some instances, the respondents' expressed dissatisfaction with the amount of salary or income they received indicates more about their ambition to get ahead than it does about the size of their salary or income per se. Actually, some respondents with the highest earnings, such as physicians, entrepreneurs, and corporate managers, expressed about the same degree of satisfaction or dissatisfaction as did some of the lowest-paid professionals, such as teachers, nurses, and social workers. It seems that their evaluation of their salaries or earnings was primarily influenced by what they perceived as norms for others in their particular positions and not for workers in American society generally. The measure of their overall satisfaction or dissatisfaction with salary had direct reference to norms in their particular occupations, or more specifically, the income of others they regard as their peers.

Choice of Occupation

Another measure of occupational success is the extent to which incumbents are satisfied with their choice of life's work or career. In this respect our respondents are very successful because 85 percent reported that they like the work in which they are primarily engaged, and would select the same occupation again if they had to do it over. When asked the extent to which they are satisfied with their chosen careers, the respondents answered as follows:

Very satisfied	38%
Satisfied	47%
Not satisfied	11%
Very dissatisfied	4%
	100%

Perhaps the most convincing indication that the respondents are reasonably satisfied with their career choices is the fact that while 32 percent did express the right of their children to select their own careers, 42 percent would encourage their children to select the same occupations in which they, the parents, are engaged. However, about 26 percent would like to see their children select a different occupation from theirs. Those who would not like their children to follow the same occupation agree with several who explained that their children have a much wider spectrum of occupations from which to choose than they did, and they have pragmatically concluded that their children should take full advantage of the new, expanding employment opportunities and not be encumbered by traditions of the past which have severely limited blacks' occupational options. Thus, a fifty-six–year–old male high school principal reasoned: "When I was in school Negro boys had very few respectable jobs open to them.... Today our children can reasonably hope to get whatever jobs they are trained for by the time they are adults. They should prepare for the jobs white people have always had."

Again, 13 percent of the respondents predict that better opportunities will open up for blacks in all occupations in the future, and 66 percent predicted that opportunities for success in their own occupations will continue to expand for blacks. They also feel that those who get the proper training and are willing to work hard will have equal chances of success regardless of race.

Job Qualifications

Generally speaking, the respondents in this study are very well satisfied with their occupational choices and advancement (see Table 23). Fully 97 percent feel well qualified for the work in which they are engaged; about half (47 percent) believe that they are even better qualified than are their immediate white peers, and only 3 percent feel less well qualified than their white peers. The others (50 percent) feel that they are as well qualified as their white peers. A significant 20 percent feel overqualified for the positions they hold.

Upon close examination, we find that those who feel overqualified for the positions they hold are usually (78 percent) those who are engaged in non-professional (white-collar) or lower-level professional occupations and are still struggling to achieve higher professional or managerial status.

Table 23
Qualifications Compared with White Co-Workers

Qualifications	Male	Female	Total
Much more qualified	24%	29%	27%
Somewhat more qualified	25%	18%	20%
Equally qualified	50%	51%	50%
Somewhat less qualified	1%	1%	2%
Much less qualified	0%	1%	1%

One outstanding characteristic of the respondents' careers is the fact that they have been stable, dependable employees. The median number of years they have held their present positions is ten. This may be why so many feel that they are succeeding. That is, most feel occupationally secure. Though they are generally young (the median age is forty-three), 57 percent believe that opportunities for promotion or advancement in their present positions are very good; 43 percent express some degree of uncertainty or skepticism about future advancement. However, 61 percent expressed satisfaction with their advancement so far. The others (39 percent) expressed some degree of dissatisfaction with the rate of their advancement. Most of those expressing dissatisfaction (34 percent of the total) attribute the "slowness" of their occupational advancement to their being black.

One respondent voiced the feeling of others when he wrote:

> Even in the most democratic situations, such as we have in certain large corporations, there is a definite, often invisible ceiling on blacks' advancement. Even the most acceptable blacks can only expect to progress so far—then they are likely to encounter too much opposition to make more progress.

It would be very difficult to determine precisely the extent to which the attitude expressed above is real or the figment of some paranoid syndrome resulting from centuries of oppression experienced by black Americans. Actually, some expert observers, such as William J. Wilson, would hold that the extent to which race is a determinant of blacks' occupational success is much overrated;[23] yet as William I. Thomas insisted, "If men define situations as real, they are real in their consequence."[24] Thus, it may be that black college graduates who are convinced that their upward occupational movement is limited may be condemning themselves to the outcome of their own prophecy. That is, they may not be moving up because they don't believe they can; they won't because they cease to try.

Insofar as the great majority of our respondents are concerned, there is general optimism about their future; they tend to feel that there is no enduring artificial racial ceiling. There is every reason to predict that more and more of them will go beyond the job ceilings other, more pessimistic black professionals perceive as real and enduring.

Future Outlook

At least 67 percent of the respondents plan to make a career of their present jobs; 14 percent are still uncertain, and 19 percent are already planning to change jobs as soon as some other better job is available.

Among those who are pessimistic or uncertain about their occupational future are those who report that even though future advancements or promotions are unlikely, they now have the best jobs available to black persons with their particular preparation, experience, and social clout. Their decision to remain in their present positions is based primarily upon the belief that a better job will be difficult to find.

In explaining their pessimism about their future careers, several respondents cited a growing national conservatism, or "an unsympathetic national administration." Thirty-two percent of them concur that the future job outlook for the black college educated is dim and worsening. As one respondent put it, "The growth of the black middle class—the black professional class—has been abruptly stopped. If this racist situation continues there will be no jobs for them. The future looks bleak."

The statement above is not unique. It calls attention to a dimension of occupational insecurity expressed in one way or another by many, perhaps most, black college graduates with whom I have talked. Some feel trapped by several U.S. Federal Court decisions which deliberately support the doctrine of "the last hired, the first fired." This policy, Hooks insisted "represents a roll back, a retreat, unequivocally in the enforcement of civil rights."[25] Therefore, even among the most successful respondents, there is often a feeling of job insecurity which stems from more or less continuous fluctuations in the American economy that have resulted in some serious, maybe permanent, cutbacks in professional and managerial jobs. College-educated blacks have been compelled to realize that they are likely to experience the same patterns of discrimination as are other blacks in the labor market. Actually, the threat to blacks who hold key professional jobs in human service agencies and programs sponsored directly or indirectly by the federal government is especially imminent due to drastic cutbacks in financial support. Also, production freezes and unusually stringent budgets of some private corporations have resulted in commensurate degrees of job attrition, including permanent loss of certain professional and managerial jobs. Ordinarily blacks in such positions are more insecure than their white peers because most will have been the last hired.

While a large proportion of our respondents do enjoy a comfortable degree of job security, others are always mindful that they are the most vulnerable when their corporations or agencies encounter financial setbacks or changing policies which might lead to a reduction in professional or white-collar jobs.

Occupational Status

When asked to evaluate their overall occupational status, those in our sample responded as follows:

Very satisfactory	66%
Somewhat satisfactory	25%
Unsatisfactory	9%
	100%

Upon close examination we find that satisfaction or dissatisfaction with occupational status is due to a variety of factors. Basically it is an attitude, often very subtle, and usually stems from perceived, more or less intangible aspects of the work environment: feeling wanted or rejected, respected or disesteemed, belonging or an outsider, contributor or non-contributor. Thus, 54 percent of those who are "very satisfied" with their occupational status indicated that they feel that they are an important part of the enterprise or occupation in which they are employed. The others (46 percent) expressed satisfaction with the quality of work they perform and felt respected by their peers. These are the high morale workers who regard their occupation as an integral part of their personal life and social identity. To them the basic question is not "What do you do?" but "Who are you?"

Those who indicated considerable dissatisfaction with their occupational status (9 percent) gave a number of reasons. Among the reasons most often cited were unsatisfactory salary, slow promotions, racism, and "the boss."

Those who expressed strong dissatisfaction with their occupational status feel that they deserve more recognition. This attitude, regardless of the amount of salary or the formal position itself, seems to be the key determinant of the degree of job satisfaction. Actually, research has shown that a primary function of salary raises and promotions is that they validate earned status and respect on the part of management. Thus a keen observer of job satisfaction concluded:

> Most of us want the satisfaction that comes from being recognized as people of worth by our friends and work associates. Money is only a small part of this social recognition....We all want tangible evidence of our social importance. We want the feeling of security that comes not so much from the amount of money we have in the bank as from being accepted as a member of a group.[26]

As we review the careers of the respondents, we are compelled to conclude that as a highly selected, representative group, they are having some significant success. They have, indeed, come a long way from their socioeconomic origins and from the occupational statuses of their parents. They are truly pioneers in blacks' movement toward the mainstream of this nation's economic life.

Through long, persistent efforts and faith in the democratic process, the respondents, as representatives of black college graduates at large, have emerged as convincing evidence that insofar as this nation is concerned the principles inherent in the American Creed are still viable and function as influential norms in American culture. They still believe that a good education, hard work, and excellent skills in racial diplomacy are the most effective means of getting ahead in American society. In this respect, they are quintessential Americans.

NOTES

1. Gunnar Myrdal, *An American Dilemma* (New York: Harper and Row, 1944; reprint, New York: Pantheon Books, 1975), pp. 60–67.

2. Ibid., p. 587.

3. Ibid., p. 61.

4. William H. Exum, "Climbing the Crystal Stair," *Social Problems* 30 (April 1983): 383–385.

5. The UNCF counted 2,742 recruiters representing a cross section of the corporate world who visited UNCF colleges during the 1973–1974 academic year. See United Negro College Fund, *Annual Statistical Report of the Member Institutions, 1974*, p. 48.

6. Robert W. Brocksbank, "The Bomb in Their Desks," paper presented at the Conference on Liberal Learning and Careers, Philadelphia, Penn., December 3, 1981.

7. Ibid.

8. U.S. Department of Commerce, Bureau of the Census, *The Social and Economic Status of the Black Population in the United States, 1970–1978*, Series p–23, no. 80 (1978), p. 75.

9. Ibid., p. 62.

10. National Commission on Excellence in Education, *A Nation at Risk: The Imperative for Educational Reform*, (Washington, D.C.: U.S. Department of Education, April 1983), p. 8.

11. See a documentation of this by Lawrence D. Maloney, "Success! The Chase is Back in Style Again," in *U.S. News and World Report*, October 3, 1983, 60–63.

12. Discussed by James Lawrence, "The Space Program...Disallowed Black Folks," *National Leader*, September 8, 1983, 7.

13. Myrdal, *An American Dilemma*, p. 29.

14. David Fyten, "The Way We Were," in *Tulanian* 55 (Fall 1984): 20.

15. See a summary of black corporate board members in Donald C. Walker, ed., *1983 Blackbook* (Chicago: National Publications, 1983), p. 3.

16. For further information on Peter Eisenberg's study, see Edmund Newton, "Taking over City Hall," *Black Enterprise* 13 (June 1983): 158–159.

17. See Charles V. Hamilton, "On Politics and Voting: Messages and Meanings," in National Urban League, *The State of Black America 1983*, p. 271.

18. Floyd B. Dickens, Jr., and Jacqueline B. Dickens, *The Black Manager: Making It in the Corporate World* (New York: Amaco, 1982), p. 284.

19. Ibid., pp. 284–286.

20. For profiles of a wide range of success patterns "American style," see Bryant S. Mason, "In the Middle of the Action," *Black Enterprise*, 13 (August 1982): 50–52; and Maloney, "Success!"

21. Comparable data have been adapted from U.S. Department of Commerce, Bureau of the Census, *Money, Income and Poverty Status of Families and Persons in the United States: 1980*, Current Population Reports, Consumer Income, Series p–60, no. 127, August 1981.

22. David H. Swinton, "The Economic Status of the Black Population," National Urban League, *The State of Black America 1983*, pp. 45–88, especially pp. 73, 145–147.

23. William Julius Wilson, *The Declining Significance of Race* (Chicago: University of Chicago Press, 1980). This book emphasizes this central point.

24. William I. Thomas, *The Unadjusted Girl* (Boston: Little, Brown, 1923), pp. 41–43.

25. "Civil Rights Heads Differ on N.O. Police Settlement," *Louisiana Weekly* newspaper (January 15, 1983): 1, 13. For a comprehensive summary of key anti-affirmative action court decisions, see Ted Gest, et al., "Justice Under Reagan," *U.S. News and World Report*, 99, no. 16, pp. 60–62.

26. F. J. Roethlisberger, *Management and Morale* (Cambridge, Mass.: Harvard University Press, 1941), pp. 11–12.

6 Social Life

The black college graduates constituting the sample for this study, very much like the American middle class in general, may be classified as joiners. They seem to have great faith in the efficacy of social organizations to solve social problems and promote individual, racial, and social class interests. They were asked "In how many different organizations do you hold membership?" The distribution of their answers can be seen in Table 24.

There are several hundred more or less formal black organizations (local, state, regional, and national) in the United States. At least 164 are national in terms of their membership. It is estimated that more than 150 of the national organizations hold annual national conventions.[1]

As will be noted in another connection, each of the black organizations provides opportunities for the identification and development of leaders and for sustained black unity and cooperation. Each is part of what turns out to be an effective network which facilitates regular communication among mostly black college graduates. Essentially the many organizations are bound together by one overriding concern: blacks' all-out struggle for equality. Hence, each of the organizations will have some major part of its general program or activities dedicated to blacks' survival and advancement in American society.

The respondents' pronounced proclivity to join organizations and engage in a wide variety of social, religious, fraternal, sororal, business, professional, political, community, and civil rights organizations and programs, at considerable financial and personal costs, underscores the key difference which sets them apart, as a group, from the black masses, or underclass, where very few individuals belong to any formal organization except, per-

Table 24
Membership in Social Organizations

Number of Organizations	Male	Female	Total
None	9%	11%	10%
Only one	12%	18%	16%
Two–four	60%	57%	58%
Five or more	19%	14%	16%

haps, the church.[2] This fact has been often noted as a basic reason why the largely unorganized black masses tend to wield little or no effective social power or influence over the private and public organizations and agencies which directly or indirectly affect or actually determine their general welfare. Few of those who constitute the black non-college underclass are involved in the planning and programs of relevant local social organizations or have sufficient indigenous organized clout to exert much pressure upon other "outside" organizations to act in their behalf.

Conversely, perhaps the main reason why black college graduates ordinarily have significant success as individuals and as a distinct, recognized social class is the fact that they are relatively well organized and have highly developed skills in the use, or manipulation, of organized social power in their own behalf.

The specific purposes or goals of the organizations in which the respondents hold membership range all the way from those for voter registration and the election of black candidates for public office to those specifically designed to establish, enhance, validate, and celebrate the high social status of successful individuals and families who belong to black society.[3]

It is true, as E. Franklin Frazier argued, that some organizations among the black college-educated are avowedly designed to set forth and promote social class exclusiveness and snobbery based upon what may be regarded as quite superficial differences, such as skin color, the size or location of one's residence, or one's associates. However, the great majority of our respondents seem to be joiners of what may be deemed worthwhile, even essential, organizations dedicated to civic betterment, racial advancement, and the general welfare. Even the purely social organizations are likely to have some program dedicated to racial advancement or some form of education, health, housing, political unity, and so forth.

For instance, all of the most exclusive, class-conscious black organizations characteristically legitimize or attempt to justify their existence on the basis of their regular support of such essential black organizations as the UNCF, the NAACP, the NUL, and the Association for the Study of Black History and Culture. Consequently, membership in a number of black organizations bespeaks one's belonging insofar as civil rights and democracy are concerned; it is an important mark of respectability which may be a result of, or may lead to, upward social mobility. As a result there is usually a rather long list of candidates waiting for membership in the more prestigious black social organizations. When these more established organizations are slow in accepting members who are "eligible," those who deem themselves eligible but not accepted often establish new organizations similar to the ones already in existence.

Some of our respondents apparently engage in selective joining as a main avenue of upward social mobility, which might even lead to career advancement. Thus, several of them submitted solid evidence to verify their active membership in twenty or more different organizations representing various areas of the social, economic, business, political, and educational life of their particular communities and the nation at large. Many of them are pioneering members in erstwhile all-white organizations (institutions, voluntary groups, powerful boards, and commissions).

It should be noted in this connection that blacks' membership in traditionally white organizations, especially those that wield significant social power, is still generally regarded as a major achievement. This achievement is recognized and lauded throughout the black community. It is usually cited as a measure of blacks' ambition and progress in American society. When we closely review the usual accolades showered upon blacks who are accepted as members of influential white groups, it can be detected that the real or basic virtues extolled are hard work, a good education, faith in the democratic process, and superb racial diplomacy. In other words, the black community, and the larger community generally, will likely regard the first or only black member in white organizations as a successful person.

Very often blacks who are deemed acceptable in some particular erstwhile white organization will likely be recommended to other such organizations that are open, so to speak, for a limited number of black members. As a result, a relatively few "acceptable" blacks tend to monopolize such memberships in a variety of white organizations.

As a rule, blacks in white organizations quickly emerge as designated spokespersons for blacks' interest whether or not they desire to do so, or for that matter, whether they are capable of doing so. Some even become informal power brokers between established white organizations and the black population at large, or some narrow, special-interest black groups. Indeed, black college graduates through their own organizations are constantly demanding representation in white organizations and appointments to powerful white-dominated commissions and committees where major social, political, economic, and administrative decisions are made.

Incidentally, the "representative" or "power broker" role occasionally accorded a few highly selected blacks in some powerful white organizations today is regarded by blacks as a much higher status than it was during the heyday of Jim Crow, when certain white organizations would recognize selected blacks and legitimize them as leaders in order to control other blacks through them.

In many instances, black members in white organizations are likely to perform a subtle though very important reciprocal legitimizing function. Not only does the prestige or social power of the particular white organizations rub off on them and enhance their personal social status, but they, in turn, often enhance the public image and authority of the white organizations in question by becoming convincing symbols of these organizations' commitment to the principle of equal opportunity, their belief in the democratic process, and their honest concern for the general welfare.

In a word, it is now more or less expected that key, powerful, mainstream, erstwhile white organizations, such as local chambers of commerce, political parties, and the United Way, include selected blacks. They can hardly claim legitimacy in communities with relatively large black populations unless they have at least a token number of black members.

Black organizations are demanding that black members be included in organizations which wield significant social power. They are very likely to insist that concerned blacks withdraw support or patronage from business enterprises, political factions, and civic groups which do not have recognized black members in decision-making positions.

As mentioned above, undoubtedly the most socially influential, respectable status accorded a few, very highly selected blacks in white organizations is "member of the board of directors" of major public and private corporations, commissions, committees, and agencies. Such membership ordinarily carries with it a number of ascribed, inherent benefits and privileges which are light-years away from the legendary, informal Uncle Tom role whites have customarily accorded a few selected, faithful black leaders throughout American history. Basically, the essential role of Uncle Tom has been that of helping white power figures preserve the racial status quo. The absolute reverse role is usually expected of "black representatives" today. They are generally perceived as formal innovators whose essential role is to assist certain white-controlled organizations in their efforts to broaden their policies and practices regarding the place of minorities and women generally, and black Americans specifically. Yet the role expected of the "accepted black" has always tended to retain at least one inherent, central characteristic: the black member or spokesperson has been always expected to establish meaningful communication between white authority figures and black leadership or at least selected black organizations.

For whatever reason different erstwhile white groups may have for admitting or actually recruiting black members, several of our respondents emphasized the belief that such membership provides them important opportunities to contribute to blacks' chances for survival and advancement in this country. One respondent expressed it this way:

> Now that I and other Negro leaders can work as equals with quality white people we don't have to stand alone in the civil rights struggle as Negroes had to do twenty years ago. Now we can speak directly to white people who are able to help us with our problems. We can now work *within* the system for needed changes.

According to information provided by the respondents, the practice of including black college graduates on the boards of directors of certain powerful community organizations or institutions is becoming rather widespread. About 12 percent of the respondents report serving on boards of institutions which must receive broad community support, such as hospitals, schools, the United Way, political factions, and so forth. One of their major functions on these boards is that of educating white members about the needs of the black community and dealing effectively with race relations issues. In a sense, the black "representative" is expected to be an expert on the black experience and able to interpret it for powerful white members.

Blacks who are deemed acceptable members by powerful white groups are usually in the position of the proverbial "tightrope walker." On the one hand, fellow blacks expect them to give white power figures a positive impression of the black community and of certain black individuals and institutions. For them the black member is a sort of ambassador who is expected to gain white support for black causes. Fellow blacks usually expect constructive social changes in their behalf and are ever vigilant to see that this is done. For instance, in some key cities where blacks have significant political clout, a few of them have been appointed to business planning organizations or committees. Fellow blacks who have been customarily frustrated by the process of establishing and maintaining stable, lucrative businesses fully expect black members to negotiate sizeable "set aside" funds and broaden opportunities for ambitious black businesspersons. When the designated black member does not produce for the special-interest groups, or for the black community at large, he or she is likely to be criticized as a modern Uncle Tom who sells out to powerful whites.

On the other hand, fellow white members of the organizations and their constituencies are likely to exert about the same degree of vigilance as does the black community. They are anxious to see how their black members behave when crucial racial or race-related issues are in question. They are likely to evaluate black members according to how dependable they prove to be in supporting and promoting status quo issues and efforts. As a respondent stated:

> I was the first black ever to serve on the Board of Directors of
> ——— corporation. It has been a great honor and I have learned
> much, yet I knew from the very beginning that I was selected
> because they believed I would be safe—not because they thought
> I would be an innovator, or a militant Negro.

All in all, the respondents in this study who hold membership in formerly all-white organizations are convinced that they are able to contribute to a better understanding of both the black experience and the democratic process. They feel that they are truly making some difference in their communities and that they are pioneers in another promising process of racial desegregation.

Let us turn now to a more specific discussion of a few major organizations which constitute the basic social life of our respondents.

THE BLACK CHURCH

The black church is the most important institution founded by black Americans. Originally it represented a delicate, unique, functional blending of highly selected African religious and magical traits with certain complementary traits from the Judeo-Christian heritage of the white slave masters. Du Bois argued that the black church was the first institution founded by Afro-American slaves and antedates even the black family in the United States.[4]

In a very real sense, then, the black church is the fountainhead of blacks' social life. All major black institutions and organizations either grew directly out of it, such as colleges, insurance companies, and a number of "secret orders," or lodges, or were indirectly nurtured by it, such as the primary organizations constituting the civil rights movement. Among the latter have been the NAACP, the NUL, and the Southern Christian Leadership Conference (SCLC). None could have developed as they have without church support. Benjamin L. Hooks, president of the NAACP, acknowledged:

> The NAACP has maintained the closest possible relationship
> with churches. . . . Indeed, the progress made by the Association
> over the years has been possible in considerable part due to
> the support that it has received from churches, their members
> and friends. . . . More than 7,500 churches and religious groups
> are Life Members and some are also Golden Heritage Members
> of the NAACP.[5]

Throughout the twentieth century, the black church has given to civil rights organizations and many racial uplift efforts strong financial and social support and trained their leaders on all levels from the local, grass-roots leaders to those on the state, regional, and national scenes. Consequently, church membership on the part of blacks goes far beyond religion per se. It also indicates a great deal about the individual's social identity, social class status, and his or her relationship to blacks' struggles, hopes, and various unique historical experiences.

Membership in some church has been generally expected of black adults, especially those in prominent and leadership positions. In some instances the particular church to which one belongs is a reliable indicator of that person's or family's overall social status in the larger community. There is a strong tendency for the black masses, or those of the black underclass, to gravitate toward the more informal, esoteric, spiritualist denominations, sects, and churches; while the more affluent, college-educated blacks tend to join the more formal, ritualistic, traditional religious denominations and churches.[6]

It must be remembered, however, that it is not at all uncommon to find a particular church congregation composed of individual members and families from just about all socio-economic segments in the black community where it is located. Actually, some of the most prestigious churches in any given community may include in their congregations individuals and families of rather humble origins and achievements (unlettered and poor) who were the founders and who experienced the development of their churches' social mobility from more or less esoteric, mass-oriented institutions to become the highest-status black churches in their respective communities. A respondent in this study writes:

> I was one of the dozen or so founders of my church over fifty years ago. I have served in every office in the church and even preached on a few occasions. We did not have a college graduate as pastor during the first twenty-three years. Since we got our first seminary-trained pastor other educated people have joined our church. Now most of our members are educated or have children in college. We have become a highfalutin church.

The social class mixture in some black churches dramatically underscores the rapid social mobility characteristic of blacks at large. Frequently, there are wide social status differences even between parents and children, among siblings, and among the rank-and-file members of the same church. Nevertheless, so far as I have been able to ascertain, there seems to be very little inter–social class conflict in comprehensive social class churches. Some pastors of such churches report that non-college members and the college-educated members usually establish a kind of spiritual symbiosis whereby certain chores are assumed by the better educated (those requiring special training, such as director of music, community relations, and so forth); most other chores are left to the less well educated.

This recognition of multi–social class congregations extends also to the form and content of worship services. A respondent in this study claims:

> I really preach three different types of sermons every Sunday: one directed at the group of seminary students who come to hear me; the second is aimed at the 25 percent or more of my members who are business and professional people, and the third is directed at ordinary members, or the "Aunt Janes," who come to enjoy themselves.

The fact that many college-educated individuals remain in churches which also include lower-class members provides an excellent opportunity for a high level of cooperation among persons of different social classes. Instead of simply changing from lower-class to upper-class churches, the upwardly mobile participants in this study have been more likely to remain in their original denominations and try to elevate their standards in terms of more universal theological premises, as opposed to narrow esoteric premises, a more realistic otherwordly, temporal orientation, and a more rational, better-planned form of worship generally.[7]

DENOMINATIONAL AFFILIATIONS OF THE RESPONDENTS

It may be advisable to reiterate that some black religious denominations, particularly the Baptists and Methodists, may have different churches representing different social classes insofar as the composition of their congregations are concerned. Therefore, any one of the traditional denominations might have both the highest-status and the lowest-status churches in the same community. Consequently, it would be quite arbitrary to rank any particular black religious denomination per se above or below the social status of some other denominations: a specific church may be well-known for its educated, affluent, professional-class membership, while another church in the same denomination may be regarded as the church of the masses. In other words, it may be that in any given large black community there will be a particular church which is regarded as the high-status or leading church because it has a significant number of college-educated members. Yet a church so designated may, in fact, represent any one of the traditional black Protestant denominations.

The respondents in this study were asked to indicate "What, if any, is your religious affiliation?" Their responses are summarized in Table 25. Several things may be concluded from the data in Table 25.

The sample colleges, though most were founded by church bodies and some still maintain their denominational ties, practice open religious enrollment in the recruitment of their students. Students (in this instance, graduates) representing all traditional religious faiths are more or less

Table 25
Denominational Affiliation

Baptist	43%
Catholic	10%
United Methodist	10%
Other Methodist(s)	14%
United Church of Christ	3%
Other Protestants	10%
Other sects	7%
None	3%

evenly distributed among them. And so far as I have been able to ascertain, none of the colleges has engaged in any systematic efforts to proselytize students from other faiths. Consequently, "students in these colleges generally remain in the denomination of their parents."[8]

The tendency for college-educated blacks to remain in the denominations of their parents makes for social stability and growth on the part of the various individual black denominations. They have been able to maintain their effectiveness even during times of dangerous racial crises and rapid social changes. Thus, under various socio-economic conditions experienced by blacks, the church at large has continued to function as a major transmitter and enricher of the black cultural heritage and the primary center for racial organization and cooperation.

Traditionally, the black church, constituting several different denominations and esoteric religious sects, has strongly fostered the preservation of blacks' individual dignity and pride. It has promoted racial unity, vis-à-vis unequal intraracial social mobility which constantly threatens to divide the black community into self-conscious, separate, uncooperating, even disruptive social classes, and it has been always in the midst of blacks' struggle for survival and advancement.

In many communities, North and South, where blacks have faced prolonged periods of dire poverty, racial intimidation, and white aggression, the black church has been their social, moral, and spiritual bulwark. It has performed these functions by being flexible in terms of its structural and theological commitments and its basic mission. That is, the black church per se has taken various stances as it deemed necessary to confront the most imminently threatening problems faced by its constituents during given crises. For instance, it has manifested itself as essentially spiritual and otherworldly when the practical problems encountered by its members, or black people as a whole, were apparently insurmountable, such as was slavery; legally recognized Jim Crow, which was established to relegate blacks forever to subcitizenship and disesteem; and institutionalized racism, which has been cunningly designed to impede blacks' economic, political, and social advancement.

When such deeply rooted, universally sanctioned problems have threatened the very survival of the race by undermining the hope and faith blacks have had in a better life, black preachers often elected to ignore such problems and focus the attention of their congregations upon loftier or spiritual things. In this way their followers have been able to escape for a while the torment, frustrations, shattered dreams, and the hopelessness inherent in their particular situations. The black preacher knew that suffering, if prolonged, would certainly drain his people of the will to persevere and continue the necessary struggle for individual and racial survival and advancement. Therefore, more or less unwittingly many black congregations, representing traditional religious denominations and a proliferation of religious sects or cults, characteristically espoused an otherworldly, spiritualistic stance at the expense of the everyday, temporal concerns of their members and other blacks.

The emphasis placed upon a strict otherworldly theology is deeply rooted in blacks' traditional religion. It must be understood as a logical consequence of their unique experiences in the United States. The black church was conceived against a background of slavery and segregation which challenged blacks' very humanity. When their present condition seemed hopeless, black religion produced a gospel of future hope and a theology of the suffering servant; at the same time, it also spun a corollary protest movement against the social order that oppressed them.[9] These two themes, the otherworldly (which some call the "pie-in-the-sky" theme) and the black liberation theme, have constantly haunted and disturbed the black church. A major issue has often been the church's division regarding the particular stance it would take.

To reinforce the black church's otherworldly theme were some definite restrictions white racists once placed upon blacks' religious services. Even after the slaves were emancipated and until recent decades, black churches in certain white communities in the South where racism was rampant were expected to bow to the doctrine of white supremacy. Black preachers fully understood that they were not to disturb their followers by reminding them of the injustices and indignities they suffered. Black preachers like their white counterparts were expected to mute the protest or liberation theme in their sermons and encourage their followers to respect in every way the white supremacy norms which were firmly established by law and custom. Preachers who violated these norms simply did not remain very long as pastors. They were not allowed to question the sanctity of the biracial status quo which prevailed throughout the social system.

Because of an unfortunate, mean combination of peculiar, insurmountable problems blacks encountered in a racist society and the doctrine of white supremacy, which was ruthlessly defended by the total white community for several decades after emancipation, the black church cautiously chose to emphasize the suffering-servant or otherworldly theme in its religion. When the protest or liberation theme did surface, it was usually so veiled in metaphors that it often lost its real meaning.[10] As an example of this the renowned scholar and preacher Benjamin E. Mays vividly described a black preacher who was his childhood pastor:

> The Reverend Marshall's preaching was highly other-worldly, emphasizing the joys of heaven and the damnation of hell. [He] ...taught the people to be honest and upright, the Gospel he preached was primarily an opiate to enable them to endure and survive the oppressive conditions under which they lived at the hands of the white people in the community. I never heard him utter one word against lynching. If he had, he would probably have been run out of the community—or lynched.[11]

As Mays reflected upon the reason his pastor bowed to white supremacy expectations, he concluded: "I am not necessarily condemning the use of religion as an opiate. Sometimes an opiate is good medicine. Sometimes it may be good in religion."[12]

Today the protest, or black liberation theme, is no longer muted because black churchgoers fear white retaliation. Actually, since the turbulent civil rights activities in the 1960s when several black churches were bombed and burned, the black church, with some notable exceptions, has become radicalized.[13]

Much of the emphasis the black church now gives to the liberation theme is due to the prodding and leadership of some college graduates who were involved in the 1960s civil rights movement. The graduates constituting the sample for this study are still challenging their local churches and the black church at large to become involved in the solution of problems blacks continue to suffer, directly and indirectly, due to racism. Some advocate that the church conduct voter registration drives and engage in political action. One respondent complained, "On the whole the black church still bears the 'mark of oppression' of former centuries when it was taking root in a segregated, racist South. It is now time to be concerned about how their members are living here on earth."

There are at least two basic reasons for the persistent dominance of the otherworldly, suffering-servant theme in black religion: first, it is central to blacks' religious belief; it is not simply an avenue of escape from unpleasant, mundane realities. It is also a theological principle which sustains them in this world and gives them hope of immortality, which is fundamental to Christianity and common to all races espousing it. And second, blacks still face many complex, apparently insurmountable problems and many feel the need to escape from their reality from time to time.

College-educated members of black churches generally argue that their churches still give lopsided attention to the suffering-servant theme and have too little concern for the black liberation theme. They are among the leaders who contend that the black church should spearhead voter registration drives and become actively involved in blacks' concern for better schools, health care, businesses, housing, jobs, and dignity. They have insisted that such mundane concerns are logical because blacks' oppression in the United States is a cardinal sin, and the church has a moral and ethical duty to oppose it. This spirit was eloquently expressed by King in his now-famous "Letter from a Birmingham Jail." In that apologia, King called for all religious leaders to join the fight for black liberation and to actively resist "unjust laws," which he defined as follows:

> Any law that uplifts human personality is just. Any law that degrades human personality is unjust. All segregation statutes are unjust because segregation distorts the soul and damages personality. I submit that an individual who breaks a law that conscience tells him is unjust, and willingly accepts the penalty by staying in jail to arouse the conscience of the community over its injustices, is in reality expressing the very highest respect for law.[14]

In support of this position Lawrence N. Jones, dean of the Howard University Divinity School, insists that "young and middle-class blacks today are asking for social relevance of the church, and want the church to exercise its role in human terms, in addition to a clear proclamation of the gospel.... [They] expect, if not demand, churches to become 'active agents of social change'."[15]

The black liberation theme, generally advocated by the college graduates in this study, was cogently enunciated by the National Committee of Black Churchmen. They stated that "Black Theology is a theology of Black Liberation. It seeks to plumb the black condition in the light of God's revelation in Jesus Christ, so that the Black community can see that the Gospel is commensurate with the achievement of Black humanity."[16]

According to a variety of sources, including our respondents, college-educated members of the black church are among the leaders of those who are attempting to get their individual churches and the black church as an institution to become more relevant to the serious, practical problems faced by black people in the United States. They would have the church provide a ready platform for social analysis and protest.

Under the leadership and proddings of some college-educated members, the black church has been cautiously shifting toward a more balanced concern with the otherworldly, suffering-servant theme and the more practical, mundane liberation theme. Even now, some of the most influential black churchpersons are leading the way toward the church's fuller participation in the temporal affairs of black people. The Reverend T. J. Jemison is president of the more than six million members of the National Baptist Convention U.S.A., the largest black organization in the United States. This convention publicly endorsed and pledged strong support for Jesse Jackson, 1984 candidate for president of the United States. However, there are still serious, legal questions about the extent to which the church, as such, can actively participate in partisan politics and retain its tax-exempt status. Nevertheless, the more than 30,000 black Baptist churches constituting the organization were asked to extend individual support to Jackson's bid for the presidency.[17]

Bishop Phillip R. Cousin, of the African Methodist Episcopal Church (AME), and president of the powerful interracial National Council of Churches, the nation's largest ecumenical church body made up of thirty-one denominations, with about forty million constituents, has contended that the black church can no longer afford to emphasize otherworldly theology and ignore political, economical, and sociological problems.[18]

Black college graduates, as represented in our sample, generally remain in the traditional denominations in which they were raised. Some, however, do transfer their membership to more formal, ritualistic denominations. While there is a critical dearth of reliable data on the subject, some college-educated blacks tend to transfer their membership to traditionally white churches. In discussing this phenomenon with some well-informed church leaders in this study, I was assured that only a relatively few blacks are joining white churches. One of the churchmen argued that the pre-1960s cliche is still quite apropos: "The most racially segregated hour in a given week is eleven o'clock on Sunday morning."

There are certainly several reasons why black college graduates, who are characteristically racial integrationists, do not ordinarily join white churches. Perhaps the basic reason is that religious worship is by its very nature a celebration. As a celebration it is designed to bring to meaningful focus the complex of folk experiences and the cultural heritage of a very distinct people. Generally speaking, then, blacks, who have experienced centuries of more or less complete segregation from whites and have been subjected to a great variety of unique experiences, would likely have great difficulty in finding satisfactory spiritual fulfillment in traditional white churches. Despite the fact that traditional black denominations had their roots in traditional white denominations and still adhere to essentially the same basic doctrinal and ritual precepts, there has been no strong, persistent movement to integrate the white church comparable to blacks' movement to integrate other institutions and aspects of American society. Among the varied explanations given as to why blacks choose to remain in black churches, Thomas Pettigrew, a Harvard University sociologist, insists that the black Protestant church was the first institution where

Table 26
Church Attendance of Respondents

Frequency	Male	Female	Total
Once a week or more	54%	69%	64%
About once a month	19%	13%	15%
Occasionally	17%	13%	14%
Seldom or never	10%	5%	7%

blacks could develop their own leadership and it's still one of their most important ladders to political power. Many people are unwilling to give that up just to go to church with white people.[19]

Instead of attempting to integrate white churches, there are some strong, well-thought-out efforts to organize the black church as a unified social institution. For instance, the avowed purpose of an attempt to unite all black churches under the proposed Congress of National Black Churches is to facilitate the cooperation of 65,000 black churches, with a combined membership of about twenty million blacks, as a coordinated effort to conquer growing social ills affecting blacks.

The movement toward a formal, united black church has been stimulated by black leaders' concern over the persistence of unemployment, poverty, broken homes, and crimes among blacks. The chairman of the movement, Bishop John Hurst Adams of the African Methodist Episcopal Church, defined the organization's essential mission in this "temporal" statement: "Economic development is a high priority among us. We're not going to be free so long as we're financed by someone else. Black denominations have a big responsibility."[20] Another leader, Richard Barber, concluded: "Unless we take full responsibility for economic strategy and planning, no one is going to do it for us."[21]

CHURCH ATTENDANCE

As can be seen in Table 26, not only do the college graduates in our sample tend to retain membership in traditionally black churches, but they are also more likely to be active church members than are Americans generally. The Gallup Poll reported that just 69 percent of Americans held membership in a church or synagogue in 1980 compared with 90 percent of those in our sample; and nationwide, just 40 percent of adults attend religious services regularly compared with 64 percent of our respondents.[22]

Some social scientists have noted that there is a strong tendency for college-educated, upwardly mobile blacks to leave the religious denominations of their childhood and join higher- and higher-status churches as they clamor for integration into the white world. For instance, a noted,

Table 27
Respondents' Involvement in Church Activities

Extent of Involvement	Male	Female	Total
National officer	5%	3%	4%
Local leader	28%	23%	25%
Active member	32%	45%	41%
Inactive member	22%	19%	20%
Not affiliated	13%	10%	10%

highly respected scholar concluded, "There is a tendency for middle-class Negroes to sever their affiliation with the Baptist and Methodist churches and join the Presbyterian, Congregational, and Episcopal churches...in order to satisfy the desire for status."[23]

The use of religious denominations as a social ladder, as noted in the statement above, has not been characteristic of our respondents. While some have certainly moved from given denominations to what might be regarded as higher-status denominations, characteristically they are more likely to choose other alternatives. Some elect to remain in the same denomination of their childhood and seek membership in a higher-status church in that denomination. Others choose to remain in their original churches and attempt to raise the social status of those churches in preference to seeking some other leading churches whose prestige may rub off on them. About 70 percent of the respondents in this study are actively involved in the affairs of their churches. The churches in which the respondents are members are primarily (74 percent) in the denominations which have a long history of mass black membership. At least 43 percent are Baptist, and 24 percent are Methodist, and another 7 percent belong to various religious sects or cults that usually attract the socially disinherited black masses.

It appears, then, from the primary data at hand, that for the most part black college graduates characteristically remain within their childhood denominations and attempt to improve or advance the social status of their individual churches rather than use different denominations as stepping-stones to advance their own social status.

At least 29 percent of the respondents regard themselves as leaders in the black church (see Table 27). It seems, therefore, that the black church is still very much engaged in one of its most important historical missions, the discovery, training, and tempering of black leadership.

Robert L. Green calls special attention to the leadership-training emphasis of the black church. He cites for examples such noted leaders as Benjamin E. Mays, Adam Clayton Powell, Jr., Martin Luther King, Jr., and his own father whose leadership talents were developed within the influ-

Table 28
The Black Church and the Struggle for Equality

Effectiveness	
Very effective	28%
Somewhat effective	48%
Little or no effectiveness	21%
Hindered blacks' struggle	3%

ence of the black church. He points out that since major white organizations have been customarily closed to young blacks, all too often their potential leadership talents have had no opportunity to develop outside the black church. "The Church," he insists, "has been both a haven and a tough, exacting proving ground for blacks who aspire to positions of leadership and responsibility."[24] More than a fourth of our respondents are among those engaged in some leadership-training function of the black church.

Throughout the history of the black experience in the United States, the church has been a major source and main bond of blacks' social life. It has been the most important institution through which blacks of all social classes and interests have been able to coordinate their efforts for survival and advancement.

Insofar as black college graduates are concerned, they insist that the church should be even more involved in blacks' struggle for liberation. Instead of pulling away from the black church, as some scholars have suspected, there is a greater tendency for them to lead their particular churches, and the black church at large, toward a more formal, unified, tangible involvement in blacks' persistent, mundane, day-by-day problems, to go beyond mere support of blacks' liberation efforts and become the cutting-edge or leader in such efforts.[25]

"How effective would you say the black church has been in blacks' struggle for equality in the United States?" Our respondents' answers to that question are summarized in Table 28. While the college graduates in this study are far from unanimous in their evaluation of the black church's liberation efforts, the great majority (76 percent) do agree that it has been effective. At the same time, they believe that it could have been more effective than it has been. They feel that traditionally too much emphasis has been placed upon otherworldly preaching and enjoyment at the expense of active concern with temporal problems which are often exacerbated by racism. In this spirit one respondent wrote:

The church should be more concerned about the economic plight of female-headed black families. Therefore at the same time the church is dealing with the moral issues involved it should pressure the federal government to guarantee black women's right to hold decent jobs and receive equal pay for them.

The mission of the black church, according to the statement above—which seems to be representative of the general opinion of the respondents—does not suggest that the black church should abandon or mute its spiritual theme. Instead, they would like to bring about a more balanced emphasis of the spiritual and temporal themes.

About a fourth (24 percent) of the sample for this study are very critical of the black church. Most of these critics discount the effectiveness of the church in blacks' liberation. A few (3 percent) even contend that it has hindered blacks' struggle for equality in American society by its opiate effects, which have tended to make blacks too passive or too prone to accept racism and the many forms of discrimination they encounter daily.

Despite some serious criticism, the large majority of black college graduates are still devout, dependable supporters of traditional black religious denominations. The fact is, both the classes- and the masses-oriented black churches are rapidly gaining in membership. Therefore, as mentioned before, the combined membership of the ten traditional denominations is about twenty million. This makes it the largest black organization in the United States. The leadership in each of the ten largest denominations generally agree that even greater emphasis should be placed upon the church's responsibility for black liberation. Thus Jemison insists that "the black church is still the strongest organization among black people, but it has not asserted itself in the manner that I feel it should. It has not used the power of its numbers to lift the standard of living for black people."[26]

Other leading black churchpersons are now expressing full agreement with the social role of the black church as recently defined by Jemison. With such key financial backing as that being given by the Lilly Foundation of Indianapolis and the strong support and intelligent leadership of black college graduates, the black church is rapidly becoming a very effective champion of black liberation and advancement in American society.

BLACK FRATERNITIES AND SORORITIES

There are four nationally recognized black social fraternities and four social sororities. As a rule they have been indigenous to black college campuses. Only two were founded on white college campuses: Alpha Phi Alpha, the first black Greek letter fraternity, founded at Cornell University, Ithaca, New York, in 1906, and Kappa Alpha Psi, founded at Indiana University, Bloomington, Indiana, in 1911.

Since 1906 the membership of these Greek letter organizations has pro-

Table 29
Membership in Greek Letter Organizations

Status of Membership	Male	Female	Total
Active leader	22%	17%	19%
Active member	17%	17%	18%
Inactive member	32%	31%	31%
Never member	29%	35%	32%

liferated, so that at the present time "there are some 5,000 chapters in the United States and abroad of the four fraternities and four sororities. They have a combined membership of almost a half million men and women."[27]

While the black church provides the most effective network whereby blacks in all walks of life, representing all socio-economic classes, may identify, communicate, and cooperate, black Greek letter organizations provide the most effective means whereby black college students and graduates can preserve a common identity and cooperate in the pursuit of common goals. They are essentially middle class oriented.

Although black Greek letter organizations have been widely criticized for what some believe to be exclusiveness, snobbishness, and elitism, they seem to have almost irresistible appeal to black college students and graduates. This can be seen in Table 29.

There are, of course, many quite logical reasons why such a large proportion of black college students would seek membership in Greek letter organizations. Many of them come from humble socio-economic backgrounds, and these organizations and their membership provide them an excellent opportunity to associate as equals with fellow students from much more affluent backgrounds. Also, as members of any one of the organizations, students can vicariously identify with the black middle class by becoming "brothers" or "sisters" to successful, even renowned members, past and present, who serve as role models and lend legitimacy to their middle-classness.

Black students from affluent backgrounds often join Greek letter organizations primarily because of a family tradition or a felt need to reinforce their own middle-class status. There are, to be sure, individuals with other more specific motives for joining such organizations. These motives may range all the way from a personal desire to substitute the fraternity's or sorority's family-type intimacy ("brothers" and "sisters") for their partially broken consanguineous relationships to a conscious desire to use fraternity or sorority connections as a stepping-stone in their upward social and career mobility.

Some of the main motives for joining Greek letter organizations in college persist during the years following college. Actually some of the vague, unstructured motives for joining during the college years eventually develop into well-thought-out, formal schemes to achieve personal, social, and career ends. There are a number of promising ways a particular Greek letter organization might promote the personal ambitions of individual members. Through their magazines, newsletters, and local, regional, and national meetings, certain loyal members who have achieved some unusual success may be cited and honored for their endeavors. Such members may be singled out for a measure of hero or heroine status which could result in both ego and career enhancement.

In addition, membership in a particular Greek letter organization may result in a quality of unity among black college graduates which has important psychological and tangible implications. For instance, the avowed raison d'être of a prestigious graduate Greek letter organization, Sigma Pi Phi Fraternity ("Boule"), founded in 1912, is so stated: "The chief purpose of this organization is ... to bind men of like qualities, tastes and attainments into a close sacred union, that they might know the best of one another."[28]

At the time Sigma Pi Phi Fraternity was founded, there were very few black college graduates in the United States, and they were widely scattered. That fraternity proposed to break down their isolation and facilitate opportunities for them to meet regularly and exchange information, ideas, and points of view calculated to redound to mutual intellectual development and leadership.

At present some members of black Greek letter organizations are using them for much more pragmatic purposes. Several examples of this new pragmatism were cited in a recent article by Pat King. The article analyzes a form of networking increasingly characteristic of members of Greek letter organizations.[29] Essentially, it is a process whereby members engage in mutual aid services. They assist one another in finding and succeeding in jobs and by extending such courtesies as helping to find homes for members who move into their communities.

All of the black social fraternities and sororities have well-organized community and national programs carefully designed to serve several needs of black people. Some have special programs to promote not only the health, economic, intellectual, and moral welfare of their own members but also to provide certain vital human services for other blacks in their particular communities who stand in need of them. In short, black Greek letter organizations are training and providing a significant proportion of expert leadership in a variety of other organizations and programs whose basic objectives are the improvement of the quality of life in the community, especially in the black community. The programs they sponsor or in which they are important participants include such areas as mental and physical

Table 30
Political Party Preference

Democratic party	90%
Republican party	4%
Other or Independent	6%

health, family welfare, education, the establishment and growth of black businesses, the development of leaders, voter registration, and informal, yet quite substantive, support of black political candidates.[30]

At least 19 percent of our respondents regard themselves as active leaders in one of the eight undergraduate or graduate Greek letter organizations. Many of them, as mentioned above, are also leaders in various non-Greek letter organizations and activities in the communities where they live. They supply much of the effective black leadership to be discussed subsequently.

COMMUNITY PARTICIPATION

POLITICAL PARTICIPATION

While many of the black college educated channel most of their community and national organizational participation through the church and Greek letter organizations, others are deeply involved in other types of special-interest organizations.

It may be that blacks' actual growing participation in political organizations and activities marks a new fundamental, most promising step toward black liberation which has been hitherto almost closed to them. The significant breach in the more or less total disenfranchisement of blacks in the South was made by the 1965 Civil Rights Act which guaranteed blacks the right to vote. Since then blacks have become an increasingly important element in the political life of this nation, especially in their local communities. It is interesting, however, that there is still a persistent tendency for blacks to continue the practice of bloc voting and loyalty to one political party. Respondents were asked about their political party identification. Their replies are summarized in Table 30. During the last fifty years, blacks have manifested about the same kind of loyalty to the Democratic party which they did regarding the Republican party during the previous fifty years. The college graduates in this study are among the most vocal critics of the radical conservatism of the Republican party, and regardless of age, sex, occupation, or place of residence, they overwhelm-

Table 31
Political Views

	Male	Female	Total
Radical	4%	5%	5%
Liberal	49%	42%	46%
Moderate	42%	46%	43%
Conservative	5%	7%	6%

ingly identify with the Democratic party in preference to other political parties, pointedly the Republican party.

The respondents were asked to describe their central political views; their replies are summarized in Table 31. Those who described themselves as "radical" are not distributed equally among all age groups. Thus, only about 3 percent are under thirty, and 74 percent of those who regard themselves as radical are forty years of age and over. Some of them, no doubt, developed their assumed or basic radical stance during their college years in the 1960s when it was fashionable for students to be regarded as radical. However, the great majority of our respondents now see themselves as politically stable, middle-class individuals who are liberal enough to seek significant changes in the existing, white-dominated socio-economic and political status quo, but would like to see certain needed changes effected in an orderly, controlled manner. So only about 5 percent classify themselves as radicals, and despite what has been several years of a conservative national government, just 6 percent see themselves as politically conservative.

It is interesting to note that in spite of social class differences between the black college educated and the black masses, their political views merge. The black underclass tends to vote for the same political candidates as do the black college educated, or middle class. Furthermore, in cities throughout the United States, wherever the black college educated have run for public office, the increase in political participation among the black masses has been unprecedented. This has been especially pronounced in such cities as Atlanta and New Orleans where the political lethargy of the black masses was once a problem of major concern to leaders. In these and other cities which now have highly educated black mayors and several other college-educated blacks in public office, the black masses have manifested constant, aggressive support and grass-roots leadership.[31]

The political clout resulting from the united efforts of the black masses and the black middle class gives greater security to both black and white politicians who would champion certain black causes or interests once

previously ignored by them. Even some major non-political black organizations, embracing both the black college educated and the black masses,
risked in 1985 their tax-exempt status by taking definite political positions
on partisan political matters. It is safe to conclude that the black community
throughout the United States has now become politicized.

Very often the most influential black political leaders are precisely those
who were civil rights activists on college campuses during the turbulent
civil rights upheaval of the 1960s, when radicals frequently carried the day.
In this context moderates may be counted either with liberals or conservatives. Most (51 percent) regard themselves as liberals and moderates with
almost half (49 percent) classifying themselves as moderates and conservatives. This raises an interesting question: Can a people, half of whom
are moderates and conservatives, really hope to achieve the radical dream
of equality enunciated by Martin Luther King, Jr.? Indeed, there must be
some doubt that those who regard themselves as moderates and conservatives would support or participate in the kinds of radical political action
that may be necessary for blacks to achieve the liberation and equality
prophesied in "The Dream" and which was epitomized in the 1960s civil
rights movement. For instance, instead of viewing the political efforts of
the Reverend Jesse Jackson as a next logical step in blacks' liberation bid,
some prominent civil rights leaders not only balked at supporting him as
a presidential candidate in 1984 but denounced his aspirations to attempt
it. Some attempted to explain or rationalize their decision to refrain from
supporting Jackson in terms of truisms inherent in traditional, separatist,
status quo politics: "Only blacks will support a black presidential candidate"; "A third party or black candidate will split the normal voter response
so that the less desirable candidate will win"; or "The time is not right for
a black presidential candidate."

It might be instructive to point out here that several noted scholars have
discovered that individuals who subjectively identify with a particular group
or social class, the "reference group" syndrome, to which they actually do
not belong, are likely to modify their beliefs, values, and behavior to accord
with those of the reference group rather than to accord with those of the
group to which they, in fact, do belong.[32] Consequently, those who regard
themselves as moderates or conservatives are, in effect, identifying with
some powerful status quo champions who have traditionally opposed or
tempered their stand on blacks' thrust for advancement in American society. Hence the moderate and conservative political stances on the part
of some respondents might indicate an increasing dilemma on the part of
the more affluent, college-educated blacks who are developing a substantial
stake in preserving the political status quo on the one hand, while still
holding onto essentially black interests and the need for basic social changes
on the other. Actually, this dilemma is inherent in the reasoning of the so-

called black conservative scholars who have received wide public and professional attention during the Republican administration of the 1980s.

For instance, there was a long period of time when all segments of the black population, regardless of education, economic status, or residence, had at least one basic thing in common: they experienced about the same degree and kinds of racial segregation. Today this is not so. There are some blacks, especially among the more affluent college-educated, who are not ordinarily subjected to the second-class citizenship status of the black masses. They are functionally integrated into mainstream American society and are generally insulated from the inconveniences and disesteem experienced by the black masses. Consequently, their political identification and attitudes may be divided between what they conceive to be good for them from the point of view of their reference group, the white middle-class, and from the point of view of their actual membership group, the black population at large. Thus some conservative black scholars attempt to resolve this nagging dilemma by postulating a theory of "The Declining Significance of Race." This theory may be employed to interpret the perennial, unique problems of blacks resulting from their own negligence and lack of creativity, rather than in terms of blacks' long struggle to overcome various subtle and blatant forms of racism which made the nature and outcomes of their efforts quite different from those of non-blacks.

CIVIL RIGHTS ORGANIZATIONS AND ACTIVITIES

As pointed out above, just about all black organizations, regardless of their main purpose or mission, generally have some program, committee, or special activity consciously designed to contribute to the survival and advancement of black Americans, to enhance, promote, and preserve the black socio-cultural heritage. In spite of the contribution members make indirectly to blacks' liberation efforts through church and social groups, the basic, indispensable contributions to blacks' civil rights movement come mainly through organizations whose central purpose is black advancement.

Organizations whose main purpose is to promote blacks' civil rights are divided into three types.

THE BLACK CAUCUS

Black caucuses are established by black members in predominantly white organizations. They are typically found in professional, political, and business groups. They usually arise when the black members in these groups feel that they are not given equal recognition or granted equal participation in the activities of the larger group and that the legitimate concerns of blacks at large are not being properly addressed by the group in question.

The most influential of these caucuses is the Congressional Black Caucus, which includes all of the twenty-one black Congresspersons (1985). It serves as a catalyst for positive legislation concerning the complex economic, educational, and social issues affecting black Americans. The Congressional Black Caucus is so structured that it is possible for each of its members to function as a sort of Congressperson at large. That is, since blacks have only a mere token number of congressional representatives, with most states having no black Congressperson, members of the Black Caucus often function in behalf of important black concerns and not merely as representatives of their limited Congressional districts.

PARALLEL BLACK ORGANIZATIONS

Parallel black organizations are founded to maximize blacks' occupational and professional advancement outside of the main parent organizations which are controlled by white members. The best examples of such organizations are the National Bar Association and the National Medical Association. Generally, blacks are dues-paying members in the American Medical Association and the American Bar Association, the parent organizations, as well as the parallel organizations.

Parallel black organizations grow out of the felt need on the part of black businesspersons and professionals to address certain problems or issues concerning blacks that are more or less ignored or underemphasized by their predominantly white parent professional bodies.

CIVIL RIGHTS ORGANIZATIONS

The most direct and effective way of promoting black equality in a variety of socio-economic areas of American life is the support of established civil rights organizations per se. Among the most representative of the civil rights organizations are the NAACP, the NUL, the SCLC, and the National Council of Negro Women, Inc. (NCNW). The central, avowed aim, the raison d'être, of these organizations is to advance the socio-economic and political status of black Americans.

The extent to which the respondents in this study are involved in direct civil rights organizations and activities is indicated in Table 32.

Seventy percent of the college graduates of primary concern here are personally engaged to some extent in civil rights activities. At least 3 percent regard themselves as leaders. In all, about 50 percent feel that through such activities they are making some significant contributions to the advancement of blacks in American society. Even those who do not regard themselves as leaders frequently point out that they have contrib-

Table 32
Direct Civil Rights Involvement

Degree of Involvement	Male	Female	Total
Leader	6%	1%	3%
Active member	55%	41%	47%
Occasionally involved	16%	23%	20%
Not involved	23%	35%	30%

uted directly to better race relations or to blacks' advancement in some very concrete situations. They generally feel that their undergraduate colleges have prepared them well for such a role. They were taught to work toward a racially integrated, democratic American society. The lessons they learned about the values, principles, and structures of mainstream society apparently make them effective participants in the process of social change designed to improve the quality of life in the black community.

Finally, it should be pointed out that civil rights for black Americans have been so basically important that the support of civil rights organizations is expected of the college educated. Frequently, they are called upon as consultants or leaders for various civil rights efforts. The fact is, active participation in civil rights efforts is a main source of legitimacy for black leaders. For example, when a black person is being considered for a top position in almost any area of American life, particularly some position where he or she may be regarded as a spokesperson for the black community, a very critical review of that persons' civil rights affiliations and activities will certainly follow. Not only do blacks in all walks of life demand and expect successful blacks to be involved in some area of the civil rights movement, but they also expect their continual involvement as they move up the occupational and social ladder. This is especially true of upwardly mobile blacks with active political aspirations.

EVALUATION OF SOME SELECTED
BLACK ORGANIZATIONS

Since the respondents usually hold membership in several different types of black organizations, they were asked to evaluate a few basic organizations in terms of their overall contribution to blacks' advancement. Their responses are summarized in Tables 33 and 34.

Data in Tables 33 and 34 underscore, again, blacks' faith in the effectiveness of organizations as reliable instruments for positive social change and for the advancement of blacks' social status in American society. Actually, several of the respondents volunteered that it would be a great

Table 33
Evaluation of Selected Black Organizations vis-à-vis Blacks'
Advancement

Evaluations	The Black Church	Black Colleges	NAACP	NUL	Black Business	Other Organizations
Very effective	28%	51%	46%	25%	9%	3%
Somewhat effective	48%	43%	48%	60%	42%	18%
Not very effective	21%	6%	6%	15%	48%	38%
Hindered	3%	0%	0%	0%	1%	41%

Table 34
Ranking of Selected, Most Effective Black Organizations vis-à-vis
Blacks' Advancement

Rankings	Most Effective
NAACP	47%
Black colleges	30%
The black church	21%
NUL	3%
Black businesses	1%
Others	1%
	103%

*Over 100% because of a few multiple answers

mistake if blacks were to diminish support of their organizations because some erstwhile white organizations and institutions are now open to them.

One respondent summarized this idea when he wrote, "The struggle for basic human rights and respect for blacks in this country goes on. It really gets more complicated and difficult as time passes. We simply must become better organized and supportive of one another if we hope to succeed in this struggle."

Because the respondents have so much faith in the potential influence of soundly established, well-managed black organizations in the struggle for equality, they often tend to be impatient, critical, and even outraged when a particular key black organization or institution fails to perform at the level of proficiency or effectiveness of which it is believed to be capable. This critical evaluation is reflected in the data above regarding some selected, or key, organizations in the black community.

THE BLACK CHURCH

The black church is, without doubt, the most comprehensive (including all socio-economic classes), ubiquitous, wealthy, and socially powerful institution controlled by blacks. While it is the oldest and the most strongly supported black institution, it still comes in for constant examination and broad criticism. Much of the criticism comes because people expect too much from the church. Blacks' very survival and advancement have been always critical issues which have been constantly contested by hostile forces in the larger white community. The church, literally as well as symbolically, is regarded as a refuge and a center of their togetherness vis-à-vis such threatening forces. Consequently, black people have too often insisted that the black church should go far beyond its religious and moral mission and become actively involved in temporal matters that may affect them, directly and indirectly. Despite their continuing loyalty to the church and their significant leadership in it, just 28 percent of the respondents give it an unqualified or "very effective" rating insofar as its role in black liberation is concerned, and only 21 percent regarded the church as the "most effective" institution in blacks' struggle for equal civil rights.

At least 69 percent indicated that the church might have been "more effective" in the civil rights movement, with 3 percent insisting that it has even impeded blacks' socio-economic progress. As a rule, those who insist that the church has impeded blacks' progress base their argument upon the premise that the black church has traditionally functioned as an "opiate," by emphasizing an otherworldly theology and adjustment to racial discrimination, rather than as a catalyst and leader in the civil rights movement.

Despite the criticism aimed at the black church there is ample evidence that the college educated, who are frequently leaders in their own churches, have constantly influenced their churches to adopt an increasingly liberal concern with civil rights issues. Thus, beginning with Martin Luther King, Jr.'s leadership during the 1960s, the black church has become more and more concerned with the development of programs and strategies especially designed to advance the socio-economic status of black Americans.

BLACK COLLEGES

The basic mission of black colleges, as is true of all colleges, is to provide quality higher education for their students. This principle was vigorously and successfully defended during the student-faculty confrontations in the 1960s and 1970s, when students attempted to make certain black colleges social revolutionary instruments.

Black colleges generally resisted this pressure to be regarded as primarily civil rights institutions. For the most part, they steadfastly pursued their basic academic mission. It is somewhat surprising that more than half (51 percent) of the respondents, many of whom were in college during the 1960s and 1970s, rated black colleges as "very effective" civil rights proponents.

Furthermore, next to the NAACP, whose avowed purpose is to promote the advancement of blacks' civil rights, the largest proportion of the respondents (30 percent) ranked black colleges as the "most effective" champion of blacks' civil rights (see Table 34). Only 6 percent felt that black colleges have not been very effective, and none accused them of impeding blacks' civil rights. In all, 94 percent concluded that black colleges have been significantly effective in the civil rights movement and that they have been a very effective black liberation force.

A large proportion of the respondents found opportunities to characterize black colleges, particularly their own colleges (86 percent), and UNCF colleges generally (73 percent), as "essential to blacks' progress" or the most effective source of blacks' long and vital struggle for equal rights and personal dignity in American society. Among the reasons they gave for classifying black colleges as the most or the second most effective civil rights organization are the following:

1. Since education is the key to black Americans' progress, the black college has been and continues to be indispensable in blacks' fight for equality. They were almost totally responsible for the education of blacks when other colleges— especially the best white colleges—ignored them and gave all kinds of bogus, pseudo-scientific reasons for doing so. Black colleges trained black teachers who have been able to prepare black students for the world of work.

2. Black colleges constitute the grass roots of the civil rights movement; other civil rights organizations would have been impossible or ineffective without the leaders prepared in black colleges.

3. Black colleges teach black people how to stand on their own two feet and how to organize for social action. They instill the love of freedom in their students and show them how to defend it.

4. Teachers in black colleges usually work closely with students and feel that it is important for them to learn how to get along in a racist world.

There is, however, a tendency for blacks, especially the respondents, to measure and criticize black colleges for their leadership role in the civil rights movement in about the same way as they evaluate other black organizations. It is often felt that they could have been more effective than they have been. The reasons range all the way from not giving enough emphasis to the history and culture of black people to what they perceive as reluctance to take an active lead in blacks' civil rights efforts. A close examination of the various criticisms offered reveals that, here again, is a tendency to expect too much of black colleges. They are often expected to go far beyond the business of giving their students an excellent education. Some fully expect them to function primarily as active civil rights organizations.

THE NAACP

The NAACP was founded in 1909 when the post–Civil War status of blacks had deteriorated to what might have been its nadir in American society. Reconstruction had failed. The castelike status of blacks seemed rather fixed. The South was then in full charge of its own system of race relations firmly based upon the doctrine of white supremacy. It was regarded as a sacred right of all white individuals and organizations to employ whatever means necessary to enforce racial segregation and discrimination. Consequently, white southern leaders and spokespersons proved to be quite ingenious in their ability to create new, ever more effective methods of "keeping blacks in their place," on the very bottom rung of the socioeconomic ladder.

From the beginning, then, the NAACP has been pointedly involved in helping blacks acquire basic civil rights within the overall framework of the Constitution of the United States. Over the decades, it has been blacks' most effective, dependable watchdog and champion of their civil rights. Since its founding there has been no significant period of time when the NAACP did not have some case before the courts dealing with an extension of the civil rights of black Americans. Actually, there have been times when the NAACP was regarded as more or less synonymous with blacks' civil rights movement. It became the major symbol of blacks' struggle for equality.

Almost half (46 percent) of the respondents feel that the NAACP has been a very effective civil rights organization, and 94 percent indicated that it has been significantly effective. Also, the largest proportion of them (47 percent) rated the NAACP as the most effective organization in the area of civil rights. As a civil rights organization it is ranked far above any other organization in the black community, including colleges and the church.

During the last five years or so there has been increasing criticism of the NAACP. Some black conservatives have accused the NAACP of being too rooted in the past and advocating principles out of keeping with present reality. They claim that it tends to misread signs of a new society now being born. They propose new, more relevant organizations dedicated to black liberation and progress. It is claimed that at this stage in American history the established civil rights organizations, as represented by the NAACP and the NUL, are actually impeding the advancement of black Americans. Therefore, Dan J. Smith, a black economist, contends that "black Civil Rights organizations need to be brought closer in line with genuine currents of black thinking. Many of these organizations have taken stances on a number of issues ... that appear, if the polls are correct, to be vastly different from the way a majority of black Americans feel."[33]

The conservatives' criticism of the NAACP is not generally shared by the respondents in this study. Only 6 percent indicated that they felt that the NAACP had not been very effective in blacks' civil rights efforts, and none felt that it had impeded blacks' progress. Overall, then, the NAACP is ranked above all other organizations as an effective civil rights advocate.

Only about 2 or 3 percent of the sample suggested that some new civil rights organizations should be established to replace the traditional organizations. Those proposed would be mostly local and limited to the championship of narrow, special-interest issues and not as comprehensive as the NAACP and the NUL. Generally speaking, in spite of some very pointed, maybe valid, criticism, the vast majority of our respondents would still prefer to work through the NAACP (94 percent), black colleges (94 percent), and the NUL (85 percent) for the advancement of blacks' civil rights and progress. Only 3 percent of the respondents would rate the other civil rights organizations as "very effective," and some 41 percent feel that some of them really function to impede blacks' movement toward equality in American society.

BLACK BUSINESSES

As pointed out before, the black community at large expects all of its institutions and leaders to make some appropriate contribution to the civil rights movement or to blacks' sustained efforts to achieve equality. Therefore, blacks, who have always experienced both relative and absolute economic deprivation in the United States, tend to expect black businesses not only to contribute to their efforts to achieve equality but to take a leading role in it.

The fact is that blacks on all socio-economic levels have generally placed great hope in the redeeming role of black-owned business enterprises. They have hoped that black businesses would develop to the point where they would be able to provide high-status jobs for blacks and thus considerably decrease their dependency upon white employers. For instance, in 1926 a national black fraternity, Phi Beta Sigma, adopted as its major project that of stimulating and supporting the growth of "bigger and better Negro businesses."

In general, blacks have been disappointed by what some perceive as the very lethargic growth and development of black-owned business enterprises. A 1977 federal government study of minority-owned businesses found that there were about 231,000 black enterprises, which constituted only 3 percent of all established business enterprises in the United States.

Further, just 40,000 (or 17 percent) of the black businesses had any paid employees outside of the immediate family, and only 113 had as many as

100 or more employees. "The total aggregate receipts came to a disappointing $8.7 billion, which combined would only rank it as the 37th largest company in the United States."[34]

All in all, black-owned businesses are not regarded as making a great impact on blacks' struggle for equal economic opportunity primarily because they do not provide a significant number of jobs for blacks, whose unemployment rates are constantly near or above what would be regarded as the economic depression level in the general American society. It is, thus, in this context that only 9 percent of our respondents agree that black businesses have been "very effective" in blacks' advancement, and a mere 1 percent ranked black businesses as "most effective" among certain selected black organizations. Furthermore, some (1 percent) expressed their disappointment with black businesses with the bitter denunciation that they have functioned to hinder or impede blacks' efforts to achieve equality. The largest proportion of the respondents (48 percent) concur that black businesses "have not been very effective."

The rather poor civil rights rating given black businesses may be due to several interrelated things. Among them are the following:

1. Throughout the centuries of American history, black people have been oppressed by the economic system in this nation. Few, indeed, have had any reasons to believe that business per se has dealt well with them. Black slavery, modified peonage, or methods of flagrant economic discrimination have always been prevalent. It is not surprising, then, that many blacks have inherited a negative image of white businesses in general.

The great majority of blacks think of the white world of business as basically conservative and essentially anti-black. At best, the rank-and-file black American is likely to regard the world of business with some degree of suspicion or trepidation.

2. Black businesses have been given a poor rating because certain business enterprises have been overlooked. For instance, black-owned newspapers and magazines are certainly among the strongest businesses in the black community. They have characteristically offered significant employment, especially for black professionals, and have always promoted essential intraracial communication, racial unity, and pride, and have functioned as dependable, staunch defenders of the civil, economic, and general human rights of black Americans.

3. Blacks seem to expect more from black businesses than they are able to deliver. Black businesses are handicapped and disadvantaged to about the same degree as are blacks as a race. Black enterprises experience about the same types of discrimination as do individual blacks and other black institutions.

In a systematic study of its readers *The Black Enterprise* in its Tenth Anniversary Issue points out some of the disadvantages experienced by black businesses. Lynda M. Hill concludes that "because black companies have not cornered many markets, they always seem to blend into the white background, over-shadowed by the corporate giants, forgotten, and sometimes betrayed."[35]

For whatever reasons, black businesses are usually relatively small and financially weak. Only a few are able to provide a significant number of badly needed jobs and to give substantial financial support to black institutions and efforts.

4. Black business enterprises must be, like all other businesses, profit-seeking. Therefore, their primary aim is not human services. They can hardly match the degree of altruism expected of such voluntary organizations as compose the civil rights movement. To succeed, then, black businesses are likely to adopt somewhat the same basic conservatism of successful white businesses. To the extent that they do this, they are apt to draw the same measure of criticism as do white businesses at large.

Finally, evidence on hand strongly supports the conclusion that the great majority of black college graduates (some 94 percent, in this sample), regardless of sex, age, geographic location, occupation, or income, have at one time or another, engaged in direct or indirect civil rights activities designed to establish or promote the advancement of blacks toward equality. Though it is often subtle and sub rosa, black college graduates as a group are more or less constantly engaged in an all-out effort to become equal, integrated participants in mainstream American society. Only a few of our so-called "separatist" respondents (2 percent) expressed any faith that blacks can achieve equality outside of mainstream American life.

Blacks' passionate, unquenchable desire to achieve equality in mainstream American society has functioned as the race's most effective focus of unity; it has pervaded all black organizations and modified all aspects of their social life. In a very real sense, it has been their "magnificent obsession." Preparing black youths to achieve this common goal is the ultimate raison d'être of the black colleges.

NOTES

1. Edmund Newton, "Suite Success," *Black Enterprise*, February 1984, 52.

2. Daniel C. Thompson, *Sociology of the Black Experience* (Westport, Conn.: Greenwood Press, 1974) p. 160. See also Daniel C. Thompson and Barbara G. Thompson, "The Black Underclass: A Continuing Saga," *The Black Southerner*, vols. 1 and 2 (Fall 1983 and Winter 1984), pp. 21–24, 48–53.

3. See E. Franklin Frazier, *Black Bourgeoisie* (New York: Collier Books, 1962), pp. 162–172.

4. See W.E.B. Du Bois, *The Souls of Black Folk* (reprint; Nashville, Tenn.: Fisk University Press, 1979), pp. 159–161.

5. Benjamin L. Hooks, "The NAACP and the Church Are Indeed Partners in Progress," *Crisis* 89 (November 1982): 5.

6. Alphonso Pinkney, *Black Americans* (Englewood Cliffs, N.J.: Prentice-Hall, 1969), pp. 124–130.

7. For the historical development of this practice, see John Hope Franklin, *From Slavery to Freedom* (New York: Vintage Books, 1969), pp. 404–406. See also Daniel C. Thompson, *Private Black Colleges at the Crossroads* (Westport, Conn.: Greenwood Press, 1973), pp. 7, 137–145.

8. Thompson, *Private Black Colleges at the Crossroads*, pp. 70, 137–145.

9. Clifton F. Brown, "Black Religion 1968" in Pat Romero, ed., *In Black America* (Washington, D.C.: United Publishing Corp., 1968), pp. 345–348.

10. See Daniel C. Thompson, "The Rise of the Negro Protest," *Annals of the Academy of Political and Social Science* 357 (January 1965): 18–29.

11. Benjamin E. Mays, *Born to Rebel: An Autobiography* (New York: Charles Scribner's Sons, 1971), pp. 14–16.

12. Ibid., p. 16.

13. Daniel C. Thompson, "Radicalizing the Black Church," in James S. Gadsen, ed., *Experiences, Struggles, and Hopes of the Black Church* (Nashville, Tenn.: Tidings, 1975), pp. 33–35.

14. Martin Luther King, Jr., "Letter from A Birmingham Jail," *Christian Century* 80, pp. 146–147.

15. Quoted material found in Henry Duval, "Youth Demanding Change in the Black Church," *Crisis* 89 (November 1982): 11.

16. Major T. Jones, *Black Awareness: A Theology of Hope* (New York: Abingdon Press, 1971), p. 14.

17. Jeannye Thornton, "Blacks Turn to the Church in Political Drive," *U.S. News and World Report*, February 6, 1984, 45–46.

18. David E. Anderson, "Church Council's New President: A Positive Signal to Black Churches," *National Leader*, January 5, 1984, 14.

19. Quoted in "Segregation in Churches: Why It Still Thrives," *U.S. News and World Report* November 29, 1976, 16. See also Charles E. Cobb, "A Message to Black Preachers," *Crisis* 89 (November 1982): 12.

20. "Black Churches Unite to Conquer Growing Social Ills," *Times Picayune* (New Orleans), December 12, 1982, 21.

21. Ibid, p. 21.

22. Gallup Poll, January 25, 1981, and March 19, 1981.

23. E. Franklin Frazier, *The Negro Church in America* (New York: Schocken Books, 1964), p. 79.

24. Robert L. Green, "Growing Up Black, Urban and in the Church," *Crisis* 89 (November 1982): 14–16.

25. Henry Duval, "Youth Demanding Change in the Black Church," *Crisis* 89 (November 1982): 11.

26. Gallup Poll, January 25, 1981, and March 19, 1981.

27. Pat King, "New Wave Networking," *Black Enterprise* 14 (December 1983): 87–92.

28. Charles H. Wesley, *History of Sigma Pi Phi: First of Negro American Greek-Letter Fraternities* (Washington, D.C.: Association for the Study of Negro Life and History, 1954), p. 26.

29. King, "New Wave Networking," pp. 89–92.

30. See Robert Gillard, "Alpha to Omega," *Black Collegian* 5 (November/Decem-

ber 1974): 42–48, 50, for comments by former president of Alpha Phi Alpha fraternity, Ernest N. Morial, who is now (1985) mayor of New Orleans.

31. See Pinkney, *Black Americans*, pp. 114–118.

32. See Richard Centers, *The Psychology of Social Classes: A Study of Class Consciousness* (Princeton, N.J.: Princeton University Press, 1949), pp. 27–29.

33. Thomas Sowell, et al., eds., *The Fairmont Papers* (San Francisco: Institute for Contemporary Studies, 1980), p. 104.

34. Robert B. Hill, "The Economic Status of Black Americans," *The State of Black America 1981* (New York: National Urban League, 1977), p. 38.

35. Lynda B. Hill, "Black Business," *Black Enterprise*, August 10, 1980, 72.

7 Social Class

The black middle class, which is quite similar to the middle class in American society at large, may be described as a rather loosely organized, yet very distinct, status-conscious, socio-economic category of the American population. Generally speaking, the black middle class is composed of individuals and families who are regarded by the black community as successful in terms of their educational, occupational and income attainments.

Those who are accorded middle-class status are characteristically engaged in occupations which require at least a high school or college education or are engaged as owners or managers of relatively stable, successful business enterprises. In all instances, the annual income of middle-class individuals and families is expected to be comfortably above the national median, and their overall style of life is expected to be in more or less sharp contrast to that which is ordinarily regarded as characteristic of the black lower classes in American society.

EDUCATION

The most estimable, legitimizing source, the very fountainhead of the black middle class, has been education, or more specifically, black colleges. While one's occupation and income have been always important intervening variables, the key most deterministic factor in measuring social success among blacks has been education. It is, then, altogether understandable that the rapid growth and expansion of the black middle class during the last twenty years or so, even when defined entirely by the median annual family income in 1980 dollars (the U.S. Department of Commerce defines "middle class" as families with an annual income of $15,000–$34,999), have been neatly parallel to the increase and variety of the college-educated segment in the black population.

For instance, in 1960 there were 192,344 black college students in the United States. Today there are over a million. This fivefold growth in the number of college-educated blacks is almost precisely commensurate with the growth, diversity, and complexity of the black middle class, however it may be defined. That is, whether we define "middle class" in terms of the relative rank of occupations, the amount of income, style of life, or the degree of social influence, only about 5 or 6 percent of the black population could have been classified as middle class in 1960. This proportion has increased about 5 or 6 times since then. Today approximately 25–30 percent of the black population of the United States may be classified as middle class.

COMPLEXITY OF THE BLACK MIDDLE CLASS

In addition to the fact that the black middle class is considerably larger today than it was before 1960, it is also significantly more complex. For instance, prior to the 1960s the range of occupations in which blacks were normally engaged was quite narrow. For the most part, even highly qualified blacks were systematically excluded from just about all professional and managerial positions in mainstream American society. Those who held middle-class occupations were usually restricted to the black community and were engaged primarily in jobs related to religion, education, health, and small businesses, plus federal jobs, especially postal services.

Since the 1960s and the explosive civil rights movement, which was led primarily by black college students and graduates, some of the most deeply rooted, stubborn barriers to equal education and equal job opportunities have been removed. Consequently, at this time the black middle class includes about the same range of occupational groups as does the white middle class. For example, until twenty or so years ago top black educators, pastors of leading churches, a mere handful of independent professionals, and a few successful businesspersons constituted the black middle class. The new, greater variety of occupations now open to highly qualified blacks has made it necessary to redefine the status hierarchy in local black communities throughout the United States. The rapid growth and increasing complexity of the black middle class have led to a state of flux which challenges traditional status rankings based upon much more limited academic choices and a narrow range of available occupations and incomes.[1]

SOCIAL CLASS INTERESTS

Closely related to the expanding educational and occupational opportunities of black Americans, which have resulted in an increase in the size and complexity of the black middle class during this generation, there is a great deal of speculation about its present inherent nature and the degree to which its basic interests are similar to those of the traditional black middle class or that of the black population at large.

Prior to the 1960s, the black "genius," whatever might have been his or her particular talents or potential, was indeed "imprisoned in the Negro problem."[2] There were very few opportunities for professional and managerial positions in the rigidly segregated black community, and blacks were just about completely barred from such positions in mainstream American society. Therefore, the collective social interests of black Americans, regardless of the amount of education they might have acquired, were very well focused. Whatever may have been their social class differences, all blacks had at least one basic, frustrating thing in common: they had to deal with deeply rooted white racism which was intricately designed to relegate all blacks to an inferior socio-economic status. Consequently, blacks' main interest, their overriding, primary collective goal was the removal of legal and traditional barriers to equal citizenship in American society. There was no significant difference among them regarding that goal. It was the rallying point for the powerful civil rights movement which, during the 1960s, brought together "the economically deprived, poorly educated masses of blacks...and the black middle class."[3]

Now that just about all legal barriers to equal citizenship have been removed and the ranges of blacks' education and job opportunities have been significantly expanded, the economic, social, and political differences among blacks are beginning to surface and proliferate. Already black unity on certain key local and national issues is much more difficult to attain than was the case previously. The age of innocence in intraracial and interracial relations is rapidly passing. It is not now uncommon to have prominent black intellectuals and spokespersons differ sharply among themselves on key issues affecting blacks. Also, some highly respected middle-class blacks have openly indicated that they place their professional, political, and business interests above purely "black interests." Some have run the risk of becoming functionally alienated from the black masses because they obviously place their social class interests above black interests per se. This phenomenon is most convincingly exemplified in the political arena, where some middle-class blacks reason that it is in their best interest to support candidates and issues which are unpopular or even anathema to the black masses.

SOCIAL CLASS OF RESPONDENTS

Respondents were asked to indicate their social class identity. Their replies are summarized in Table 35.

Only a few (3 percent) of the respondents identified themselves with the upper class. This is in keeping with facts gathered by all studies of social class identification in the United States. There are not many Americans, regardless of their affluence, who select "upper class" as most appropriate for describing their social position in the class structure.[4] Actually, most Americans, as is true in this study, choose to identify with the middle class. Accordingly, 90 percent of our respondents regard themselves as middle class.

SOCIAL CLASS CRITERIA

The criteria for stratifying any given society have too often proven to be quite subjective and arbitrary. This has been especially true of studies where individuals were requested to rank themselves.[5] It is generally difficult to determine whether individual respondents are comparing themselves to others in their actual membership groups, those in their particular communities, other blacks, some prestigious reference group they admire or respect, or to certain individuals and families whom they regard as relatively unsuccessful.

About 2 or 3 percent of the respondents identified themselves with the lower class, despite the fact that they all are college graduates, hold white-collar or professional jobs, and have incomes considerably above the national average. The truth is, 41 percent of those who identified themselves as lower class have annual median family incomes of $25,000 or more.

At least 73 percent of the respondents were born to parents of humble means, who could be classified as lower-class people. Further, 38 percent have one or more non-college siblings who hold blue-collar or common labor jobs. It is likely that some of these respondents have identified with the lower class because of their continuing loyalty to their parents, siblings, and childhood friends who may still be objectively classified as lower class.

A small number of the respondents, about 5 percent, indicated that they are "uncertain" about their social class status. If we generalized from findings of a previous study (Daniel C. Thompson, "The Black Elite," *Boulé Journal* 39 [Summer 1976], pp. 10–18), we may assume that the "uncertains" are those either too modest to specify their social class as "upper" or who cannot decide because of certain inherent status conflicts. For instance, a highly successful physician confided: "Insofar as my profession and education are concerned, you could say that I am upper class. However when

I compare my status with the truly rich physicians in this country, I am at best middle class."

Also, a prominent, reputedly wealthy businessman in our sample insisted:

> When I compare myself with other black people in this city, where most are having a hard time just to make ends meet, and where so many are unemployed or get very poor wages, you might say I am upper class. However when I compare myself with white persons who inherit millions from their families, or who are able to become millionaires in a short time, then I consider myself a poor man.

As I reflect upon the forty or more formal and informal interviews I have had with graduates of black colleges during the course of this study, some of the most successful and eminent among them shift away from black reference groups toward white reference groups when evaluating their success or social status. That is, the greater the measure of success they achieve, the more likely they are to compare themselves with their white peers rather than their black peers per se.

In deference to the overall greater success of their white reference groups, some of the most successful of our respondents were evidently too modest to rank themselves as upper class. Instead they either ranked themselves as middle class or truthfully indicated that they were uncertain about their social class status.

Furthermore, some who indicated that they were uncertain about their social class status might have been influenced by the basic principles of equality inherent in American culture. Their responses may be a disclaimer of the concept of "social stratification" per se, which definitely implies that some people and families are better or superior.

Black college graduates with whom I have discussed the issue of social classes characteristically become somewhat confused and argumentative. Even when they acknowledge their own high social class status, they are likely to be very careful not to boast about it. For example, one respondent, who described himself as a "self-made man all the way," insisted:

> The worst thing that can happen to blacks at this point in time would be to put too much emphasis upon superficial class dif- ferences. We are divided too much as it is. We must find ways to cooperate. We cannot afford to look down on others because we have a better education and get a little fatter pay check.

According to data in Table 35, the female respondents are slightly more class-conscious than are the males: a somewhat smaller proportion tend to identify with the lower class, and a larger proportion regard themselves

Table 35
Social Class Identification

Social Classes	Male	Female	Total
Upper class	1%	4%	3%
Upper middle class	18%	19%	18%
Middle class	54%	55%	55%
Lower middle class	19%	17%	17%
Lower class	4%	1%	2%
Uncertain	4%	4%	5%

as upper class. Yet by and large, whether the respondent is male or female, young or old, their attitudes toward social class are remarkably similar: while few deny their high social status, few boast about it.

NATURE OF THE BLACK MIDDLE CLASS

Graduates of black colleges are quintessential representatives of the black middle class in American society. The fact is, black colleges have functioned as the origin of this social class as we know it today.

In this particular formulation, the black upper class and the middle class merge, and as one they articulate a central, overriding value—success, which sets certain individuals and families apart from the great masses. Success in education and occupation is the primary, determining virtue.

EDUCATION

Historically, blacks have taken the idea—now the UNCF slogan—"a mind is a terrible thing to waste" very seriously. For many complex reasons blacks have always emphasized the efficacy of a good education. Somehow they came to believe that if they acquired an education equal to that acquired by whites, they would, ipso facto, become equal citizens. While this approach to first-class citizenship has proven to be too simplistic and naive, it has had some very far-reaching positive influence upon blacks' advancement toward equality. The vast majority of black spokespersons and leaders still cling to this theory as the most promising in blacks' struggle for survival and advancement in American society. As a result, while 83 percent of the graduates of UNCF-related colleges came from high schools where academic standards were too often low, 77 percent have now attended graduate or professional schools. Some of the graduate universities they have attended are among the most prestigious, high-ranking in the world.

SOCIAL MOBILITY

On the whole, college-educated blacks are very ambitious. On their way up the social ladder they have, as a group, had to struggle against just about all conceivable odds. In their epic struggle to survive and advance they have had to employ all available strategies to be able to compete successfully with their white peers whose socio-economic circumstances were often more fortunate.

The success of the black college graduates in this study is no accident or social fluke. One reason for their success is that black colleges deliberately and systematically prepare their students to deal effectively with problems stemming from poverty and racism. Blacks who have succeeded in overcoming the complex of ordinary and unique problems they encountered are understandably proud of their achievements and usually challenge black youth to follow in their footsteps. Indeed, in this way, they serve to raise the social status of the entire race.

OCCUPATION

Informed observers generally agree that one of the most serious problems black Americans have always encountered is that of employment or earning a living. Here, again, the black middle class, on the whole, functions as worthy role models for youths from poor families.

From 78 to 82 percent of the black college graduates in this study hold higher statuses and better-paying jobs than did either of their parents. They have convincingly refuted the cliche that "the apple does not fall far from the tree." They have not allowed their humble beginnings to be an insurmountable psychological or social barrier in their bid for success. The black middle class is actually composed of individuals from all major social and economic segments in the black community. Fully 94 percent of them hold white-collar and professional jobs. Their annual median family income is between $32,000 and $35,000, compared to the median income of their original families, which was less than $10,000 in 1980 dollars.

STRUCTURE OF THE BLACK MIDDLE CLASS

The black middle class, with which 90 percent or more of the graduates of black colleges identify, is not a monolith. Upon close examination, we find that it is composed of individuals and families representing four quite distinct, yet interrelated, social worlds: the upper stratum, the rank and file, the upwardly mobile, and the downwardly mobile.

THE UPPER STRATUM

In communities throughout the United States, especially in cities with large black populations, there are certain black families which have been regarded as upper class for three or more generations.[6]

The life-styles of this upper stratum may vary all the way from disciplined austerity to blatant, conspicuous consumption and display of wealth. All tend, however, to have some basic characteristics in common:

1. They usually belong to high-status churches, in which they are regarded as leaders.

2. Family members have membership in a number of prestigious social, professional, and civic organizations which provide them regular opportunities to associate with other upper-stratum individuals.

3. They are extremely ambitious for their children. Many send their children to expensive, prestigious preparatory schools and expect them to go on to "the best" colleges and graduate schools.

Every effort is made to see that their children come to know other upper-class black children, and internalize upper-class values and attitudes.

4. Adults, male and female, are likely to hold at least one graduate or professional degree from some high-ranking university. Some are likely to be among the first blacks to graduate from erstwhile white universities.

5. As a rule, certain stable members of the upper stratum attempt to develop some significant degree of national unity through a network of prestigious professional or business organizations, fraternities or sororities, and exclusive social connections. Such individuals are often regarded as the core of the black leadership class and sometimes get a great deal of national publicity when they are listed as being among "the most influential 100 blacks" in the United States.

6. Much emphasis is placed upon being accepted as belonging to the upper stratum. Upwardly mobile individuals often find the process of getting acceptance confusing and frustrating because the criteria governing acceptability are usually very unclear and inconsistent. In addition to such requirements as a college education, professional employment, and considerable financial success, the criteria may also include any number of personal subtleties, such as skin color, the personality characteristics of the would-be member, his or her attitudes regarding a variety of issues, values, and traditions, plus private attitudes toward the aspirant on the part of key persons who already belong.

THE RANK AND FILE

This segment of the black middle class is by far the largest. It centers on successful individuals rather than around families. It is composed of individuals representing a wide range of occupations from top independent professionals to ordinary white-collar workers.

All evidence indicates that most, perhaps 85 percent, of the members of this social world are first-generation middle class. There are two distinct subsocial worlds within this larger social world: the upwardly mobile and the downwardly mobile.

THE UPWARDLY SOCIAL MOBILE

This element in the black middle class is ordinarily composed of the younger members of the rank and file who are more or less obsessed with the desire to get ahead in their occupations and to become recognized as leaders or spokespersons. They generally have the proper credentials for occupational success and leadership; much of their striving is for acceptance by those with established social power and influence.

Characteristically, individuals who fit into this category challenge traditional institutions and established procedures. They are usually among the most vocal advocates of social changes. They have been referred to as Young Turks who regularly attempt to take over the leadership of social organizations in the black community. They often insist that older, more conservative black organizations and leaders are out of step with modern times and are alienated from the black masses.

At the same time, another faction of the upwardly mobile element employs a fundamentally different strategy: the overzealous support of those in positions of authority and influence. Instead of attempting to get ahead by putting down those in authority, they adopt all-out efforts to curry recognition and social favors from persons in top professional and social positions. They sometimes offer them unstinting support and loyalty. They tend to over-identify with those in authority and promise to enhance the status quo. Thus despite their lower-class origins, some become consummate social class diplomats who manage to ascend the social class ladder all the way to the top.

THE DOWNWARDLY MOBILE

Just about all black communities have a number of individuals and families who were once regarded as the black upper class and the most respected black leaders. They functioned as models of respectability and success. For the most part, they were pastors of the leading black churches, educators, a few physicians and dentists, small business people, and heads of various social organizations.

While most of the leaders were college-educated, the range of good jobs was very narrow, and chances for success in mainstream white society were all to often nonexistent.

Since the 1960s and 1970s the range of occupations available to college-educated blacks has been considerably widened and there are some unprecedented chances for success in mainstream American society. Some of the new positions now occupied by blacks supersede those held by the traditional black middle class. Consequently, the pre–1960s' bases for stratifying the black community have been broadened to include such high-status positions as certified public accountants; corporate managers; franchise business persons; wealthy entertainers; local, state, and nationally elected public officials, including mayors, judges, and state and national representatives; blacks in high positions in erstwhile white institutions; and a few who serve on powerful corporate boards and commissions.

In short, the social class structure in the black community today is very definitely in a state of flux as it makes room in "social space" for several new, high status positions. It is not only necessary for blacks to restructure social classes within the black community per se, but it is now obvious that as desegregation becomes more and more a reality, the hierarchy of social statuses and social classes in the larger community will also reflect an interracial character. That is, the class structures in the white and black communities must converge so that a common value system will prevail for all.

Black college graduates are already challenging the legality, even the logic, of exclusive white upper-class clubs which symbolize a segregated white stratified society, as opposed to a black stratified society. They are insisting that such a social division does not make sense in an open, democratic society where blacks are succeeding in direct competition with whites. This challenge to exclusive upper-class white clubs or organizations is taking place in cities throughout the United States. It has been emphasized in regards to the very celebrated, erstwhile totally segregated Daughters of the American Revolution, which finally yielded to relentless social and legal pressure. Recently it announced that it will now accept qualified black and other minority women into its exclusive membership.[7]

EVALUATION OF THE BLACK MIDDLE CLASS

The black middle class is somewhat amorphous in the sense that it is composed of individuals and heads of families who are characteristically college graduates engaged in such diverse occupations as entrepreneurs, managers, physicians, dentists, lawyers, educators, ministers, insurance executives, contractors, publishers, government bureaucrats, and a wide variety of white-collar services. The styles of life of the black middle class also vary greatly. Upon close inspection their values are seen to reflect what is universally regarded as basic American values. Some observers have referred to this social class as being "more than 100 percent American." They are anxious to be socially correct.

In some fundamental respects the culture of the black middle class is markedly different from that of the black underclass.[8] Yet despite the differences, there is reliable evidence that some, even the more affluent blacks, attempt to hold onto substantial ties with the black masses. Their motives for doing this may range all the way from the desire to exploit connections with the black masses, upon whom many depend for their economic success, to the very altruistic desire to render services to the poor and socially disadvantaged blacks in their communities.

SELF-EVALUATION

Respondents were asked to evaluate the extent to which the black middle class actually contributes to the survival and advancement of the less fortunate black masses. Since all of the respondents are themselves middle class, theirs is a sort of self-evaluation.

The distribution of their responses is as follows:

Black middle class persons

are helping, but need to do more	53%
are doing very little	27%
give very valuable help	15%
only exploit blacks	5%
	100%

As a rule, our respondents were very critical of the relationship between the more successful black middle class and the black masses. Some of them said, in effect, that there is a growing, very serious alienation between the black middle class and the black masses. A female respondent, who is a successful psychiatrist (income over $50,000 a year) in a large city, insisted that

> When young blacks are in college they like to sound off about all of the great services they plan to provide the poor and wretched in the black community. When they actually become qualified to follow through on their undergraduate commitment, we find them too busy going to the bank to worry about the plight of their black brothers and sisters.

The statement above reflects a feeling on the part of many that successful, educated blacks have a moral duty to help less fortunate blacks. Thus, 5 percent of our respondents very bitterly denounced the black middle class generally as exploiters of the black masses.

Respondents who had an opportunity to speak freely on the subject usually separated themselves from those who do little or nothing to serve the black poor. Some of them eagerly called attention to the fact that they carefully set aside days during which much of their time and expertise are bestowed upon the poor without cost. At the same time, they usually acknowledged that they probably should do more.

An interesting phenomenon emerged out of the respondents' criticism of the black middle class' relationship to indigent blacks. They generally singled out those in some other professions as being negligent. Ultimately, however, the buck stopped with the black family and the public school. Parents and teachers were most often criticized for the prevalence of poverty and antisocial and socially reprehensible behavior on the part of many lower-class blacks.

Surprising, indeed, was the tendency of some respondents to blame the victim for his own victimization and almost completely ignore injustices which are literally built into the American social system where racism, economic exploitation, and blatant inequalities are inherent in the black experience. They tended to insist that the poor must assume total responsibility for their own plight.

The respondents, as a group, sense some serious social class strains among black Americans. This is quite similar to observations made by certain black intellectuals who hold that such strains have already become so severe that the college-educated, middle-class blacks are virtually alienated from the black masses and can no longer speak for them.[9]

Whatever degree of alienation that might exist between the black middle class and the black masses is likely to be exacerbated by the tendency for more and more successful blacks to live and work in white communities, essentially in white worlds. The black masses sometimes express the fear that such individuals and families are likely to adopt the basic values and opinions associated with middle-class whites, including their negative attitudes toward blacks and the poor.

As we review and evaluate the rather extensive information available on the black middle class, we must conclude that it is one of the most significant developments in the history of this nation. Whatever strains that might exist between the black middle class and the black masses can be accounted for as expected consequences of a rapidly changing American society and the very significant advancement college-educated blacks have made since 1960.

Since college-educated blacks are among the most ambitious and upwardly mobile element in American society, their children will certainly swell the ranks of the black middle class. Already there are definite indications that a much larger proportion of blacks today, compared with a generation ago, are escaping the hitherto perpetual first-generation trap where the vast majority of black children began life at "ground zero" insofar as their socio-economic heritage was concerned. Now an increasing number of successful blacks are beginning to pass on substantial social, cultural, and economic legacies to their children in the same way many white Americans have done for their children over the centuries.

As the proportion of second- and third-generation black college graduates increases, an increasingly wide socio-economic gap between the black middle class and the black masses is likely to develop. To preserve functional inter-class unity it will be necessary for the better-educated, more affluent blacks to find ways whereby the status of the masses can continue to be elevated. As it is now, while the black middle class is expanding, the great majority of non-college blacks are making little or no progress. It might become more and more difficult for black children to escape from the poverty and disesteemed status they inherit from their parents. Bernard E. Anderson points out that "many of the disadvantaged and unemployed have such low levels of basic education that it is hard to teach them skills."[10]

So far, the significant civil rights gains made since 1960 have mostly benefited the college-educated blacks. There is already a great deal of expert speculation that a permanent black underclass is developing even more rapidly than the black middle class. Certainly the most obvious and historically reliable approach to the greater social mobility of the poor is to increase the size, enhance the quality, and guarantee the economic stability of black colleges which have a long and distinguished history of preparing socially and economically disadvantaged black youth for success in American society.

The enviable record of success achieved by the black middle class on the whole, despite some very stubborn handicaps, may be due primarily to the fact that they tend to have an abiding faith in the power of education and firmly believe in the values inherent in the American Creed. When the respondents were asked to recount their "most satisfying experience," their statements amounted to a strong, unequivocal sanction of basic American values. The experiences they valued most highly had to do with wholesome family life, especially the love and charm of children; helping others who needed it; advancing the race or civil rights activities; attempts to improve race relations; academic achievements; occupational success; and acts of loyalty to their government. Actually, helping others is a central theme running throughout their listings of their "most satisfying experience."

NOTES

1. See Benjamin L. Hooks, "A Profile of Black America," *Crisis* 90 (December 1983): 4; and William C. Mathey, Jr., and Dwight L. Johnson, "America's Black Population 1970 to 1982," *Crisis* 90 (December 1983): 10–18.

2. Gunnar Myrdal, *An American Dilemma* (New York: Harper and Row, 1944; reprint, New York: Pantheon Books, 1975), p. 28.

3. Daniel C. Thompson, *Sociology of the Black Experience* (Westport, Conn.: Greenwood Press, 1974), pp. 11–13.

4. See Alfred Winslow Jones, "Class Consciousness and Prosperity," in Richard Bendix and Seymour M. Lipset, eds., *Class, Status and Power*, (Glencoe, Ill.: The Free Press, 1966), pp. 340–344.

5. H. H. Hyman, "The Value System of Different Classes," in Bendix and Lipset, eds., *Class, Status and Power*, pp. 426–442.

6. For profiles of some of these families, see Peter Ross Range, "Atlanta: Capital of Black-Is-Bountiful," *New York Times Magazine*, April 9, 1974, 28–29, 68–78; Alice Randall and Stanley Tretick, "Washington's Other Elite," *The Washingtonian*, May 1982, 111–119; Cathy L. Connors and John Bowen, "New York's Black Elite," *Town and Country*, September 1982, 222–229, 295–306; Lawrence Wright, "Easy Street: Houston's Black Elite," *Texas Monthly*, November 1982, 174–181, 285–292; and Marylouise Oates, "Black Society in Los Angeles," *Los Angeles Times*, June 27, 1982, 1, 12–13.

7. See "DC Council Persuades DAR to add Black Woman," *Jet*, May 7, 1984, 23.

8. See, for contrast, Daniel C. Thompson and Barbara G. Thompson, "The Black Underclass: A Continuing Saga," *Black Southerner Magazine*, vols. 1 and 2 (1983, 1984): 21–24, 48–53; also, Jack White and Joseph Boyce, "The Underclass: Enduring Dilemma," *Time Magazine*, June 17, 1974, 26–27.

9. See Thomas Sowell, et al., eds., *The Fairmont Papers* (San Francisco, Calif.: Institute for Contemporary Studies, 1980), p. 104.

10. Quote from Bernard E. Anderson cited in H. Johnson, D. T. Dingle and F. D. Brown, "New Directions for Economic Growth," *Black Enterprise*, June 1984, 204.

8 Leadership

The ancient and oft-quoted adage "like priest, like people" expresses succinctly and dramatically the essential role and universal function of leadership. It emphasizes what seems to be an eternal, ubiquitous social fact:
leadership is an inherent, indispensable status in all organized, effective
group life. Historically, leadership has been the ultimate source, the essential catalyst of institutional, racial, ethnic, and national stability and
greatness. Therefore, no race, organized group, nation, or society can expect to achieve greatness or long maintain a greatness previously achieved
without great leadership.

It is a well-documented fact that great leaders have been ultimately
associated with or involved in great historical movements, events, and
issues. However, the precise role they have played in social changes, the
exact nature of cause-effect socio-historical syndromes of which they have
been active participants, is often unclear and equivocal. Thomas Carlyle,
the great Scottish essayist and historian, wrote in 1840 that "The History
of the world is but the Biography of great men."[1] He insisted that the leader
causes things to happen in society and that in the final analysis it is the
leader who is the architect, the maker, the mover and director of significant
historical forces and events.

An example of Carlyle's argument is the contention that the charismatic
leadership of Martin Luther King, Jr., caused the civil rights revolution of
the 1950s and 1960s. Or more pointedly, the civil rights revolution, which
greatly extended the rights of black Americans, could not have happened
without him.

Other philosophers follow the reasoning of Otto von Bismarck, a principal founder of the modern German empire and chancellor from 1871 to 1890. Bismarck argued that it is not the individual leader who causes things of historical significance to happen, but rather it is the total evolving social situation and the methods of the masses which somehow conspire to produce the kind and quality of leadership demanded of the time and place. He said, "A statesman cannot create anything himself. . . . He must wait and listen until he hears the footsteps of God sounding through events; then leap up and grasp the hem of his garment."[2]

Bismarck's statement reflects a disturbing contemporary fact. Often potentially great leaders have lived rather unproductive, undistinguished, unfulfilled, even wasted lives in which there were only brief, infrequent, unfocused flashes of their true genius and social worth. At the same time, history is replete with records of truly superior, humane leadership which emerged, developed, and blossomed in backward, intellectually barren, hostile social environments when the times became ripe for social change and the masses began to demand a new social order.

The essential importance of the "social readiness," or "fullness of time," concept was demonstrated by the success of the civil rights movement during the 1950s and 1960s. During that short period of time hitherto socially dormant institutions and communities suddenly revealed a relatively large number of dedicated, courageous leaders—men, women, and children, blacks and whites—representing just about all social segments, who seemed to be waiting for the proper time and circumstances to display their leadership talents and to develop into vital instruments in bringing about long-needed social changes.

The philosophies of both Carlyle and Bismarck should be taken seriously. It is essential that key leaders have the wide, active, sustained, dedicated support of the masses of people. The success of the explosive civil rights movement of the 1950s and 1960s definitely required a high degree of sustained interaction between able, dedicated, courageous leaders and the great masses of people in the persistent pursuit of mutually shared goals, which took precedence over the pursuit of narrow personal goals.

This vital interaction between the leader and the masses was described by Martin Luther King, Jr. He observed: "Patterns of leadership are changing, and will continue to change in an attempt to keep up with mass demands. Gandhi's oft-quoted statement is so applicable today. 'There go my people, I must catch them, for I am their leader.' "[3]

Therefore, while the actual role of the leader tends to vary according to time, circumstances, and situations, leadership itself has been indispensable in the formation, development, and achievements of human groups and civilizations. Consequently, before we turn our attention to the specific group of leaders in this study, it behooves us to take a close look at the general status and social role of the leader per se.

WHAT IS A LEADER?

The concept "leader" is rather sophisticated. The word has been in the English language since about 1300 A.D. The word had a prestigious status in other languages long before then. It has been used synonymously with words meaning king, chief, president, hero, genius, outstanding achiever, shaman, rabbi, priest, minister, elder, conductor, elite, decision maker, superstar, and so forth. Furthermore, the concept "leader" has indicated or suggested several associated qualities such as intelligence, vision, originality, dependability, experience, authority, altruism, and manliness.[4]

THE CONCEPT "LEADER" AS A RESEARCH TOOL

During the last twenty years or so I have done several studies of leadership. I have had contacts with, known, and formally interviewed leaders in about all major walks of the black community. Some of the most prominent, well-established, effective leaders are not at all certain that they are leaders. Conversely, some other much less prominent, comparatively uninfluential individuals are quick to identify themselves as leaders and delight in boasting about their leadership activities.

The general confusion regarding the status and role of the leader is quite understandable because the concept is broad and connotes many different duties, privileges, responsibilities, and functions. Because of the lack of a simple, sovereign definition of "leader," we frequently discover, on the one hand, that some of the most effective and humane leaders are likely to remain virtually unrecognized and unheralded outside of their small, intimate groups. On the other hand, certain other individuals with a shrewd sense of timing and public relations become widely acclaimed, even celebrated as leaders (reminiscent of Thomas Carlyle's formulation), but are really quite unproductive and ineffective insofar as advancing the quality of life of their people or followers.

Because the concept "leader" is so varied and comprehensive, in order to study leadership objectively it is first necessary to arrive at a logical, empirical, functional definition. For this particular study of black college graduates the leader is regarded as "one who initiates, stimulates, coordinates and directs the activities of others (the followers) in the solution of some common problem(s) or the achievement of some particular social goal(s)."[5]

This particular analysis of leadership includes graduates of UNCF-related colleges who were singled out as having significant success in influencing the activities of others in their occupations, social organizations, communities, and the American society at large in the resolution of social issues or the solution of social problems. Essentially, they identify with certain definite social positions or ideologies and become representatives of their groups' norms, strategies, goals, and outlooks.

EFFECTIVE BLACK LEADERSHIP

Just about all black leaders about whom I have extensive information, especially those in this study, concur that they regard the role of black leadership as placing a heavy, even a terrible, responsibility upon the individuals. They regard the role of black leadership as more awesome or sacred than leadership in American society in general. Directly or by inference they agree that since black leaders must define, plan, and direct the issues and destinies of this nation's most maligned and persecuted minority, they should be expected to set especially high standards of preparation, wisdom, honesty, unselfishness, and empathy with the great black masses.[6] One respondent put it this way: "The condition of blacks in about every part of this society is critical. We need, we must have superstar leaders if we hope to win the desperate struggle for equal rights."

Because blacks need so much, and have so few "superstars," or authentic spokespersons, they usually expect too much from them and are super-critical of their leaders who do not perform according to the high standards set for them.

Basically, black Americans, like long-oppressed, disesteemed, perennially powerless peoples throughout history, have longed for a Messiah who would lead them to freedom, prosperity, recognition, and power. Therefore, when their leaders fall short of these unrealistic expectations the masses are likely to become disenchanted with them and often make them the brunt of scathing criticism, and label them "conservative," "selfish," "conciliatory," "reactionary," even "Uncle Tom."[7]

SOME BASIC CHARACTERISTICS OF EFFECTIVE BLACK LEADERS

One of the genuinely epic chapters in American history is that which tells of the constant challenges, failures, and successes of black leaders. Essentially, it is the story of a rare breed of leaders who blazed new trails which often led through very dangerous social, moral, spiritual, legal, economic, and political wilderness in search of equal citizenship, dignity, and opportunity.

It is amazing that throughout the ever-recurring, acute times of trouble experienced by black Americans, from slavery until this day, there have been always a few well-prepared, courageous, dedicated black leaders willing to assume the high risks of demanding blacks' rights. Generally speaking, the primary role of black leaders has been that of securing for black people the inherent citizenship rights ordinarily freely bestowed upon white people.[8]

Functionally, blacks' long, ever-dangerous, frustrating struggle for survival and advancement in American society has been the very crucible in which superior black leadership has been forged. When truly great black leadership was demanded, great black leaders tended to emerge. It seems that the greater the leadership challenge, the more positive and effective has been the leadership produced.

A careful examination and evaluation of the careers of key, effective black leaders throughout the history of the black experience (those who have been able to get things done for and with their people, such as the founding of important institutions, and organizations, and the launching of new ideas, new leadership strategies, patterns, and goals), in the actual context of their particular times and circumstances, will indeed reveal a large, rich storehouse of ingeniously designed, reliable strategies and principles they have characteristically employed to lead their people over many rough roads toward freedom and equality.[9]

1. Complete Identification with the Problems and Plight of the More Unfortunate Black Masses

While the bona fide black leadership class per se may be accurately described as elitist in terms of its education, dedication to high aims, humane values, and noteworthy achievements, it has never been elitist in terms of its membership, attitudes toward the poor, disadvantaged black masses, or its proud identification with black institutions, movements, and special causes.

The most effective black leaders have always identified with the black masses because the vast majority of them have been, themselves, products of the black lower class. Even today about 85 percent of all black leaders in this study have come from humble homes where their parents had relatively little formal education and no significant economic or political influence. Most black leaders in the past and at present are first-generation successes insofar as affluence and social power are concerned.

The inauspicious, ordinary socio-economic origins of most black leaders throughout the history of this nation have been the distinguishing mark, the respected crest which has set them apart from all other leaders in this nation. Black leaders' humble origins and education have eminently prepared them to identify with the overall, complex problems of the poor and disesteemed in an otherwise affluent and powerful American society. Even some of the most successful, influential black leaders in this study confided that they have close relatives and childhood friends who may be still classified among the poor, who live from hand to mouth in run-down, neglected, crime-ridden black ghettos. Such leaders should have little or no difficulty in understanding and articulating the dreams, hopes, strivings, and disappointments of the economically insecure and politically power-less black masses.

During the last decade or so the socio-economic status of a relatively small percentage of blacks, about 25 percent, has improved significantly. This is good in the sense that it is what blacks have been struggling to achieve since the beginning of the black experience in this country. As we have noted, this emerging black middle class is much larger, more complex, and secure than ever before. Individuals constituting this new black middle class are usually first-generation occupational successes. They are char-acteristically ambitious, intelligent citizens, well educated and justifiably proud of their achievements. Most have succeeded despite almost impos-sible odds. Many have literally fought their way up from dire poverty and the strong negative pulls of the black ghetto to positions of respect and power. Those who participated in this study concur that all of this is good because their successes are the very best proof that the American Dream can become a reality. As one respondent put it, "Successful blacks are examples of manhood and womanhood our children need so badly as role models."

As much as black people respect the successes of fellow blacks and celebrate their noteworthy accomplishments, many are afraid that some have begun to get trapped, so to speak, in their own successes. That is, they have begun to separate themselves from their real roots, the disad-vantaged black masses. A nationally prominent respondent said that "some-how the new black successes seem to be deluded into believing that they have transcended the racial barriers imposed upon other blacks."[10] He called attention to the fact that a few even argue that any normal black person can manage to overcome racial barriers and their negative con-sequences if they honestly try.

During the generations since slavery, black leaders have come to realize that often racism is directed against blacks representing every socio-eco-nomic class and every occupation in American society. All blacks regard-less of education are likely to encounter some important degree of racism. Therefore, effective black leaders have certainly continued to admonish their followers to improve themselves intellectually, socially, economically, and morally; yet they have not ceased to protest formidable barriers to advancement, or racism, over which blacks have little or no control. At the very heart of their leadership has been their urgent prodding of powerful white institutions and government on all levels to make democracy a living reality by guaranteeing blacks equality in all walks of life and by giving them the special help they will need to compete as equals with their historically more fortunate white peers.

This characteristic approach was best epitomized during the 1960s by Whitney M. Young, Jr., the late executive director of the NUL. He called for a domestic "Marshall Plan." According to this plan, blacks would be given special help in the areas of education, employment, and leadership. He regarded this as a necessary step toward rectifying centuries of injustices blacks have suffered in this society. Without this help, he insisted, the black masses would not be able to compete successfully for the fruits of equal, full citizenship.[11]

While some respondents do not agree with Whitney M. Young, Jr.'s, "compensatory doctrine," 81 percent do agree that basic American institutions, including the federal government, have a central responsibility for the improvement of the condition of the black masses. Few black leaders would agree that blacks must lift themselves totally by their own bootstraps. While they exhort blacks to strive to improve themselves, they are ever mindful that many of the basic problems suffered by blacks, and certainly some of their greatest shortcomings, were spawned by the intensely racist society in which they were reared. Very often blacks' negative adjustment to racism and deprivation are symptoms of much deeper causes, such as widespread social disesteem, lack of equal opportunity, poor schools, and a prevailing feeling of frustration, helplessness, and anger in black ghettos. Thus, most effective black leaders insist that black youths need convincing evidence that long-cherished American values are genuine and apply to them just as they do to other citizens. In short, they need to know that blacks too can succeed in American society by espousing these values. Many have real doubts.

2. Unequivocal Commitment to the Democratic Process

No doubt one of the most outstanding characteristics of black leadership throughout American history has been its consistent, firm belief that significant social reforms, particularly the advancement of blacks, can be accomplished within the framework of the democratic process. Actually, no other group of leaders has more persistently manifested the high degree of commitment to the democratic process than has black leadership. Even when blacks stand to lose by such things as an honest merit system, which may determine job entrance or upgrading, the great majority of black leaders concur with it. Thus 92 percent of the respondents only insist that the measurement should be fair, nor racially or culturally biased.

In a real sense effective black leaders have been quintessential Americans. They have continued to espouse a basic democratic ideology, to manifest a firm belief in the equality of all men, to insist upon an integrated American society, and to express strong faith in the worth, ability, and sanctity of the individual. Few successful black leaders have ever seriously challenged the authority, rightness, and practicality of the U.S. Constitution or the precepts of the American Creed.

Thus, when we carefully study the underlying ideology reflected in the speeches, writings, and organizations of effective black leaders, we will discover that almost without exception they attest to an abiding faith that personal virtues, solid achievements, and unswerving dedication to the democratic process will ultimately triumph among men and nations. This, in fact, is the raison d'être of black protest. That is, black protest has seldom focused upon major deprivations inherent in the American social system as such but rather it has been directed at what might be described as "relative deprivations," or racial inequalities. Actually, the grand strategy of black protest has been always designed to achieve goals and effectuate values that are traditionally acknowledged to be inherent in a political democracy and which are firmly established as an integral aspect of our American culture. In just about all respects black protest has been a clear endorsement of the American Creed and a reaffirmation of faith in the essential goodness of the individual and the soundness of the democratic process.

According to data to be presented forthwith, the newly emerging black leadership continues to have faith in our republican form of government and insists that it should be made to work for all segments of American society. They regard this as their central challenge. Thus, despite more than three centuries of intense racial unrest and frustrations, black leaders in this study continue to champion fundamental democratic procedures as the most promising and desirable approach to blacks' welfare and advancement.

3. Belief in Strong Black Organizations

It is well documented that just about all major social problems, such as unemployment, inadequate housing, and crime, come to focus in the black community where their rates are two to three times as high as they are in the larger community or nation. However, and this is ironic, black people control only a few, if any, organizations strong enough to deal effectively with these problems, or even to exert effective pressure upon the political process with which all of them are related to some significant degree.

The generally unorganized state of the black community has been always a source of grave concern for black leaders. They have constantly pointed out that basic social problems must be dealt with by carefully designed organizations. Therefore, despite the fact that a large proportion of black leaders may be classified as charismatic, because they are called, as it were, to their leadership positions rather than being elected or selected by designated followers or organizations, just about all of them have proceeded to establish or strengthen organizations to deal with the particular problems they have singled out as the most important. They spearheaded the establishment of many types of institutions, agencies, and organizations: schools, churches, business leagues, professional associations, farmers' cooperatives, lodges, fraternities, sororities, social clubs, alliances, ad hoc committees, black caucuses, and so on. Actually, no matter what the

Table 36
Leadership Recognition

Extent of Influence	Male	Female	Total
Certain organizations	39%	40%	39%
Local black community	15%	15%	15%
Local community at large	13%	7%	9%
Statewide	9%	4%	6%
National black community	1%	1%	1%
Nationally recognized	2%	1%	2%
Not a leader	21%	32%	28%

stated purpose of a given black organization may be, the ultimate purpose is always black advancement.

Blacks have founded and developed many special civil rights organizations, the best examples of which have been the most durable—NAACP, NUL, SCLC, and People United to Save Humanity (PUSH). These organizations coordinate blacks' overall movement for equal citizenship. While charismatic leaders have certainly made great contributions insofar as arousing a favorable public opinion, educating the black masses, and stimulating important social action, the real progress blacks have made toward first-class citizenship has been due primarily to black organizations and institutions. The charismatic leader soon finds that it is not enough to simply inspire downtrodden people and give them hope for a better tomorrow. Sooner or later the leader must also clearly define the basic social problems faced by his or her followers, give them logical priority, and propose concrete ways or strategies by which these problems can be solved. As a rule, solutions to social problems require organized efforts.

LEADERSHIP OF RESPONDENTS

The college graduates included in this study were asked, "Generally speaking, would you say that you are regarded as a leader?" Their answers are summarized in Table 36. Certainly the most significant datum in Table 36 is that the great majority of our respondents (72 percent) regard themselves as leaders on some level. This is indeed a very positive testimony that the sample colleges have effectively pursued one of their cardinal missions, the preparation of a black leadership class with a desire to rectify social wrongs, alleviate suffering and injustices, one which is able to set sound ideals and standards for the organizations, communities, and institutions in which they are involved.

Characteristically, graduates of the black colleges identify with the so-called underdog in American society and cultivate a sense of responsibility to see that their quality of life is improved. One prominent respondent writing about black colleges in a recent article concluded that "a spirit of leadership responsibility pervades the black campus."[12] The sense of leadership responsibility on black campuses has been always stimulated by two interrelated facts: at least 80 percent of the students come from homes and communities where well-prepared, articulate leadership is desperately needed, and because these campuses are relatively small, all students have opportunities, even challenges, to discover and develop their leadership talents.

Much of the respondents' leadership talents, nurtured on black college campuses during the civil rights revolution of the 1960s and 1970s, have been sharpened and effectively focused upon just about every major issue in American life. Graduates of these colleges have seriously attempted to see and interpret from the black perspective all basic issues from the quality of education in local schools to the reality of international war. Central to their thinking is the effect these issues will have on black Americans.

TYPES OF LEADERS

The particular types of leaders which will emerge from any given social situation will vary with the prevailing leadership climate, the goals to be attained, the historical nature of the problems to be dealt with, and the extent to which individual leaders have been prepared to deal effectively with the problems. Some of the most fruitful studies of leadership have been primarily concerned with individuals in government and the military who wielded great social power. Such studies generally focused upon how they wielded power over others: whether they were autocratic, democratic, laissez-faire, tyrannical, lions/foxes, heroes/supermen, formal/informal, just or unjust.

Studies which have focused upon the types of black leaders have generally emphasized race relations or the importance of blacks getting along with white Americans. They have assumed that whites hold the predominant social-power positions and that black Americans hold little or no social power. Therefore, the types of black leaders considered were often labeled "Uncle Tom," "racial diplomat," "race man," "black militant," "issues leaders," "power leaders," or "accommodation leaders." These black leaders have been traditionally associated with a biracial social system where there existed two distinct social worlds, one white, the other black, one powerful, the other powerless.[13]

TYPES OF LEADERS IN THIS STUDY

While racial segregation and discrimination are still rampant in American society, they generally exist without constitutional and moral sanctions.

Blacks' success in all areas of American life in which they are privileged to participate has completely discredited the theories and myths once used to rationalize the doctrine of white supremacy and total racial segregation. According to all available information, blacks in all walks of life summarily reject racial segregation. Fully 98 percent of the respondents in this study indicated that they are dedicated to the proposition that equality for blacks is possible only in a racially desegregated American society. Few, indeed only about 1 percent, can be classified as "racial separatists."

It is also quite interesting that even the college graduates who advocate strong, well-financed, independent black institutions, organizations, and movements usually justify them as essential instruments in blacks' efforts to achieve equality in a desegregating American society.

THE CHANGING NATURE OF BLACK LEADERSHIP

A close inspection of the leadership roles and goals of the respondents in this study during the decades before and after the 1960s reveals a continuing pattern of evolution from total racial segregation and exclusive focus upon black issues and concerns to a pattern of integrated leadership where black leaders' interests and goals are focused upon issues involving the welfare of the larger mainstream community. Their interest and responsibilities transcend purely racial boundaries.

Stage One: Segregated Black Leaders

Prior to the 1960s when racial segregation was an integral aspect of American life, black leaders, regardless of their ability or ambition, were generally restricted to only black concerns. Seldom were they expected to provide any significant measure of guidance outside the confines of the black community. Thus a former college administrator in the sample complained:

> Whites in my community had so little respect for us that even when they needed information about people connected with our campus they would hire one another to get it rather than extending us the right to supply it...There was always some white person telling Negroes what they thought and how they should run their lives.

Too often black segregated leaders had to be approved by powerful white segregationists in order to get anything done for their black followers. Usually the black community suspected the more effective among them as being "safe," in the sense that they would bow to white mores rather than insist upon black rights. A retired minister in the sample lamented, "We had no choice. We either did what the white folks wanted us to do, or we could do nothing for our people. Simply put, we were controlled. It was tough."

Some of the segregated black leaders did have considerable success and social power within their black communities and were often called upon to influence their followers to cooperate with certain plans and programs of special consequence to the larger white community.

The more or less rigid restraints white racists placed upon the scope and goals of segregated black leaders functioned to limit and compromise some of the most creative and courageous of them for at least a century after slavery. The fact is that some of the most creative thinkers and doers may be described as "compromised" leaders. They simply were not free to champion the causes in which they believed.

The Move Toward Stage Two: Interracial Black Leadership

Despite threats, intimidations, and all manner of sociological handicaps, many black institutions and organizations were founded, took firm roots, and flourished during the first hundred years after slavery. Some organized on a national level and developed into strong, persistent advocates of blacks' civil rights. Their scathing criticism of racial segregation and loud protests of inequality began to embarrass this nation during World War II when it was attempting to establish itself as leader of the free world. Though there had been always some semblance of the interracial black leaders, the role, as such, became formalized and took on a new, more dignified meaning during the decades just after World War II. Several highly educated black leaders were recognized as experts on racial issues related to national welfare. Their talents were sought out by top policymakers and their advice and counsel had an impact on decision making in many areas of American life. Top black educators, especially presidents of black colleges, were always among the most influential interracial black leaders. One of them stated in an interview, "At one time or another I have served as a consultant to five different presidents of the United States."

Interracial leaders proved to be as valuable on a local level as on a national level. In just about every large black community, black college graduates are called upon to be consultants when there are basic issues involving the black community. Thus, 72 percent of the respondents served on some committee, commission, or board dedicated to community advancement or improvement.

The services rendered to community cooperation and racial harmony by interracial experts have been especially pronounced in large school districts which experienced riots and near riots in the wake of school desegregation. A close reading of the desegregation process throughout the nation reveals that it was relatively orderly and had the greatest success in communities with strong, courageous interracial leaders and was most disruptive in communities where such leadership was weak or absent.[14]

It is obvious that interracial leaders who are heads of civil rights organizations on both the national and local levels and heads of well-established
black institutions are highly skilled racial diplomats. They, more than any
other social segment in large cities, have functioned as watchdogs of civil
rights and have constantly promoted black progress and racial harmony.
They can always be depended upon to prod white policymakers and institutions to expand their concept and practice of democracy. One of the
respondents in this study remarked that "a truly effective race relations
leader is apt to be more like Thomas Jefferson than was Jefferson himself."

Stage Three: The Integrated Black Leaders

An emerging group of distinguished black leaders, which includes about
2 or 3 percent of the respondents in this sample, is functionally integrated
into the so-called establishment, which was virtually lily-white until a decade or so ago. Essentially, these black men and women are college graduates, often professionally trained, who hold high positions in mainstream
organizations and institutions. They are members of corporate boards,
officials in large corporations, administrators of traditionally white institutions, officers of predominantly white organizations, and elected and
appointed public officials whose interest and responsibilities must necessarily transcend the black community per se.

Integrated black leaders occupy a sensitive, yet strategic position insofar
as black interests and outlook are concerned. In a real sense, they are the
selected blacks with significant authority to effectuate fundamental changes
in the racial status quo. They have the best opportunities to affect the old
biracial system and to propose constructive, new biracial experiments and
programs in socio-economic contexts.

Integrated black leaders are routinely challenged by fellow blacks to
extend some aspects of the democratic process and to help increase the
number of blacks in top jobs and decision-making positions. These leaders
occupying positions of trust and authority have a responsibility to help
blacks in their struggle toward equality in American society.

Several integrated leaders in this study concur that their strategic relationship with the white power structure poses a frustrating dilemma: the
desire to render expected services to the particular organization or enterprise which gives them leadership legitimacy and authority and the
strong desire to do something special for the advancement of black Americans. This dilemma is frequently exacerbated by the goals of some white
enterprises which are often at odds with the goal of black advancement.

For example, one respondent who sits on the board of directors of a
southern corporation wrote, "I fill a very important but awkward position.
I was appointed to help expand the corporation not to expand the employment of blacks. I want to get more black managers but my hands are
tied."

Actually, the respondents who function as integrated leaders feel that their efforts to promote black interests are closely evaluated by their white colleagues, and they try to be non-racial and fair. This is especially true of those in public office who take great care to assure everyone that they will not favor blacks over whites in appointments, promotions, and so forth.

The college graduates in this sample agree that integrated black leaders need the confidence and support of the black community if they are to perform at their best. One respondent said she felt that when a black person is included among basic community policymakers, other blacks should openly express their approval and let the larger community know that that person is supported as their representative. Without such general support some fear the integrated black leaders may eventually lose the black perspective as they become increasingly socialized into white power arrangements. When, or if, this happens, these very strategically placed black leaders might become defenders of the status quo rather than advocates of needed, overdue reforms in key areas of American life, especially those related directly to black progress. They would come off as a modern version of the ancient image of Uncle Tom. The respondents here generally applaud the success and progress certain fellow blacks have made as integrated leaders, and at least 70 percent feel that somehow black leaders must be held accountable to the black community.[15]

While the avowed conservative black leader is still rare, there is ample evidence in the data to support the fear that the radical conservatism that seems to be characteristic of American society in recent years is beginning to be reflected in the attitudes and statements of some of the most influential black leaders. This is the real basis of the dilemma facing the new black leadership today. Some are tempted to forge relationships with established white power persons and arrangements to enhance and secure their own social power, rather than perform as advocates of black progress. This is a much more uncertain path to social influence since white liberals are unorganized and seldom speak out on civil rights issues.

NEW DIRECTIONS

To get some concrete idea about the respondents' conceptions of the type of black leadership best suited to deal with the problems now faced by black Americans, they were asked to name one leader they regarded as "the most effective" in getting things done for black Americans. In all they named fifteen different individuals. Included are the heads of four major civil rights organizations, six political figures, and five nationally prominent individuals from different walks of life, a federal judge, two religious leaders, an educator, and a publisher.

The respondents' explanations strongly suggest that college-educated blacks, at least, are moving away from the notion of an all-purpose, messianic-type charismatic leader to the concept of a leadership structure which embraces a variety of able experts with different occupational perspectives and different leadership styles representing the various organizational bases found in the black community. This new approach to black leadership was called for in a conference of "conservative" black scholars.[16]

Speakers at that conference demanded a "new black leadership" with new racial and national perspectives, new alliances, and new institutional foundations as essential in the solution of the new and chronic problems facing blacks during the years ahead. They were particularly concerned about the plight of the black underclass. They tended to agree that the traditional black leadership is not properly addressing their key problems. This point of view was expressed by Martin Kilson:

> black leadership has to diversify itself....Up until the early 1970s it was basically correct to have a homogenized black leadership. The simple reason was naked racism....We are in a new era now....There is an incredibly pressing need for policy postures coming from different sectors of the black leadership....New coalitions and alliance patterns and network patterns are needed.[17]

Chuck Stone concluded that blacks need a new leadership to "formulate a coherent black strategy to deal with black pathologies: the crime, the poor health, the unemployment, mis-education." For this Stone proposes the development of "a new breed of independent black leadership."[18]

Fully 78 percent of the respondents in this study concur that the structure, goals, and strategies of black leadership need to be revised. Most feel that blacks must put a great deal more emphasis upon doing it themselves. During the years ahead blacks must assume almost total responsibility for their own advancement. Thus, they must make every effort to strengthen their institutions, seek out new alliances with other struggling groups, find better strategies for strengthening black businesses, and see that black colleges continue as the fountainhead of black advancement.

Apparently, the conservatives' demand for diversification of black leadership in behalf of the black underclass is primarily directed at established civil rights organizations. Actually, 78 percent of the respondents in this study are already engaged in diversified leadership patterns on an informal or formal basis. Their varied leadership activities have had an impact upon local communities, state, and national policy-making. For instance, in addition to their services on committees, directorships of voluntary organizations, and commissions where the plight of the poor (especially the black underclass) is of special concern, they often hold formal leadership positions where they are directly responsible for dealing with the disadvantages and problems characteristic of the poor.

A review of the respondents' leadership activities in behalf of the poor reveals that some are giving their time in community health clinics, legal aid programs, services to the aged and juvenile delinquents, free tutoring of poor children, and numerous other charitable endeavors. Twenty percent or more hold official positions which make them directly responsible for improving the quality of life of the black underclass. Some are teachers and principals of so-called inner-city schools and devote their lives to the education of disadvantaged children; others are directors of low-cost housing and endeavor to make it work best for the tenants; many are employed on all levels of the criminal justice system from basic law enforcement to federal judges where they are in positions to make and interpret public policy affecting the poor; and a large number, about 5 percent of the respondents, are heads of black churches and voluntary groups, and may be regarded as opinion leaders, who constantly seek ways to improve living conditions among the poor. For instance, some churches have built low-cost housing; other groups headed by the respondents are engaged in all-out efforts to expand and improve black-owned businesses in the hope that they will be able to expand black employment; some diverse groups and organizations work constantly to multiply black youths' chances to escape the ghetto entrapment in which they are too often permanently caught. Some respondents have organized schools for the performing arts, fine arts, and the trades.

Black leaders in general are bracing themselves for a period of national conservatism which has already threatened many public programs designed to benefit blacks, especially the poor. There has already developed a mood of self-help. Efforts are underway for black groups to assume more and more responsibility for blacks' progress. These efforts include the strengthening of all black institutions, seeking new alliances with other groups with similar goals, designing more effective techniques and strategies for strengthening political and economic ties, and insisting that blacks receive the best education available. This obligation to prepare college-educated leaders was expressed by Charles C. Teamer, Sr., general president of Alpha Phi Alpha fraternity. He defined one of the main goals of that fraternity as "to train young men for leadership. We must encourage them to become better educated, to participate in civic and community affairs on all levels and to be ready when the call for leadership is issued forth."[19]

As a distinguished social group, black college graduates as represented in this study are carrying on the tradition of what Samuel DuBois Cook called "social-ethical" leadership.

More than eighty years ago, W. E. B. Du Bois said: "In the professions they are slowly but surely leavening the Negro Church, are healing and preventing the devastation of disease, and beginning to furnish legal protection for the liberty and prosperity of the toiling masses."[20] And thirty years later Charles S. Johnson reached the following conclusion: "Negro college graduates are most likely to disturb the custom of social and racial matters and also most likely to contribute constructively to social adjustment....All in all, they are the ones who...most frequently engage in elevating the stagnant masses of their own race."[21]

In a very functional sense, then, black college graduates constitute an elite, an effective leadership class, in the vanguard of black advancement specifically and democracy generally.

NOTES

1. A. J. P. Taylor, *Bismarck: The Man and the Statesman* (New York: Alfred A. Knopf, 1955), p. 115.

2. Thomas Carlyle, *On Heroes, Hero-Worship and the Heroic in History* (New York: E. P. Dutton and Co., 1908), p. 226.

3. Daniel C. Thompson, *The Negro Leadership Class* (Englewood Cliffs, N.J.: Prentice-Hall, 1963), p. x.

4. Ralph M. Stogdill, *Handbook of Leadership* (New York: Free Press, 1974), pp. 7–16.

5. Thompson, *The Negro Leadership Class*, p. 3.

6. See "The Longest Struggle: The NAACP in Historical Perspective," *Tony Brown's Journal*, (January/March, 1984): 1–4; See also Benjamin L. Hooks, "A Profile of Black America—A Grim Picture," *Crisis* 90 (October 1981): 380–384, 392–400.

7. See Gunnar Myrdal, *An American Dilemma* (New York: Harper and Row, 1944; reprint, New York, Pantheon Books, 1975), pp. 640–641.

8. See, for instance, National Urban League, *The State of Black America 1977*. "Introduction" by former Executive Director, Vernon E. Jordan, Jr.

9. For a succinct analysis of some effective black leaders and their distinct "leadership styles," see Raymond Gavins, *The Perils and Prospects of Southern Black Leadership* (Durham, N.C.: Duke University Press, 1977).

10. For a comprehensive discussion, see Wilson, *The Declining Significance of Race* (Chicago: University of Chicago Press, 1980), pp. 167–175.

11. Whitney M. Young, Jr., *To Be Equal* (New York: McGraw-Hill, 1964), pp. 22–23.

12. Sidney J. Barthelemy, "Nurturing Leadership," in Antoine Garibaldi, ed., *Black Colleges and Universities* (New York: Praeger, 1984), p. 19.

13. See Thompson, *The Negro Leadership Class*, pp. 58–79; Elaine Burgess, *Negro Leadership in a Southern City* (Durham, N.C.: University of North Carolina Press, 1960); and Myrdal, *An American Dilemma*, chapter 34.

14. Thompson, *Sociology of the Black Experience* (Westport, Conn.: Greenwood Press, 1974), p. 210.

15. For an analysis of this, see Ronald V. Dellums,"Black Leadership for Change or Status Quo?" *Black Scholar*, 8 (January/February 1977): 2–5.

16. See Thomas Sowell et al., *The Fairmont Papers* (San Francisco: Institute for Contemporary Studies, 1981), especially pp. 119, 137, and 160.

17. Ibid., pp. 134–135.

18. Ibid., pp. 118–119.

19.   Charles C. Teamer, Sr., "Inaugural Address: A Legacy of Leadership and Service," *Sphinx* 70 (Winter 1984): 19.

20. As previously quoted, W. E. B. Du Bois, *The Souls of Black Folk* (Nashville, Tenn.: Fisk University Press, 1979; reprint) p. 103.

21. Charles S. Johnson, *The Negro College Graduate* (Durham, N.C.: University of North Carolina Press, 1938), p. 355.

9 Conclusions

Conclusions reached in this book have been validated by data gathered from 2,089 graduates of the forty-two UNCF-member colleges who responded to the mailed questionnaire designed for this study. Additionally, basic information and insights regarding the career patterns, social concerns, and leadership of black college graduates were acquired from interviews with more than forty alumni during the three-year study (1982–1985). Extensive information from a wide range of secondary sources was used to supplement and interpret responses in the context of higher education in the United States at large.

The information gathered firmly supports the following conclusions:

Graduates of the colleges in this study may be regarded as an elitist subgroup in American society because they are among the more successful individuals in the black community and because they constitute the vanguard of blacks' struggle for survival and advancement toward equality in American society.

Essentially, black college graduates today, as represented by those constituting the sample for this study, play the same social role of effective leaders and standard setters that W.E.B. Du Bois visualized for the college educated, or "The Talented Tenth" of the black population. It is also similar to what Thomas Jefferson postulated for the "natural aristocracy" or those with superior education and talents.

The elite as presented in this volume is made up of those who come from every distinct socio-economic category in the black community from which black colleges recruit the vast majority of their students. Despite some significant differences in social backgrounds, levels and fields of education, life-styles and general outlook, black college graduates share at least one basic thing in common. They are avowedly dedicated to the survival and development of black institutions and the advancement of blacks as a distinct people within the general context of a desegregating American social system. Therefore, as employed in this analysis the concept "black elite" is the opposite of the popular concept "elite," which suggests attitudes of social exclusiveness, snobbishness, and pretentiousness.

As members of a well-educated subgroup, black college graduates, such as those in this study, usually join forces or otherwise identify with organizations and individuals which champion the cause of blacks' civil rights. They insist that a basic function of government on all levels is to guarantee all citizens equal opportunity and equal protection of the law.

College-educated blacks as a rule shy away from advocating outright preferential or compensatory treatment of blacks in education or employment except in situations where it is regarded as absolutely necessary to deal specifically with race as a step toward the achievement of equality of opportunity.

While the respondents have no compunction about criticizing what they regard as unequal opportunities and other indications of racism in the United States, they are equally prone to express faith in the American Creed. They insist that if black Americans are accorded equal opportunities to participate in American society their achievements would be equal to those of any other racial or ethnic group.

The respondents' profound belief in the democratic distribution of inherent talent and potential, no doubt, stems from the fact that 80–85 percent of them have succeeded against great odds. The vast majority hold that their upward social mobility comes from hard work and a good education. Thus, they praise black colleges for recruiting students on the basis of their potential as well as on the basis of proven ability.

The flexible admission practices of black colleges are much sounder than some critics are willing to admit: 77 percent of the respondents went on to graduate study in a wide range of fields, with 54 percent earning some post-baccalaureate degree. Some of the respondents (6 percent) who had unpromising high school records went on to earn advanced degrees from some of the most prestigious, high-ranking universities in the world.

The college graduates in this study place great value upon a good job. This is true of Americans on all socio-economic levels. At the same time a good steady job has special significance for black Americans because a good job is an important milestone in some black families where few, if any, members have ever had a good job as defined by the larger white community. Also, the value the black community places upon high-status employment reflects the fact that blacks, once regarded as mere chattel, were assigned the most menial, degrading jobs.

Ever since slavery blacks have had to strive against the general practice of white employers to classify the most desirable, well-paying jobs as for "whites only," leaving the less desirable, low-status jobs for blacks. During times of high unemployment, jobs previously set aside for blacks have been often reclassified as open or for whites. Basically the employment of blacks reflects a long-standing principle inherent in the doctrine of white supremacy: all white people, in all situations, must be socially superior to all black people. Accordingly, white employers have traditionally refrained from employing blacks in situations where they would be expected to supervise white workers. When blacks secure a good job, they are likely to regard it as a personal and racial triumph, especially when they are the first blacks to secure some traditional white job.

The respondents constitute one of the most successful groups in American society. At least 76 percent hold professional or managerial positions. Ninety-seven percent regard themselves as qualified professionals in some field. This claim has validity because they were usually prepared in college for some profession, such as teaching, accounting, and social welfare services, along with their liberal arts education. Thus, those who hold positions which rank lower than professional or managerial status are likely to describe their employment as tentative or temporary.

Approximately 8 percent of the college graduates in the sample hold some kind of white-collar job. Almost half of them (46 percent) were the first blacks to hold that particular job. What might be regarded as an ordinary white-collar job in mainstream American society, such as office assistant, stenographer in a large prestigious establishment, clerk, or staff employee in a large corporation may be regarded as high-status employment in the black community where traditionally such jobs were not available. For instance, in 1960 only 16.1 percent of employed blacks held white-collar jobs. By 1972, this figure jumped to 29.8 percent. This increase in the number of blacks holding white-collar jobs suggests that a significant number were the first of their race to hold such positions.

Just 3 percent of the respondents held blue-collar and service jobs at the time of the study. All regarded their jobs as temporary or interim employment while they were waiting for some job more in keeping with their qualifications.

Only 2 or 3 percent in the sample were unemployed when they responded to the questionnaire in August 1982. By contrast, the national unemployment average was hovering around 9 percent, and the unemployment rate for black Americans was 18 percent and above. The graduates who classified themselves as unemployed were usually young (under thirty) who were waiting for their first professional appointment.

Ninety-five percent of the graduates are employed in interracial situations where they either work closely with whites or have white clients, patients, or customers. The range is from 13 percent with all black clientele to 2 percent with all white clientele.

Blacks who are employed in predominantly white situations recognize that they are in the vanguard of their race's socio-economic advancement. Though they usually feel uncomfortable as "black representatives," they are quite conscious that some, both blacks and whites, fully expect them to play that role and that their individual performance may redound to overall advancement of blacks.

In the wake of the civil rights thrust of the 1960s new employment opportunities have opened to blacks. Since the Voting Rights Act of 1965, politics and government have provided an expanded area of employment for blacks. Beginning at almost "ground zero" in most states, especially in the South where only a few blacks were even enfranchised, the number of college-educated blacks participating in the political process has increased constantly. Not only have they qualified to vote and wield considerable political clout as united or bloc voters, but over five thousand blacks also hold elective or appointive political positions. Among these are 286 mayors. About 2 percent of the respondents in this study hold public office.

Employment opportunities in the corporate world have expanded rapidly during the last twenty or so years. This area now offers high-status, well-paying jobs which previously did not exist for black college graduates. Approximately 15 percent of those in this study hold management-level positions in the corporate world. As a group they feel that they are as well qualified for the positions they hold as are their white peers. Actually, some insist that they are better qualified to deal with a variety of issues and problems related to racial matters than are their white peers. Some even regard themselves as skilled racial diplomats who are expected to establish and maintain racial harmony even in the presence of obvious racial bigotry. A few of the respondents argue that as blacks in traditionally racially segregated management positions, they are prepared to bring new insights and styles to the management process. They therefore do not feel that it should be necessary for them to follow slavishly management styles set by their white peers.

Sixty-five percent of the sample insist that the traditional work ethic is, indeed, the best means of achieving success in American society. This response indicates that they reject the various undemocratic practices characteristic of the world of work, such as "buddy cliques," "pull," and influence networks. Forty-one percent of the respondents are convinced that being black has been a handicap for them. Yet in spite of all of these undemocratic practices, they still manifest great confidence in the American system where the work ethic is a sacred tradition.

The college graduates in this sample are joiners. At least 90 percent hold membership in some organization, with 16 percent belonging to five or more organizations. While many of the organizations are purely social in nature, an examination of their avowed aims, programs, and activities reveals that just about all of the 164 different organizations make serious efforts to contribute in some way to blacks' advancement toward equality in American society.

Historically, the black church has been the glue, the primary source of unity and cooperation in the black community. All major black institutions and movements either grew directly out of the church or were indirectly nurtured by it.

Ninety-seven percent of our sample claim membership in some church. The great majority (78 percent) still identify with the denomination in which they were reared, though many have been tempted to join higher-status denominations or white congregations more comparable to their rising social status. Such loyalty to their original faiths helps to preserve the inter–social class unity in the black community. Not only do they claim membership in some church, but 93 percent also attend regularly or at least occasionally. This is in contrast to a Gallup Poll report (1980) in which only 69 percent of Americans attended churches or synagogues at all, and just 40 percent attended regularly. Further, 76 percent of our sample feel that the black church has been an important, effective instrument in blacks' long, frustrating struggle for equality. The other 24 percent are critical of the church because they are convinced that it could have done much more for blacks' advancement.

Black social fraternities and sororities provide effective communication among college-educated blacks. Sixty-eight percent of the respondents joined Greek letter organizations in college, and 37 percent are still active members. The Greek letter organizations have a total of five thousand chapters or more in the United States and abroad, and have a combined membership of approximately five hundred thousand. The heads of these organizations are always cited as top or most influential black leaders.

Members communicate through magazines, newsletters, and regular local, regional, and national meetings. This effective communication often results in a system of networking whereby "brothers" and "sisters" provide mutual aid for each other. In addition to their concerns with the welfare and strength of their particular organizations, they sponsor well-planned community-related programs carefully designed to advance the status and quality of life among the black masses.

Ninety percent of the respondents identify themselves as members of the Democratic party; only 4 percent are Republicans, and 6 percent are Independent or other. When describing their personal political views, only 5 percent claim to be radical, 46 percent liberal, 43 percent moderate, and 6 percent conservative. According to all reliable information available, the political identification and views of the college educated in this sample generally merge with those of the black masses who usually identify with the Democratic party and regard themselves as liberal or moderate when it comes to key political issues.

When asked to evaluate the various organizations to which they belong in terms of their contributions to blacks' goal of equality, the respondents ranked them as follows:

1. Black colleges
2. The NAACP
3. The black church
4. The NUL
5. Black business organizations

The college graduates in this study are quintessential representatives of the middle class in American society. They have the education, occupation, and income to afford a middle-class life-style. While at least 73 percent of them were born to parents who might be classified as lower class, 90 percent of them now regard themselves as middle class. Only 3 percent identify with the upper class, despite their having impressive upper-class credentials. The others (7 percent) identify with the lower class or indicate that they are uncertain about their social class.

The black middle class, as represented by our respondents, is not a monolith. It is, rather, in a state of dynamic change where at least four distinct elements or status groups constantly compete for recognition and influence:

1. The upper stratum, composed mainly of families which have been regarded as upper class in their particular communities for three or more generations.

2. The rank-and-file segment, a wide range of individuals and families from all socio-economic backgrounds. They constitute by far the largest segment of the black middle class, though some do not qualify in some respects. That is, they are college graduates but are underemployed, or they have less than the necessary income to support a middle-class life-style.

3. The upwardly mobile, composed mainly of younger graduates (under fifty) who are ambitious to get ahead. As a rule, they are critical of the status quo in American society in general and in black institutions in particular. They have all of the proper credentials as middle-class people and strive to acquire the leadership recognition they feel they deserve.

4. The downwardly mobile, composed primarily of those who held high social status at a time when occupational opportunities for blacks were more limited than they are today. Essentially those who comprise this group are teachers and preachers, with a few traditional independent

professionals and businesspersons. Now they feel challenged by other blacks who hold high-status jobs. Those who once regarded themselves as the highest-status people in their particular communities now must compete for that status with a new, emerging segment of the black middle class. In 1960 only 5–10 percent of the black population could be classified as middle class, while today 25–30 percent may be so classified. Thus, the black community is in a state of flux as people attempt to adjust to the new elements inherent in the class structure.

The black middle class has been criticized because some feel that the people in it are becoming alienated from the black masses and are trying too hard to imitate the white middle class. This criticism has been prevalent since E. Franklin Frazier's scathing criticism in the *Black Bourgeoisie* (1957). It is ironic that that book was published on the eve of the powerful civil rights movement which was actually led by middle-class blacks. In an evaluation of the social role of the black middle class, 60 percent of the respondents agree that it is making a significant and lasting contribution to blacks' advancement in all areas of American life.

A primary mission of the sample colleges is that of discovering and developing knowledgeable, ethical leadership. Seventy-two percent regard themselves as leaders on some level in American society. An analysis of their organizational affiliations and activities reveals at least three ideal types of leadership:

1. Intraracial leaders. The interests and influence of these leaders are generally confined to the black community, to some institution or organization with all black members. Some make very significant contributions in that they often create and maintain a high level of unity and cooperation which would not be otherwise possible. Such leaders proved to be essential to the movement headed by Martin Luther King, Jr., during the turbulent days of the 1960s when the black masses played a key, essential part in black advancement.

2. Interracial leaders. These leaders "walk in two worlds," as one respondent phrased it. This type of leader always existed in some form, even during the period of slavery. There were always blacks who were called upon to establish or maintain harmony between whites and blacks. However, it was not until after World War II that this leadership pattern became formalized. It developed in response to blacks' strong national push for equality which threatened to disrupt the biracial status quo. Outstanding black leaders, especially those who headed large, influential organizations, were called upon as consultants. Some proved to be very highly skilled racial diplomats and functioned as valuable watchdogs of blacks' civil rights. More than 28 percent of the respondents in this study are now or have been leaders in interracial activities.

3. Integrated black leaders. This is a new, emerging, segment of the black leadership class. Their leadership duties and responsibilities necessarily

transcend black interest per se. They are often administrators of traditional white institutions and agencies, serve on committees, commissions, and boards of directors in the larger community, and hold elective and appointive public offices. Some respondents who hold such leadership positions report that they often face a dilemma when they attempt to use their influence to advance the cause of blacks because their central job is to advance the cause of their enterprises which may or may not be best for blacks. One respondent wrote: "In my position as the only Negro ever on this board, I look for every opportunity to push for more blacks in the corporation. My white board members watch me closely. Any move on my part to be partial to blacks might end my influence with the board."

Some black observers fear that the dilemma of integrated black leaders may be so severe in some instances that they fail to do what they might for blacks' advancement. One of the respondents feels that there is a danger that integrated leaders will eventually become so socialized into the white experience that they might lose the black perspective. However, 71 percent of our respondents feel that blacks who are integrated into powerful white policy-making structures represent a promising vanguard of blacks making progress toward a truly democratic American society.

Some 87 percent of the respondents espouse the concept of a black leadership structure which embraces individuals representing a variety of occupations, organizations, and areas of expertise. They have moved away from the concept of a single messianic, charismatic leader, the type that often prevailed in the black community and is best represented by Martin Luther King, Jr.

Finally, the sample colleges' unswerving dedication to the preparation of students for careers and for informed, ethical leadership has paid off. Their graduates are, indeed, convincing evidence of their success.

Appendix: United Negro College Fund, Inc. Institutional Members

Atlanta University
Atlanta, Georgia

Barber-Scotia College
Concord, North Carolina

Benedict College
Columbia, South Carolina

Bethune-Cookman College
Daytona Beach, Florida

Bishop College
Dallas, Texas

Claflin College
Orangeburg, South Carolina

Clark College
Atlanta, Georgia

Dillard University
New Orleans, Louisiana

Fisk University
Nashville, Tennessee

Florida Memorial College
Miami, Florida

Huston-Tillotson College
Austin, Texas

Interdenominational Theological Center
Atlanta, Georgia

Jarvis Christian College
Hawkins, Texas

Johnson C. Smith University
Charlotte, North Carolina

Knoxville College
Knoxville, Tennessee

Lane College
Jackson, Tennessee

LeMoyne-Owen College
Memphis, Tennessee

Livingstone College
Salisbury, North Carolina

Miles College
Birmingham, Alabama

Morehouse College
Atlanta, Georgia

Morris College
Sumter, South Carolina

Morris Brown College
Atlanta, Georgia

Oakwood College
Huntsville, Alabama

Paine College
Augusta, Georgia

Paul Quinn College
Waco, Texas

Philander Smith College
Little Rock, Arkansas

Rust College
Holly Springs, Mississippi

Saint Augustine's College
Raleigh, North Carolina

Saint Paul's College
Lawrenceville, Virginia

Shaw University
Raleigh, North Carolina

Spelman College
Atlanta, Georgia

Stillman College
Tuscaloosa, Alabama

Talladega College
Talladega, Alabama

Texas College
Tyler, Texas

Tougaloo College
Tougaloo, Mississippi

Tuskegee Institute
Tuskegee Institute, Alabama

Virginia Union University
Richmond, Virginia

Voorhees College
Denmark, South Carolina

Edward Waters College
Jacksonville, Florida

Wilberforce University
Wilberforce, Ohio

Wiley College
Marshall, Texas

Xavier University
New Orleans, Louisiana

Bibliography

Anderson, David E. "Church Council's New President: A Positive Signal to Black Churches." *National Leader* (January 5, 1984).

Astin, Alexander W. *Minorities in American Higher Education*. San Francisco: Jossey-Bass, 1982.

Barthelemy, Sidney J. "Nurturing Leadership." In Antoine Garibaldi, ed., *Black Colleges and Universities*. New York: Praeger, 1984.

Baskin, Wade, ed. *Classics in Education*. New York: Philosophical Library, 1966.

Bell, Daniel. *The Coming of Post-Industrial Society*. New York: Basic Books, 1973.

———. "Meritocracy and Equality." *Public Interest* 29 (Fall 1972).

Bennett, Lerone, Jr. *Confrontation: Black and White*. Chicago: Johnson Publishing Co., 1968.

"Black Churches Unite to Conquer Growing Social Ills." *Times Picayune*. New Orleans, La., December 12, 1982.

Blackwell, James E. *The Black Community: Diversity and Unity*. New York: Dodd, Mead & Co., 1975.

———. "The Crisis Upon Us." *Social Problems* 29 (April 1982).

Blau, Peter M., and Otis Dudley Duncan. *The American Occupational Structure*. New York: Free Press, 1967.

Bond, Horace Mann. *Black American Scholars*. Detroit: Belamp, 1972.

Brawley, James P. *The Clark College Legacy*. Princeton, N.J.: Princeton University Press, 1977.

Brocksbank, Robert W. "The Bomb in Their Desks." Paper presented at the Conference on Liberal Learning and Careers, December 3, 1981, Philadelphia, Penn.

Broderick, Francis L. *W.E.B. Du Bois*. Stanford, Calif.: Stanford University Press, 1959.

Brown, Clifton F. "Black Religion 1968." In Pat Romero, ed., *In Black America*. Washington, D.C.: United Publishing Corp., 1968.

Brown, Tony. "Black College Day in Historical Perspective." *Tony Brown's Journal* (October/December, 1983): 4–13.

———. "The Longest Struggle—The NAACP in Historical Perspective." *Tony Brown's Journal* (January/March, 1984): 4–9.

Bullock, Henry A. *A History of Negro Education in the South*. Cambridge, Mass.: Harvard University Press, 1967.

Burgess, Elaine. *Negro Leadership in a Southern City*. Durham: University of North Carolina Press, 1960.

Burnley, Maureen, ed. *The Significant Difference Black Colleges Make*. New York: United Negro College Fund, June 1982.

Butler, Addie Louise Joyner. *The Distinctive College: Talladega, Tuskegee, and Morehouse*. Metuchen, N.J.: Scarecrow Press, 1977.

Carlyle, Thomas. *On Heroes, Hero-Worship, and the Heroic in History*. New York: E.P. Dutton & Co., 1908.

Centers, Richard. *The Psychology of Social Classes: A Study of Class Consciousness*. Princeton, N.J.: Princeton University Press, 1949.

"Civil Rights Heads Differ on N.O. Police Settlement." *Louisiana Weekly*, January 15, 1983.

Clark, Kenneth B. *Dark Ghetto*. New York: Harper and Row, 1965.

———. "Educational Stimulation of Racially Disadvantaged Children". In A. Harry Passow, ed., *Education in Depressed Areas*. New York: Columbia University, Teachers College Press, 1963.

Cleaver, Eldridge. "The Crisis of the Black Bourgeoisie." *Black Scholar* 4 (January 1973).

Cobb, Charles E. "A Message to Black Preachers." *Crisis* 89 (November 1982).

Coleman, James S., et al. *Equality of Educational Opportunity*. Washington, D.C.: U.S. Office of Education, Government Printing Office, 1966.

Connors, Cathy L., and John Bowen. "New York's Black Elite." *Town and Country* (September 1982): 222–229, 295–306.

Cook, Samuel DuBois. *Promises To Keep*. New Orleans, La.: Dillard University, 1974.

———. "The Socio-Ethical Role and Responsibility of the Black College Graduates." In Charles V. Willie and Ronald Edmonds, eds., *Black Colleges in America: Challenge, Development, Survival*. New York: Columbia University, Teachers College Press, 1978.

Cross, K. Patricia. *Beyond the Open Door*. San Francisco: Jossey-Bass, 1974.

"D.C. Council Persuades DAR to add Black Women." *Jet* 66 (May 1984).

Dellums, Ronald V. "Black Leadership for Change or Status Quo?" *Black Scholar* 8 (January/February, 1977): 2–5.

Dickens, Floyd B., Jr., and Jacqueline B. Dickens. *The Black Manager: Making it in The Corporate World*. New York: Amaco, 1982.

Dillard University. *Academic Orientation*. New Orleans, La. 1977.

———. *Bulletin*. 31, no. 3, February 1965.

———. *Bulletin*. 1982–1984.

Dolbeare, Kenneth M. *American Political Thought*. Monterey, Calif. Duxbury Press, 1981.

Drake, St. Clair. "Social and Economic Status of the Negro in the United States." *Daedalus* 94 (Fall 1965).

Drake, St. Clair, and Horace R. Clayton. *Black Metropolis*. New York: Harper and Row, 1945.

Dred Scott v. Sanford. 19 Howard 393 (1857).

Drimmer, Melvin. *Black History*. Garden City, N.Y.: Anchor Books, 1969.

Du Bois, W.E.B. *Dusk of Dawn*. New York: Harcourt, Brace, 1940.

———. *The Souls of Black Folk.* 1903. Reprint. Nashville, Tenn.: Fisk University Press, 1979.

———. "The Talented Tenth." In Booker T. Washington, ed., *The Negro Problem*. Reprint. New York: Arno Press, 1969.

Durkheim, Emile. *The Elementary Forms of the Religious Life*. New York: Collier Books, 1961.

Duval, Henry. "Youth Demanding Change in the Black Church." *Crisis* 89 (November 1982).

Ebony Staff. "Ten Religious Groups with Biggest Black Membership." *Ebony* 39 (March 1984).

Exum, William H. "Climbing The Crystal Stair". *Social Problems* 30 (April 1983).

Farrell, Charles S. "NCAA's New Academic Standards," *Chronicle of Higher Education*. XXV (January 26, 1983): 1, 17–19.

Fleming, Jacqueline. *Blacks in College*. San Francisco: Jossey-Bass, 1984.

Franklin, John Hope. *From Slavery to Freedom*. New York: Vintage Books, 1969.

———. *Racial Equality in America*. Chicago: University of Chicago Press, 1976.

Frazier, E. Franklin. *Black Bourgeoisie*. New York: Collier Books, 1962.

———. *The Negro Church in America*. New York: Schocken Books, 1964 and 1972.

Freeman, Richard. *The Black Elite*. New York: McGraw-Hill, 1976.

Fyten, David. "The Way We Were." *Tulanian* 55 (Fall 1984).

Gallagher, Buell G. *American Caste and the Negro College*. New York: Gordian Press, 1966.

Gallup Poll. January 25, 1981.

Gallup Poll. March 19, 1981.

Garibaldi, Antoine, ed. *Black Colleges and Universities*. New York: Praeger, 1984.

Gavins, Raymond. *The Perils and Prospects of Southern Black Leadership*. Durham, N.C.: Duke University Press, 1977.

Gest, Ted et al. "Justice Under Reagan." *U.S. News and World Report* 99, no. 16, pp. 60–62.

Gilford, Dorothy M., and Peter D. Syverson. *Doctorate Recipients from United States Universities: Summary Report 1978*. Washington, D.C.: National Academy of Sciences, 1979.

Gillard, Robert. "Alpha To Omega." *Black Collegian* 5 (November/December 1974).

Goode, William G. "Family and Mobility." In Reinhard Bendix and Seymour Martin Lipset, eds., *Class, Status, and Power*. Glencoe, Ill.: Free Press, 1966.

Grady, Henry W. *The New South and Other Addresses*. New York: Robert Bonner's Sons, 1890.

Green, Robert L. "Growing Up Black, Urban and in the Church." *Crisis* 89 (November 1982).

Gurin, Patricia, and Edgar Epps. *Black Consciousness, Identity and Achievement*. New York: Wiley, 1975.

Hamilton, Charles V. "On Politics and Voting: Messages and Meanings." In National Urban League, *The State of Black America 1983*. New York: National Urban League, 1983.

———. "The Place of the Black College in the Human Rights Struggle." *Negro Digest*, September 1967.

Harlan, Lewis. *Booker T. Washington: The Making of a Black Leader, 1856–1901*. Madison: University of Wisconsin Press, 1962.

Henry, Charles P. "Ebony Elite: America's Most Influential Blacks." *Phylon* XLII (June 1981).

Henry, William A., III. "Double Jeopardy in the Newsroom." *Time*, November 29, 1982.

Higginbotham, A. Leon, Jr. *In the Matter of Color*. New York: Oxford University Press, 1978.

Hill, Lynda M. "Black Business." *Black Enterprise*, August 10, 1980.

Hill, John R. "Presidential Perceptions: Administrative Problems and Needs of Public Black Colleges." *Journal of Negro Education* 44 (Winter 1975).

Hill, Robert B. "The Economic Status of Black Americans." In National Urban League, *The State of Black America 1981*. New York: National Urban League, 1981.

Holmes, Lorene Barnes. "Black Colleges—Miracle Workers." *Journal of Black Academia* 1 (November 1980).

Homans, George C. *The Human Group*. New York: Harcourt, Brace, 1950.

Hooks, Benjamin L. "The NAACP And The Church Are Indeed Partners In Progress." *Crisis* 89 (November 1982).

Hooks, Benjamin L. "A Profile of Black America." *Crisis* 88 (October 1981).

———. "A Profile of Black America—A Grim Picture." *Crisis* 90 (December 1983).

Hutchins, Robert Maynard, ed. "Aristotle's Politics." *Great Books of the Western World*, vol. 2. Chicago: William Benton, 1952.

Hyman, H. H. "The Value Systems of Different Classes." In Reinhard Bendix and Seymour Martin Lipset, eds., *Class, Status and Power*. Glencoe, Ill.: Free Press, 1966.

Jencks, Christopher, et al. *Inequality: A Reassessment of the Effects of Family and Schooling in America*. New York: Basic Books, 1972.

Jencks, Christopher and David Reisman. *The Academic Revolution*. Garden City, N.Y.: Doubleday and Co., 1968.

Johnson, Charles S. *The Negro College Graduate*. Durham: University of North Carolina Press, 1938.

Johnson, H., D. T. Dingle, and F. D. Brown. "New Directions for Economic Growth." *Black Enterprise*, (June 1984): 201–212.

Johnson, Tobe. "The Black College System." *Daedalus* 100 (Summer 1971).

Jones, Alfred Winslow. "Class Consciousness and Prosperity." In Reinhard Bendix and Seymour Martin Lipset, eds., *Class, Status and Power*. Glencoe, Ill.: Free Press, 1966.

Jones, Major J. *Black Awareness: A Theology of Hope*. New York: Abingdon Press, 1971.

Jordan, Vernon E., Jr. "Blacks in Higher Education: Some Reflections." *Daedalus* 104 (Winter 1975).

———. "Introduction." *The State of Black America 1977*. New York: National Urban League, 1977.

Kilson, Martin. "Black Social Classes and Intergenerational Poverty." *Public Interest* 64 (Summer 1981): 58–78.

King, Martin Luther, Jr. "Letter from a Birmingham Jail." *Christian Century* 80, pp. 767–773.

King, Pat. "New Wave Networking." *Black Enterprise* 14 (December 1983): 87–92.

Kirschner, Allan H. *UNCF 1982 Statistical Report*. New York: United Negro College Fund, 1982.

Kirschner, Alan H., Jacqueline Fleming, Kathleen Payne, and Maureen Burnley. *UNCF 1985 Statistical Report*. New York: United Negro College Fund, 1985.

Klein, Arthur Jay. *Survey of Negro Colleges and Universities*. New York: Negro University Press, 1969.

Kriss, Ronald P., Sr., et al., eds., "In Quest of Leadership." *Time*, July 15, 1974, pp. 21–70.

Larry Williams et al. v. City of New Orleans. Civil Action No. 72–629 (1982).

Lawrence, James. "The Space Program . . . Disallowed Black Folks." *National Leader*, September 8, 1983.

LeMelle, Tilden J., and Wilbert J. LeMelle. *The Black College: A Strategy for Relevancy*. New York: Praeger, 1969.

Maloney, Lawrence D. "Success! The Chase is Back in Style Again." *U.S. News and World Report*, October 3, 1983, pp. 60–63.

Mays, Benjamin E. *Born To Rebel: An Autobiography*. New York: Charles Scribner's Sons, 1971.

Mason, Bryant S. "In the Middle of the Action." *Black Enterprise* 13 (August 1982).

Mathy, William C., Jr., and Dwight L. Johnson. "America's Black Population 1970–1982." *Crisis* 90 (December 1982) 10–18.

McBay, Shirley M. "Black Students In The Sciences: A Look At Spelman College." In Charles V. Willie and Ronald R. Edmonds, eds., *Black Colleges In America*. New York: Columbia University, Teachers College Press, 1978.

McBride, David, and Monroe H. Little. "The Afro-American Elite, 1930–1940: A Historical and Statistical Profile." *Phylon* XLII (June 1981).

McNatt, Robert. "Economic Outlook for Black America: 1984." *Black Enterprise* 14 (January 1984).

Merton, Robert K. *Social Theory and Social Structure*. New York: Free Press, 1968.

Montgomery, M. Lee. "The Education of Black Children." In Nathan Wright, ed., *What Black Educators Are Saying*. New York: Hawthorn Books, 1970.

Moon, Henry Lee. *The Emergent Thought of W.E.B. Du Bois*. New York: Simon and Schuster, 1972.

Morehouse College. *Bulletin* 1983–85. Atlanta: Morehouse College.

Morris, Lorenzo. *Elusive Equality*. Washington, D.C.: Howard University Press, 1979.

Mosteller, Frederick, and Daniel P. Moynihan, eds. *On Equality of Educational Opportunity*. New York: Random House, 1972.

Myrdal, Gunnar. *An American Dilemma*. New York: Harper and Row, 1944; Reprint, New York: Pantheon Books, 1975.

National Advisory Committee on Black Higher Education and Black Colleges and Universities. *Equity for Black Americans, Vol. 1*. Washington, D.C.: U.S. Government Printing Office, 1980.

National Center for Education Statistics. *1972 Digest of Educational Statistics*. Washington, D.C.: U.S. Office of Education, 1972.

National Commission On Excellence In Education. *A Nation At Risk: The Imperative for Educational Reform*. Washington, D.C.: U.S. Department of Education, April 1983.

National Urban League. *The State of Black America, 1977*. New York: National Urban League, 1977.

———. *The State of Black America, 1980*. New York: National Urban League, 1980.

———. *The State of Black America, 1981*. New York: National Urban League, 1981.

———. *The State of Black America, 1982*. New York: National Urban League, 1982.

———. *The State of Black America, 1983*. New York: National Urban League, 1983.

Newberry, Robert. *Time Magazine*, November 29, 1982.

Newton, Edmund. "Suite Success." *Black Enterprise* 14 (February 1984).

———. "Taking Over City Hall." *Black Enterprise*. 13 (June 1983).

Oates, Marylouise. "Black Society in Los Angeles." *Los Angeles Times*, June 27, 1982, 1, 12–13.

Padover, Saul K., ed. *Thomas Jefferson on Democracy*. New York: New American Library, 1946.

Paris, Peter J. *Black Leaders in Conflict*. New York: Pilgrim Press, 1978.

Passow, A. Harry, ed., *Education in Depressed Areas*. New York: Columbia University, Teachers College Press, 1963.

Piliawsky, Monte. *Exit 13: Oppression and Racism in Academia*. Boston: South End Press, 1982.

Pinkney, Alphonso. *Black Americans*. Englewood Cliffs, N.J.: Prentice-Hall, 1969.

Plessy v. Ferguson, 163 U.S. 1138 (1896).

Proctor, Samuel D. "Survival Techniques and the Black Middle Class." In Rhonda L. Goldstein, ed., *Black Life and Culture in the United States*. New York: Thomas Y. Crowell Co., 1971.

Randall, Alice, and Stanley Tretick. "Washington's Other Elite." *The Washingtonian*, May 1982, 111–119.

Range, Peter Ross. "Atlanta: Capital of Black-Is-Bountiful." *New York Times Magazine*, April 9, 1974.

Raspberry, William. "Whites Interested in Creating Black Leaders." *National Leader*, January 5, 1984.

Reissman, Leonard. *Class In American Society*. Glencoe, Ill.: Free Press, 1959.

Robertson, Ian, ed. *The Social World*. New York: Worth, 1981.

Roethlisberger, F. J. *Management and Morale*. Cambridge, Mass.:Harvard University Press, 1941.

Roethlisberger, F. J., and William J. Dickson. *Management and the Workers*. Cambridge, Mass.: Harvard University Press, 1959.

Schulke, Flip, ed. *Martin Luther King, Jr.* New York: W. W. Norton, 1976.

"Segregation in Churches: Why it Still Thrives." U.S. News and World Report, November 29, 1976.

Smith, Charles U. "Problems and Possibilities of the Predominantly Negro College." *Journal of Social and Behavioral Sciences* 13 (1968).

Smith, Donald H. *Admission and Retention of Black Students at Seven Predominantly White Universities*. Washington, D.C.: U.S. Government Printing Office, December 1979.

Southern Regional Education Board. *New Careers and Curriculum Changes*. Atlanta: Southern Regional Education Board, 1968.

Sowell, Thomas. *Black Education: Myths and Tragedies*. New York: David McKay Company, Inc., 1972.

———— et al., eds. *The Fairmont Papers*. San Francisco: Institute for Contemporary Studies, 1981.

Stogdill, Ralph M. *Handbook of Leadership*. New York: Free Press, 1974.

Stone, Chuck. "The Imperative for Change." In Thomas Sowell, ed., *The Fairmont Papers*. San Francisco: Institute for Contemporary Studies, 1980.

Swinton, David H. "The Economic Status of the Black Population." In National Urban League, *The State of Black America, 1983*. New York: National Urban League, 1983.

Taylor, A.J.P. *Bismarck: The Man and the Statesman*. New York: Alfred A. Knopf, 1955.

Teamer, Charles C., Sr. "Inaugural Address: A Legacy of Leadership and Service." *Sphinx* 70 (Winter 1984).

Therstrom, Stephan. "Class Mobility In A Nineteenth Century City." In Reinhard Bendix, and Seymour Martin Lipset, eds., *Class, Status, and Power*. Glencoe, Ill.: Free Press, 1966.

Thomas, William I. *The Unadjusted Girl*. Boston: Little, Brown & Co., 1923.

Thompson, Barbara Guillory. "The Black Family: A Case For Change and Survival In America." Ph.D. diss. Tulane University, New Orleans, 1974.

————. "The Career Patterns of Negro Lawyers in New Orleans." Masters thesis, Louisiana State University, Baton Rouge, 1960.

Thompson, Daniel C. "Black College Faculty and Students: The Nature of Their Interaction." In Charles V. Willie and Ronald R. Edmonds, eds., *Black Colleges in America: Challenge, Development, Survival*. New York: Columbia University, Teachers College Press, 1978.

————. "Black Colleges: Continuing Challenges." *Phylon* 40 (Summer 1979).

————. "The Black Elite." *The Boulé Journal* 39 (Summer 1976): 10–18.

————. *The Negro Leadership Class*. Englewood Cliffs, N.J.: Prentice-Hall, 1963.

————. *Private Black Colleges at the Crossroads*. Westport, Conn.: Greenwood Press, 1973.

————. "Radicalizing The Black Church." In James S. Gadsden, ed., *Experiences, Struggles, and Hopes of the Black Church*. Nashville, Tenn.: Tidings, 1975.

————. "The Rise of the Negro Protest." *Annals of The Academy of Political and Social Science*. 357 (January 1965): 18–29.

————. "Social Class Factors in Public School Education As Related To Desegregation." *American Journal of Orthopsychiatry* 26 (July 1956).

————. *Sociology of the Black Experience*. Westport, Conn.: Greenwood Press, 1974.

————. "Teaching The Culturally Disadvantaged." In Floyd Rinker, ed., *Speaking about Teaching*. New York: College Entrance Examination Board, 1967.

Thompson, Daniel C., and Barbara G. Thompson, "The Black Underclass: A Continuing Saga." *The Black Southerner* 1 and 2 (Fall 1983 and Winter 1984).

Thornton, Jeannye. "Blacks Turn to the Church in Political Drive." *U.S. News and World Report*, February 6, 1984.

Trow, Martin. *Teachers and Students*. New York: McGraw-Hill, 1975.

United Negro College Fund. *Annual Statistical Report of the Member Institutions, 1974*.

————. *Research Report* IV (May 1980).

U.S. Department of Commerce, Bureau of the Census. Current Population Reports. *Money, Income and Poverty Status of Families and Persons in the United States: 1980.* Consumer Income Series 127 (August 1981): 60.

U.S. Department of Commerce; *The Social and Economic Status of the Black Population in the United States, 1970–1978,* 80 (1978): 23.

Walker, Donald C., ed. *1983 Blackbook.* Chicago: National Publications Agency, 1983.

Watson, Bernard. "Education: A Matter of Grave Concern." In National Urban League, *The State of Black America 1980.* New York: National Urban League, 1980.

Webster, David S. "America's Highest Ranked Graduate Schools, 1925–1982." *Change Magazine,* May/June 1983, 15–24.

Wesley, Charles H. *History of Sigma Pi Phi: First of Negro American Greek-Letter Fraternities.* Washington, D.C.: Association for the Study of Negro Life and History, 1954.

White, Jack, and Joseph Boyce. "The Underclass: Enduring Dilemma." *Time,* June 17, 1974, 26–27.

Who's Who Among Black Americans, 1980–1982. North Miami, Fla.: Educational Book Publishing, 1984.

Willie, Charles V. "Black Students In Higher Education." *American Sociological Review* 7 (1981).

Willie, Charles V., and Donald Cunnigen. "Black Students In Higher Education." *Annual Review of Sociology* 7 (1980): 177–198.

Willie, Charles V., and Arline S. McCord. *Black Students at White Colleges.* New York: Praeger, 1972.

Willie, Charles V., and Ronald R. Edmonds, eds. *Black Colleges in America: Challenge, Development, Survival.* New York: Columbia University, Teachers College Press, 1978.

Wilson, William Julius. *The Declining Significance of Race.* Chicago: University of Chicago Press, 1980.

Wright, Lawrence. "Easy Street: Houston's Black Elite." *Texas Monthly,* November 1982, 174–181, 285–292.

Wright, Nathan, Jr., ed. *What Black Educators Are Saying.* New York: Hawthorn Books, 1970.

Wright, Stephen J., Benjamin E. Mays, Hugh M. Gloster, and Albert W. Dent. "The American Negro College: Four Responses and A Reply." *Harvard Educational Review.* 37 (1967): 451–467.

Yankelovitch, Daniel. "Who Gets Ahead in America." In Ian Robertson, ed., *The Social World.* New York: Worth Publishers, 1981.

Young, Kimball, and Raymond Mack. *Sociology and Social Life.* New York: American Book Co., 1965.

Young, Whitney M., Jr. *To Be Equal.* New York: McGraw-Hill, 1964.

Index

About the Author

DANIEL C. THOMPSON, Professor Emeritus of Sociology, Dillard University, has taught at Clark College, Howard University, and Stanford University, and served as Director of the Leadership Training Program for the U.S. Office of Education. Among his books are *The Negro Leadership Class*, *Sociology of the Black Experience*, and *Private Black Colleges at the Crossroads* (Greenwood Press, 1974, 1973).